"TILL HE COME."

"TILL HE COME."

COMMUNION MEDITATIONS

AND

ADDRESSES

BY

C. H. SPURGEON.

(Not published in *The Metropolitan Tabernacle Pulpit.*)

Christian Focus Publications Limited

© Christian Focus Publications Ltd 1989

ISBN 1 871676 002

Christian Focus Publications

Houston   Tain
Texas   Ross-shire

Printed and bound in Scotland

PREFATORY NOTE.

———————◆———————

For many years, whether at home or abroad, it was Mr. Spurgeon's constant custom to observe the ordinance of the Lord's supper every Sabbath-day, unless illness prevented. This he believed to be in accordance with apostolic precedent; and it was his oft-repeated testimony that the more frequently he obeyed his Lord's command, "This do in remembrance of Me," the more precious did his Saviour become to him, while the memorial celebration itself proved increasingly helpful and instructive as the years rolled by.

Several of the discourses here published were delivered to thousands of communicants in the Metropolitan Tabernacle, while others were addressed to the little companies of Christians,—of different denominations, and of various nationalities,—who gathered around the communion table in Mr. Spurgeon's sitting-room at Mentone. The addresses cover a wide range of subjects; but all of them speak more or less fully of the great atoning sacrifice of which the broken bread and the filled cup are the simple yet significant symbols.

Mr. Spurgeon had intended to publish a selection of his Communion Addresses; so this volume may be regarded as another of the precious literary legacies bequeathed by him to his brethren and sisters in Christ who have yet to tarry a while here below. It is hoped that these sermonettes will be the means of deepening the spiritual life of many believers, and that they will suggest suitable themes for meditation and discourse to those who have the privilege and responsibility of presiding at the ordinance.

CONTENTS.

MYSTERIOUS VISITS.

AN ADDRESS TO A LITTLE COMPANY AT THE COMMUNION TABLE AT MENTONE.

" Thou hast visited me in the night."—*Psalm* xvii. 3.

MYSTERIOUS VISITS.

———

IT is a theme for wonder that the glorious God should visit sinful man. "What is man, that Thou art mindful of him? and the son of man, that Thou visitest him?" A divine visit is a joy to be treasured whenever we are favoured with it. David speaks of it with great solemnity. The Psalmist was not content barely to *speak* of it; but he wrote it down in plain terms, that it might be known throughout all generations: "*Thou hast visited me in the night.*" Beloved, if God has ever visited you, you also will marvel at it, will carry it in your memory, will speak of it to your friends, and will record it in your diary as one of the notable events of your life. Above all, you will speak of it to God Himself, and say with adoring gratitude, "Thou hast visited me in the night." It should be a solemn part of worship to remember and make known the condescension of the Lord, and say, both in lowly prayer and in joyful psalm, "Thou hast visited me."

To you, beloved friends, who gather with me about this communion table, I will speak of my own experience, nothing doubting that it is also yours. If our God has ever visited any of us, personally, by His Spirit, two results have attended the visit: *it has been sharply searching*, and *it has been sweetly solacing*.

When first of all the Lord draws nigh to the heart,

the trembling soul perceives clearly the searching character of His visit. Remember how Job answered the Lord: "I have heard of Thee by the hearing of the ear : but now mine eye seeth Thee, wherefore I abhor myself, and repent in dust and ashes." We can read of God, and hear of God, and be little moved ; but when we feel His presence, it is another matter. I thought my house was good enough for kings ; but when the King of kings came to it, I saw that it was a hovel quite unfit for His abode. I had never known sin to be so "exceeding sinful " if I had not known God to be so perfectly holy. I had never understood the depravity of my own nature if I had not known the holiness of God's nature. When we see Jesus, we fall at His feet as dead ; till then, we are alive with vainglorious life. If letters of light traced by a mysterious hand upon the wall caused the joints of Belshazzar's loins to be loosed, what awe overcomes our spirits when we see the Lord Himself! In the presence of so much light our spots and wrinkles are revealed, and we are utterly ashamed. We are like Daniel, who said, " I was left alone, and saw this great vision, and there remained no strength in me : for my comeliness was turned in me into corruption." It is when the Lord visits us that we see our nothingness, and ask, " Lord, what is man ? "

I do remember well when God first visited me ; and assuredly it was the night of nature, of ignorance, of sin. His visit had the same effect upon me that it had upon Saul of Tarsus when the Lord spake to him out of heaven. He brought me down from the high horse, and caused me to fall to the ground ; by the brightness of the light of His Spirit He made me grope in conscious blindness; and in the brokenness of my heart I cried, "Lord, what wilt Thou have me to do?" I felt that I had been rebelling against the Lord, kicking against the pricks, and doing evil even as I could; and my soul was filled with anguish at the discovery. Very searching was the glance of the eye of Jesus, for it revealed my sin, and caused me to go out and weep bitterly. As when the Lord visited Adam, and called him to stand naked before Him, so was I stripped of all my righteousness before the face of the Most High. Yet the visit ended not there; for as the Lord God clothed our first parents in coats of skins, so did He cover me with the righteousness of the great sacrifice, and He gave me songs in the night. It was night, but the visit was no dream: in fact, I there and then ceased to dream, and began to deal with the reality of things.

I think you will remember that, when the Lord first visited you in the night, it was with you as with Peter when Jesus came to him. He had been toiling with his net all the night, and nothing had come of it; but when the Lord Jesus came into his boat, and bade him launch out into the deep, and let down his net for a draught, he caught such a great multitude of fishes that the boat began to sink. See! the boat goes down, down, till the water threatens to engulf it, and Peter, and the fish, and all. Then Peter fell down at Jesus' knees, and cried, "Depart from me; for I am a sinful man, O Lord!" The presence of Jesus was too much for him: his sense of unworthiness made him sink like his boat, and shrink away from the Divine Lord. I remember that sensation well; for I was half inclined to cry with the demoniac of Gadara, "What have I to do with Thee, Jesus, Thou Son of God most high?" That first discovery of His injured love was overpowering; its very hopefulness increased my anguish; for then I saw that I had slain the Lord who had come to save me. I saw that mine was the hand which made the hammer fall, and drove the nails that fastened the Redeemer's hands and feet to the cruel tree.

> "My conscience felt and own'd the guilt,
>   And plunged me in despair;
> I saw my sins His blood had spilt,
>   And help'd to nail Him there."

This is the sight which breeds repentance: "They shall look upon Him whom they have pierced, and mourn for Him." When the Lord visits us, He humbles us, removes all hardness from our hearts, and leads us to the Saviour's feet.

When the Lord first visited us in the night, it was very much with us as with John, when the Lord visited him in the isle that is called Patmos. He tells us, "And when I saw Him, I fell at His feet as dead." Yes, even when we begin to see that He has put away our sin, and removed our guilt by His death, we feel as if we could never look up again, because we have been so cruel to our best Friend. It is no wonder if we then say, "It is true that He has forgiven me; but I never can forgive myself. He makes me live, and I live in Him; but at the thought of His goodness I fall at His feet as dead. Boasting is dead, self is dead, and all desire for anything beyond my Lord is dead also." Well does Cowper sing of—

> "That dear hour, that brought me to His foot,
>   And cut up all my follies by the root."

The process of destroying follies is more hopefully performed at Jesus' feet than anywhere else. Oh, that the Lord would come again to us as at the first, and like a consuming fire discover and destroy the dross which now alloys our gold! The word *visit* brings to us who travel the remembrance of the government officer who searches our baggage; thus doth the Lord seek out our secret things. But it also reminds us of the visits of the physician, who not only finds out our maladies, but also removes them. Thus did the Lord Jesus visit us at the first.

Since those early days, I hope that you and I have had many visits from our Lord. Those first visits were, as I said, sharply searching; but the later ones have been *sweetly solacing*. Some of us have had them, especially in the night, when we have been compelled to count the sleepless hours. "Heaven's gate opens when this world's is shut." The night is still; everybody is away; work is done; care is forgotten, and then the Lord Himself draws near. Possibly there may be pain to be endured, the head may be aching, and the heart may be throbbing; but if Jesus comes to visit us, our bed of languishing becomes a throne of glory. Though it is true "He giveth His beloved sleep," yet at such times He gives them something better than sleep, namely, His own presence, and the fulness of joy which comes with it. By night upon our bed we have seen the unseen. I have tried sometimes not to sleep under an excess of joy, when the company of Christ has been sweetly mine.

"Thou hast visited me in the night." Believe me, there are such things as personal visits from Jesus to His people. He has not left us utterly. Though He

be not seen with the bodily eye by bush or brook, nor
on the mount, nor by the sea, yet doth He come and
go, observed only by the spirit, felt only by the heart.
Still he standeth behind our wall, He showeth Himself
through the lattices.

> " Jesus, these eyes have never seen
>   That radiant form of Thine !
> The veil of sense hangs dark between
>   Thy blessed face and mine !
>
> " I see Thee not, I hear Thee not,
>   Yet art Thou oft with me,
> And earth hath ne'er so dear a spot
>   As where I meet with Thee.
>
> " Like some bright dream that comes unsought,
>   When slumbers o'er me roll,
> Thine image ever fills my thought,
>   And charms my ravish'd soul.
>
> " Yet though I have not seen, and still
>   Must rest in faith alone ;
> I love Thee, dearest Lord ! and will,
>   Unseen, but not unknown."

Do you ask me to describe these manifestations of
the Lord ? It were hard to tell you in words : you
must know them for yourselves. If you had never
tasted sweetness, no man living could give you an
idea of honey. Yet if the honey be there, you can
" taste and see." To a man born blind, sight must be
a thing past imagination ; and to one who has never
known the Lord, His visits are quite as much beyond
conception.

For our Lord to visit us is something more than for
us to have the assurance of our salvation, though that
is very delightful, and none of us should rest satisfied

unless we possess it. To know that Jesus loves me, is one thing; but to be visited by Him in love, is more.

Nor is it simply a close contemplation of Christ; for we can picture Him as exceedingly fair and majestic, and yet not have Him consciously near us. Delightful and instructive as it is to behold the likeness of Christ by meditation, yet the enjoyment of His actual presence is something more. I may wear my friend's portrait about my person, and yet may not be able to say, "Thou hast visited me."

It is the actual, though spiritual, coming of Christ which we so much desire. The Romish church says much about the *real* presence; meaning thereby, the corporeal presence of the Lord Jesus. The priest who celebrates mass tells us that he believes in the *real* presence, but we reply, "Nay, you believe in knowing Christ after the flesh, and in that sense the only real presence is in heaven; but we firmly believe in the real presence of Christ which is spiritual, and yet certain." By spiritual we do not mean unreal; in fact, the spiritual takes the lead in real-ness to spiritual men. I believe in the true and real presence of Jesus with His people : such presence has been real to my spirit. Lord Jesus, Thou Thyself hast visited me. As surely as the Lord Jesus came really as to His flesh to Bethlehem and Calvary, so surely does He come really by His Spirit to His people in the hours of their communion with Him. We are as conscious of that presence as of our own existence.

When the Lord visits us in the night, what is the effect upon us? When hearts meet hearts in fellowship of love, communion brings first peace, then rest, and then joy of soul. I am speaking of no emotional excitement rising into fanatical rapture; but I speak of sober fact, when I say that the Lord's great heart touches ours, and our heart rises into sympathy with Him.

First, we experience *peace*. All war is over, and a blessed peace is proclaimed; the peace of God keeps our heart and mind by Christ Jesus.

> " Peace ! perfect peace ! in this dark world of sin ?
> The blood of Jesus whispers peace within.

> " Peace ! perfect peace ! with sorrows surging round ?
> On Jesus' bosom nought but calm is found."

At such a time there is a delightful sense of *rest ;* we have no ambitions, no desires. A divine serenity and security envelop us. We have no thought of foes, or fears, or afflictions, or doubts. There is a joyous laying aside of our own will. We *are* nothing, and we *will* nothing : Christ is everything, and His will is the pulse of our soul. We are perfectly content either to be ill or to be well, to be rich or to be poor, to be slandered or to be honoured, so that we may but abide in the love of Christ. Jesus fills the horizon of our being.

At such a time a flood of great *joy* will fill our minds. We shall half wish that the morning may never break again, for fear its light should banish the superior light of Christ's presence. We shall wish that we could glide away with our Beloved to the place where He feedeth among the lilies. We long to hear the voices of the white-robed armies, that we may follow their glorious Leader whithersoever He goeth. I am persuaded that there is no great actual distance between earth and heaven : the distance lies in our dull minds. When the Beloved visits us in the night, He makes our chambers to be the vestibule of His palace-halls. Earth rises to heaven when heaven comes down to earth.

Now, beloved friends, you may be saying to yourselves, " *We* have not enjoyed such visits as these." You may do so. If the Father loves you even as He loves His Son, then you are on visiting terms with Him. If, then, He has not called upon you, you will be wise to call on Him. Breathe a sigh to Him, and say,—

> " When wilt Thou come unto me, Lord ?
> Oh come, my Lord most dear !
> Come near, come nearer, nearer still,
> I'm blest when Thou art near.
>
> " When wilt Thou come unto me, Lord ?
> I languish for the sight ;
> Ten thousand suns when Thou art hid,
> Are shades instead of light.
>
> " When wilt Thou come unto me, Lord ?
> Until Thou dost appear,
> I count each moment for a day,
> Each minute for a year."

"As the hart panteth after the water-brooks, so panteth my soul after Thee, O God !" If you long for Him, He much more longs for you. Never was there a sinner that was half so eager for Christ as Christ is eager for the sinner ; nor a saint one-tenth so anxious to behold his Lord as his Lord is to behold him. If thou art running to Christ, He is already near thee. If thou dost sigh for His presence, that sigh is the evidence that He is with thee. He is with thee now : therefore be calmly glad.

Go forth, beloved, and talk with Jesus on the beach, for He oft resorted to the sea-shore. Commune with Him amid the olive-groves so dear to Him in many a night of wrestling prayer. If ever there was a country in which men should see traces of Jesus, next to the Holy Land, this Riviera is the favoured spot. It is a land of vines, and figs, and olives, and palms ; I have called it " Thy land, O Immanuel." While in this Mentone, I often fancy that I am looking out upon the Lake of Gennesaret, or walking at the foot of the Mount of Olives, or peering into the mysterious gloom of the Garden of Gethsemane. The narrow streets of the old town are such as Jesus traversed, these villages are such as He inhabited. Have your hearts right with Him, and He will visit you often, until every day you shall walk with God, as Enoch did, and so turn week-days into Sabbaths, meals into sacraments, homes into temples, and earth into heaven. So be it with us! Amen.

UNDER HIS SHADOW.

A BRIEF SACRAMENTAL DISCOURSE DELIVERED AT MENTONE TO ABOUT A SCORE BRETHREN.

"He that dwelleth in the secret place of the most High shall abide under the shadow of the Almighty."—*Psalm* xci. 1.

UNDER HIS SHADOW.

———

I MUST confess of my short discourse, as the man did of the axe which fell into the stream, that it is borrowed. The outline of it is taken from one who will never complain of me, for to the great loss of the Church she has left these lower choirs to sing above. Miss Havergal, last and loveliest of our modern poets, when her tones were most mellow, and her language most sublime, has been caught up to swell the music of heaven. Her last poems are published with the title, "Under His Shadow," and the preface gives the reason for the name. She said, "I should like the title to be, 'Under His Shadow.' I seem to see four pictures suggested by that : under the shadow of a rock in a weary plain ; under the shadow of a tree ; closer still, under the shadow of His wing ; nearest and closest, in the shadow of His hand. Surely that hand must be the pierced hand, that may oftentimes press us sorely, and yet evermore encircling, upholding, and shadowing."

"Under His Shadow," is our afternoon subject, and we will in a few words enlarge on the Scriptural plan which Miss Havergal has bequeathed to us. Our text is, "He that dwelleth in the secret place of the most High shall abide *under the shadow* of the Almighty." The shadow of God is not the occasional resort, but the constant abiding-place, of the saint. Here we find not only our consolation, but our habitation. We ought never to be 'out of the shadow of God. It is to dwellers, not to visitors, that the Lord promises His protection. " He that *dwelleth* in the secret place of the most High shall abide under the shadow of the Almighty : " and that shadow shall preserve him from nightly terror and ghostly ill, from the arrows of war and of pestilence, from death and from destruction. Guarded by Omnipotence, the chosen of the Lord are always safe ; for as they dwell in the holy place, hard by the mercy-seat, where the blood was sprinkled of old, the pillar of fire by night, the pillar of cloud by day, which ever hangs over the sanctuary, covers them also. Is it not written, " In the time of trouble He shall hide me in His pavilion, in the secret of His tabernacle shall He hide me " ? What better security can we desire ? As the people of God, we are always under the protection of the Most High. Wherever we go, whatever we suffer, whatever may be our difficulties, temptations, trials, or perplexities, we are always " under the shadow of the Almighty." Over all who maintain their fellowship with God the most tender guardian care is extended. Their heavenly Father Himself interposes between them and their adversaries. The experience of the saints, albeit they are all under the shadow, yet differs as to the form in which that protection has been enjoyed by them, hence the value of the four figures which will now engage our attention.

I. We will begin with the first picture which Miss Havergal mentions, namely, THE ROCK sheltering the weary traveller :—" *The shadow of a great rock in a weary land* " (Isaiah xxxii. 2).

Now, I take it that this is where we begin to know our Lord's shadow. He was at the first to us *a refuge in time of trouble.* Weary was the way, and great was the heat ; our lips were parched, and our souls were fainting ; we sought for shelter, and we found none ; for we were in the wilderness of sin and condemnation, and who could bring us deliverance, or even hope ? Then we cried unto the Lord in our trouble, and He led us to the Rock of ages, which of old was cleft for us. We saw our interposing Mediator coming between us and the fierce heat of justice, and we hailed the blessed screen. The Lord Jesus was unto us a covering for sin, and so a covert from wrath. The sense of divine displeasure, which had beaten upon our conscience, was removed by the removal of the sin itself, which we saw to be laid on Jesus, who in our place and stead endured its penalty.

The shadow of a rock is remarkably cooling, and so was the Lord Jesus eminently comforting to us. The shadow of a rock is more dense, more complete, and more cool than any other shade ; and so the peace which Jesus gives passeth all understanding, there is none like it. No chance beam darts through the rock-shade, nor can the heat penetrate as it will do in a measure through the foliage of a forest. Jesus is a complete shelter, and blessed are they who are " under His shadow." Let them take care that they abide there, and never venture forth to answer for themselves, or to brave the accusations of Satan.

As with sin, so with sorrow of every sort : the Lord is the Rock of our refuge. No sun shall smite

us, nor any heat, because we are never out of Christ.
The saints know where to fly, and they use their
privilege.

> "When troubles, like a burning sun,
> Beat heavy on their head,
> To Christ their mighty Rock they run,
> And find a pleasing shade."

There is, however, something of awe about this
great shadow. A rock is often so high as to be
terrible, and we tremble in presence of its greatness.
The idea of littleness hiding behind massive greatness
is well set forth; but there is no tender thought of
fellowship, or gentleness: even so, at the first, we
view the Lord Jesus as our shelter from the consuming
heat of well-deserved punishment, and we know little
more. It is most pleasant to remember that this is
only one panel of the four-fold picture. Inexpressibly
dear to my soul is the deep cool rock-shade of my
blessed Lord, as I stand in Him a sinner saved; yet
is there more.

II. Our second picture, that of THE TREE, is to
be found in the Song of Solomon ii. 3 :—*"As the
apple tree among the trees of the wood, so is my Beloved
among the sons. I sat down under His shadow with
great delight, and His fruit was sweet to my taste."*
Here we have not so much refuge from trouble as
special *rest in times of joy.* The spouse is happily
wandering through a wood, glancing at many trees,
and rejoicing in the music of the birds. One tree
specially charms her: the citron with its golden fruit
wins her admiration, and she sits under its shadow
with great delight; such was her Beloved to her, the
best among the good, the fairest of the fair, the joy of

her joy, the light of her delight. Such is Jesus to the believing soul.

The sweet influences of Christ are intended to give us a happy rest, and we ought to avail ourselves of them: "I sat down under His shadow." This was Mary's better part, which Martha well-nigh missed by being cumbered. That is the good old way wherein we are to walk, the way in which we find rest unto our souls. Papists and papistical persons, whose religion is all ceremonies, or all working, or all groaning, or all feeling, have never come to an end. We may say of their religion as of the law, that it made nothing perfect; but under the gospel there is something finished, and that something is the sum and substance of our salvation, and therefore there is rest for us, and we ought to sing, " I sat down."

Dear friends, is Christ to each one of us a place of sitting down? I do not mean a rest of idleness and self-content,—God deliver us from that; but there is rest in a conscious grasp of Christ, a rest of contentment with Him as our all in all. God give us to know more of this! This shadow is also meant to yield perpetual solace, for the spouse did not merely come under it, but there she sat down as one who meant to stay. Continuance 'of repose and joy is purchased for us by our Lord's perfected work. Under the shadow she found food; she had no need to leave it to find a single needful thing, for the tree which shaded also yielded fruit; nor did she need even to rise from her rest, but sitting still she feasted on the delicious fruit. You who know the Lord Jesus know also what this meaneth.

The spouse never wished to go beyond her Lord.

She knew no higher life than that of sitting under the Well-beloved's shadow. She passed the cedar, and oak, and every other goodly tree, but the apple-tree held her, and there she sat down. "Many there be that say, who will show us any good? But as for us, O Lord, our heart is fixed, our heart is fixed, resting on Thee. We will go no further, for Thou art our dwelling-place, we feel at home with Thee, and sit down beneath Thy shadow." Some Christians cultivate reverence at the expense of childlike love; they kneel down, but they dare not sit down. Our Divine Friend and Lover wills not that it should be so; He would not have us stand on ceremony with Him, but come boldly unto Him.

> " Let us be simple with Him, then,
>   Not backward, stiff or cold,
>   As though our Bethlehem could be
>   What Sina was of old."

Let us use His sacred name as a common word, as a household word, and run to Him as to a dear familiar friend. Under His shadow we are to feel that we are at home, and then He will make Himself at home to us by becoming food unto our souls, and giving spiritual refreshment to us while we rest. The spouse does not here say that she reached up to the tree to gather its fruit, but she sat down on the ground in intense delight, and the fruit came to her where she sat. It is wonderful how Christ will come down to souls that sit beneath His shadow; if we can but be at home with Christ, He will sweetly commune with us. Has He not said, "Delight thyself also in the Lord, and He shall give thee the desires of thine heart"?

In this second form of the sacred shadow, the sense of awe gives place to that of restful delight in Christ. Have you ever figured in such a scene as the sitter beneath the grateful shade of the fruitful tree? Have you not only possessed security, but experienced delight in Christ? Have you sung,—

> " I sat down under His shadow,
> Sat down with great delight;
> His fruit was sweet unto my taste,
> And pleasant to my sight"?

This is as necessary an experience as it is joyful: necessary for many uses. The joy of the Lord is our strength, and it is when we delight ourselves in the Lord that we have assurance of power in prayer. Here faith develops, and hope grows bright, while love sheds abroad all the fragrance of her sweet spices. Oh! get you to the apple-tree, and find out who is the fairest among the fair. Make the Light of heaven the delight of your heart, and then be filled with heart's-ease, and revel in complete content.

III. The third view of the one subject is,—THE SHADOW OF HIS WINGS,—a precious word. I think the best specimen of it, for it occurs several times, is in that blessed Psalm, the sixty-third, verse seven :—

"*Because Thou hast been my help, therefore in the shadow of Thy wings will I rejoice.*"

Does not this set forth our Lord as *our trust in hours of depression?* In the Psalm now open before us, David was banished from the means of grace to a dry and thirsty land, where no water was. What is much worse, he was in a measure away from all conscious enjoyment of God. He says, " Early will I seek Thee. My soul thirsteth for Thee." He sings

rather of memories than of present communion with
God. We also have come into this condition, and
have been unable to find any present comfort. "Thou
hast been my help," has been the highest note we
could strike, and we have been glad to reach to that.
At such times, the light of God's face has been withdrawn, but our faith has taught us to rejoice under the
shadow of His wings. Light there was none; we
were altogether in the shade, but it was a warm shade.
We felt that God who had been near must be near us
still, and therefore we were quieted. Our God cannot
change, and therefore as He was our help He must
still be our help, our help even though He casts a
shadow over us, for it must be the shadow of His own
eternal wings. The metaphor is, of course, derived
from the nestling of little birds under the shadow of
their mother's wings, and the picture is singularly
touching and comforting. The little bird is not yet
able to take care of itself, so it cowers down under
the mother, and is there happy and safe. Disturb a
hen for a moment, and you will see all the little
chickens huddling together, and by their chirps
making a kind of song. Then they push their heads
into her feathers, and seem happy beyond measure
in their warm abode. When we are very sick and
sore depressed, when we are worried with the care of
pining children, and the troubles of a needy household, and the temptations of Satan, how comforting
it is to run to our God,—like the little chicks run to the
hen,—and hide away near His heart, beneath His
wings. Oh, tried ones, press closely to the loving
heart of your Lord, hide yourselves entirely beneath
His wings! Here awe has disappeared, and rest

itself is enhanced by the idea of loving **trust.** The little birds are safe in their mother's love, and we, too, are beyond measure secure and happy in the loving favour of the Lord.

IV. The last form of the shadow is that of THE HAND, and this, it seems to me, points to *power and position in service.* Turn to Isaiah xlix. 2 :—

" And He hath made my mouth like a sharp sword; in the shadow of His hand hath He hid me, and made me a polished shaft; in His quiver hath He hid me."

This undoubtedly refers to the Saviour, for the passage proceeds :—"And said unto me, Thou art my servant, O Israel, in whom I will be glorified. Then I said, I have laboured in vain, I have spent my strength for nought, and in vain : yet surely my judgment is with the Lord, and my work with my God. And now, saith the Lord that formed me from the womb to be His servant, to bring Jacob again to Him, though Israel be not gathered, yet shall I be glorious in the eyes of the Lord, and my God shall be my strength. And He said, It is a light thing that thou shouldest be My servant to raise up the tribes of Jacob, and to restore the preserved of Israel : I will also give thee for a light to the Gentiles, that thou mayest be My salvation unto the end of the earth." Our Lord Jesus Christ was hidden away in the hand of Jehovah, to be used by Him as a polished shaft for the overthrow of His enemies, and the victory of His people. Yet, inasmuch as it is Christ, it is also all Christ's servants, since as He is so are we also in this world ; and to make quite sure of it, we have the same expression in the sixteenth verse of the fifty-first chapter, where, speaking of His people, He says, " I have covered thee in the shadow of Mine hand." Is not this an excellent minister's text ? Every one of you who will speak a word for Jesus shall have a share in it. This is where those who are workers for Christ should long to be,—" in the shadow of His hand," to achieve His eternal purpose. What are any of God's servants without their Lord but weapons out of the warrior's hand, having no power to do anything ? We ought to be as the arrows of the Lord which He shoots at His enemies ; and so great is His hand of power, and so little are we as His instruments, that He hides us away in the hollow of His hand, unseen until He darts us forth. As workers, we are to be hidden away in the hand of God, or to quote the other figure, " in His quiver hath He hid me : " we are to be unseen till He uses us. It is impossible for us not to be known somewhat if the Lord uses us, but we may not aim at being noticed, but, on the contrary, if we be as much used as the very chief of the apostles, we must truthfully add, " though I be nothing." Our desire should be that Christ should be glorified, and that self should be concealed. Alas ! there is a way of always showing self in what we do, and we are all too ready to fall into it. You can visit the poor in such a way that they will feel that his lordship or her ladyship has condescended to call upon poor Betsy ; but there is another way of doing the same thing so that the tried child of God shall know that a brother beloved or a dear sister in Christ has shown a fellow-feeling for her, and has talked to her heart. There is a way of preaching, in which a great divine has evidently displayed his vast learning and talent ; and there is another way of preaching, in which a faithful servant of Jesus Christ, depending upon his Lord, has spoken in his Master's name, and left a rich unction behind. Within the hand of God is the place of acceptance, and safety; and for service it is the place of power, as well as of concealment. God only works with those who are in His hand; and the more we lie hidden there, the more surely will He use us ere long. May the Lord do unto us according to His word, "I have put My words in thy mouth, and I have covered thee in the shadow of My hand." In this case we shall feel all the former emotions combined: awe that the Lord should condescend to take us into His hand, rest and delight that He should deign to use us, trust that out of weakness we shall now be made strong, and to this will be added an absolute assurance that the end of our being must be answered, for that which is urged onward by the Almighty hand cannot miss its mark.

These are mere surface thoughts. The subject deserves a series of discourses. Your best course, my beloved friends, will be to enlarge upon these hints by a long personal experience of abiding under the shadow of the Almighty. May God the Holy Ghost lead you into it, and keep you there, for Jesus' sake!

UNDER THE APPLE TREE.

" I sat down under His shadow with great delight, and His fruit was sweet to my taste."—*Solomon's Song* ii. 3:

UNDER THE APPLE TREE.

CHRIST *known should be Christ used.* The spouse
knew her Beloved to be like a fruit-bearing tree,
and at once she sat under His shadow, and fed upon
His fruit. It is a pity that we know so much about
Christ, and yet enjoy Him so little. May our experience keep pace with our knowledge, and may that
experience be composed of a practical using of our
Lord! Jesus casts a shadow, let us sit under it : Jesus
yields fruit, let us taste the sweetness of it. Depend
upon it that the way to learn more is to use what you
know ; and, moreover, the way to learn a truth
thoroughly is to learn it experimentally. You know
a doctrine beyond all fear of contradiction when you
have proved it for yourself by personal test and trial.
The bride in the song as good as says, "I am certain
that my Beloved casts a shadow, for I have sat under
it, and I am persuaded that He bears sweet fruit, for I
have tasted of it." The best way of demonstrating
the power of Christ to save is to trust in Him and be
saved yourself ; and of all those who are sure of the
divinity of our holy faith, there are none so certain as
those who feel its divine power upon themselves. You
may reason yourself into a belief of the gospel, and
you may by further reasoning keep yourself orthodox ;
but a personal trial, and an inward knowing of the
truth, are incomparably the best evidences. If Jesus
be as an apple tree among the trees of the wood, do

not keep away from Him, but sit under His shadow, and taste His fruit. He is a Saviour; do not believe the fact and yet remain unsaved. As far as Christ is known to you, so far make use of Him. Is not this sound common-sense?

We would further remark that *we are at liberty to make every possible use of Christ.* Shadow and fruit may both be enjoyed. Christ in His infinite condescension exists for needy souls. Oh, let us say it over again: it is a bold word, but it is true,—as Christ Jesus, our Lord exists for the benefit of His people. A Saviour only exists to save. A physician lives to heal. The Good Shepherd lives, yea, dies, for His sheep. Our Lord Jesus Christ hath wrapped us about His heart; we are intimately interwoven with all His offices, with all His honours, with all His traits of character, with all that He has done, and with all that He has yet to do. The sinners' Friend lives for sinners, and sinners may have Him and use Him to the uttermost. He is as free to us as the air we breathe. What are fountains for, but that the thirsty may drink? What is the harbour for but that storm-tossed barques may there find refuge? What is Christ for but that poor guilty ones like ourselves may come to Him and look and live, and afterwards may have all our needs supplied out of His fulness?

We have thus the door set open for us, and we pray that the Holy Spirit may help us to enter in while we notice in the text two things which we pray that you may enjoy to the full. First, *the heart's rest in Christ:* "I sat down under His shadow with great delight." And, secondly, *the heart's refreshment in Christ:* "His fruit was sweet to my taste."

I. To begin with, we have here THE HEART'S REST IN CHRIST. To set this forth, let us notice the character of the person who uttered this sentence. She who said, "I sat down under His shadow with great delight," was one who *had known before what weary travel meant, and therefore valued rest ;* for the man who has never laboured knows nothing of the sweetness of repose. The loafer who has eaten bread he never earned, from whose brow there never oozed a drop of honest sweat, does not deserve rest, and knows not what it is. It is to the labouring man that rest is sweet ; and when at last we come, toilworn with many miles of weary plodding, to a shaded place where we may comfortably sit down, then are we filled with delight.

The spouse had been seeking her Beloved, and in looking for Him she had asked where she was likely to find Him. "Tell me," says she, "O Thou whom my soul loveth, where Thou feedest, where Thou makest Thy flock to rest at noon." The answer was given to her, "Go thy way forth by the footsteps of the flock." She did go her way ; but, after a while, she came to this resolution : "I will *sit down* under His shadow."

Many of you have been sorely wearied with going your way to find peace. Some of you tried cere- monies, and trusted in them, and the priest came to your help ; but he mocked your heart's distress. Others of you sought by various systems of thought to come to an anchorage ; but, tossed from billow to billow, you found no rest upon the seething sea of speculation. More of you tried by your good works to gain rest to your consciences. You multiplied

your prayers, you poured out floods of tears, you
hoped, by almsgiving and by the like, that some
merit might accrue to you, and that your heart might
feel acceptance with God, and so have rest. You
toiled and toiled, like the men that were in the vessel
with Jonah when they rowed hard to bring their ship
to land, but could not, for the sea wrought and was
tempestuous.   There was no escape for you that way,
and so you were driven to another way, even to rest
in Jesus. My heart looks back to the time when I
was under a sense of sin, and sought with all my soul
to find peace, but could not discover it, high or low,
in any place beneath the sky ; yet when "I saw one
hanging on a tree," as the Substitute for sin, then my
heart sat down under His shadow with great delight.
My heart reasoned thus with herself,—Did Jesus
suffer in my stead ? Then I shall not suffer. Did He
bear my sin ? Then I do not bear it. Did God
accept His Son as my Substitute ? Then He will
never smite *me*. Was Jesus acceptable with God as
my Sacrifice ? Then what contents the Lord may
well enough content me, and so I will go no farther,
but " sit down under His shadow," and enjoy a
delightful rest.

She who said, " I sat down under His shadow with
great delight," *could appreciate shade, for she had been
sunburnt.* Did we not read just now her exclamation,
—" Look not upon me, for I am black, because the
sun hath looked upon me "? She knew what heat
meant, what the burning sun meant ; and therefore
shade was pleasant to her. You know nothing
about the deliciousness of shade till you travel in a
thoroughly hot country ; then you are delighted with

it. Did you ever feel the heat of divine wrath ? **Did the great Sun**—that Sun without variableness or shadow of a turning—ever dart upon you His hottest rays,—the rays of his holiness and justice ? Did you cower down beneath the scorching beams of that great Light, and say, " We are consumed by Thine anger"? If you have ever felt *that*, you have found it a very blessed thing to come under the shadow of Christ's atoning sacrifice. A shadow, you know, is cast by a body coming between us and the light and heat ; and our Lord's most blessed body has come between us and the scorching sun of divine justice, so that we sit under the shadow of His mediation with great delight.

And now, if any other sun begins to scorch us, we fly to our Lord. If domestic trouble, or business care, or Satanic temptation, or inward corruption, oppresses us, we hasten to Jesus' shadow, to hide under Him, and there " sit down " in the cool refreshment with great delight. The interposition of our blessed Lord is the cause of our inward quiet. The sun cannot scorch *me*, for it scorched *Him*. My troubles need not trouble me, for He has taken my trouble, and I have left it in His hands. " I sat down under His shadow."

Mark well these two things concerning the spouse. She knew what it was to be weary, and she knew what it was to be sunburnt ; and just in proportion as you also know these two things, your valuation of Christ will rise. You who have never pined under the wrath of God have never prized the Saviour. Water is of small value in this land of brooks and rivers, and so you commonly sprinkle the roads with it ; but I warrant you that, if you were making a day's march over burning sand, a cup of cold water would be worth a king's ransom ; and so to thirsty souls Christ is precious, but to none beside.

Now, when the spouse was sitting down, restful and delighted, *she was overshadowed.* She says, " I sat down *under His shadow.*" I do not know a more delightful state of mind than to feel quite overshadowed by our beloved Lord. Here is my black sin, but there is His precious blood overshadowing my sin, and hiding it for ever. Here is my condition by nature, an enemy to God ; but He who reconciled me to God by His blood has overshadowed that also, so that I forget that I was once an enemy in the joy of being now a friend. I am very weak ; but He is strong, and His strength overshadows my feebleness. I am very poor ; but He hath all riches, and His riches overshadow my poverty. I am most unworthy ; but He is so worthy that if I use His name I shall receive as much as if I were worthy : His worthiness doth overshadow my unworthiness. It is very precious to put the truth the other way, and say,— If there be anything good in me, it is not good when I compare myself with Him, for His goodness quite eclipses and overshadows it. Can I say I love Him ? So I do, but I hardly dare call it love, for His love overshadows it. Did I suppose that I served Him ? So I would ; but my poor service is not worth mentioning in comparison with what He has done for me. Did I think I had any degree of holiness ? I must not deny what His Spirit works in me ; but when I think of His immaculate life, and all His divine perfections, where am I ? What am I ? Have you not sometimes felt this ? Have you not been so over-

shadowed and hidden under your Lord that you
became as nothing? I know myself what it is to feel
that if I die in a workhouse it does not matter so long
as my Lord is glorified. Mortals may cast out my
name as evil, if they like; but what matters it since
His dear name shall one day be printed in stars
athwart the sky? Let Him overshadow me; I
delight that it should be so.

The spouse tells us that, when she became quite
overshadowed, then. *she felt great delight*. Great "*I*"
never has great delight, for it cannot bear to own a
greater than itself, but the humble believer finds his
delight in being overshadowed by his Lord. In the
shade of Jesus we have more delight than in any
fancied light of our own. The spouse had *great*
delight. I trust that you Christian people do have
great delight; and if not, you ought to ask yourselves
whether you really are the people of God. I like to
see a cheerful countenance; ay, and to hear of raptures
in the hearts of those who are God's saints! There
are people who seem to think that religion and gloom
are married, and must never be divorced. Pull down
the blinds on Sunday, and darken the rooms; if you
have a garden, or a rose in flower, try to forget that
there are such beauties: are you not to serve God as
dolorously as you can? Put your book under your
arm, and crawl to your place of worship in as mournful a manner as if you were being marched to the
whipping-post. Act thus if you will; but give me
that religion which cheers my heart, fires my soul, and
fills me with enthusiasm and delight,—for that is
likely to be the religion of heaven, and it agrees with
the experience of the Inspired Song.

Although I trust that we know what delight means, I question if we have enough of it to describe ourselves as *sitting down* in the enjoyment of it. Do you give yourselves enough time to sit at Jesus' feet? *There* is the place of delight, do you abide in it? Sit down under His shadow. " I have no leisure," cries one. Try and make a little. Steal it from your sleep if you cannot get it anyhow else. Grant leisure to your heart. It would be a great pity if a man never spent five minutes with his wife, but was forced to be always hard at work. Why, that is slavery, is it not? Shall we not then have time to commune with our Best-beloved? Surely, somehow or other, we can squeeze out a little season in which we shall have nothing else to do but to sit down under His shadow with great delight! When I take my Bible, and want to feed on it for myself, I generally get thinking about preaching upon the text, and what I should say to you from it. This will not do; I must get away from that, and forget that there is a Tabernacle, that I may sit personally at Jesus' feet. And, oh, there is an intense delight in being overshadowed by Him! He is near you, and you know it. His dear presence is as certainly with you as if you could see Him, for His influence surrounds you.

Often have I felt as if Jesus leaned over me, as a friend might look over my shoulder. Although no cool shade comes over your brow, yet you may as much feel His shadow as if it did, for your heart grows calm; and if you have been wearied with the family, or troubled with the church, or vexed with yourself, you come down from the chamber where you have seen your Lord, and you feel braced for the battle of life, ready for its troubles and its temptations, because you have seen the Lord. "I sat down," said she, "under His shadow with *great delight.*" How great that delight was she could not tell, but she sat down as one overpowered with it, needing to sit still under the load of bliss. I do not like to talk much about the secret delights of Christians, because there are always some around us who do not understand our meaning; but I will venture to say this much— that if worldlings could but even guess what are the secret joys of believers, they would give their eyes to share with us. We have troubles, and we admit it, we expect to have them; but we have joys which are frequently excessive. We should not like that others should be witnesses of the delight which now and then tosses our soul into a very tempest of joy. You know what it means, do you not? When you have been quite alone with the heavenly Bridegroom, you wanted to tell the angels of the sweet love of Christ to you, a poor unworthy one. You even wished to teach the golden harps fresh music, for seraphs know not the heights and depths of the grace of God as you know them.

The spouse had great delight, and we know that she had, for this one reason, that *she did not forget it.* This verse and the whole Song are a remembrance of what she had enjoyed. She says, "I sat down under His shadow." It may have been a month, it may have been years ago; but she had not forgotten it. The joys of fellowship with God are written in marble. "Engraved as in eternal brass" are memories of communion with Christ Jesus. "Above fourteen years ago," says the apostle, "I knew a man." Ah, it was worth remembering all those years! He had not told his delight, but he had kept it stored up. He says, " I knew a man in Christ above fourteen years ago (whether in the body, I cannot tell ; or whether out of the body, I cannot tell :) " so great had his delights been. When we look back, we forget birthdays, holidays, and bonfire-nights which we have spent after the manner of men, but we readily recall our times of fellowship with the Well-beloved. We have known our Tabors, our times of transfiguration-fellowship, and like Peter we remember when we were "with Him in the holy mount." Our head has leaned upon the Master's bosom, and we can never forget the intense delight ; nor will we fail to put on record for the good of others the joys with which we have been indulged.

Now I leave this first part of the subject, only noticing how beautifully natural it is. There was a tree, and she sat down under the shadow : there was nothing strained, nothing formal. So ought true piety ever to be consistent with common-sense, with that which seems most fitting, most comely, most wise, and most natural. There is Christ, we may enjoy Him, let us not despise the privilege.

II. The second part of our subject is, THE HEART'S REFRESHMENT IN CHRIST. " His fruit was sweet to my taste." Here I will not enlarge, but give you thoughts in brief which you can beat out afterwards. *She did not feast upon the fruit of the tree till first she was under the shadow of it.* There is no knowing the excellent things of Christ till you trust Him. Not a single sweet apple shall fall to the lot of those who are outside the shadow. Come and trust Christ, and

then all that there is in Christ shall be enjoyed by
you. O unbelievers, what you miss! If you will
but sit down under His shadow, you shall have all
things; but if you will not, neither shall any good
thing of Christ's be yours.

*But as soon as ever she was under the shadow, then
the fruit was all hers.* "I sat down under His
shadow," saith she, and then, "His fruit was sweet to
my taste." Dost thou believe in Jesus, friend? Then
Jesus Christ Himself is thine; and if thou dost own
the tree, thou mayest well eat the fruit. Since He
Himself becomes thine altogether, then His redemption
and the pardon that comes of it, His living power,
His mighty intercession, the glories of His Second
Advent, and all that belong to Him are made over to
thee for thy personal and present use and enjoyment.
All things are yours, since Christ is yours. Only
mind you imitate the spouse: *when she found that the
fruit was hers, she ate it.* Copy her closely in this.
It is a great fault in many believers, that they do not
appropriate the promises, and feed on them. Do not
err as they do. Under the shadow you have a right
to eat the fruit. Deny not yourselves the sacred
entertainment.

Now, it would appear, as we read the text, that
she obtained this fruit without effort. The proverb
says, "He who would gain the fruit must climb the
tree." But she did not climb, for she says, "I sat
down under His shadow." I suppose the fruit dropped
down to her. I know that it is so with us. We no
longer spend our money for that which is not bread,
and our labour for that which satisfieth not; but we
sit under our Lord's shadow, and we eat that which

is good, and our soul delights itself in sweetness.
Come Christian, enter into the calm rest of faith, by
sitting down beneath the cross, and thou shalt be fed
even to the full.

The spouse rested while feasting : she sat and ate.
So, O true believer, rest whilst thou art feeding upon
Christ! The spouse says, "I sat, and I ate." Had
she not told us in the former chapter that the King
sat at His table? See how like the Church is to her
Lord, and the believer to his Saviour! We sit down
also, and we eat, even as the King doth. Right
royally are we entertained. His joy is in us, and
His peace keeps our hearts and minds.

Further, notice that, _as the spouse fed upon this fruit,
she had a relish for it._ It is not every palate that
likes every fruit. Never dispute with other people
about tastes of any sort, for agreement is not possible.
That dainty which to one person is the most delicious
is to another nauseous ; and if there were a com-
petition as to which fruit is preferable to all the rest,
there would probably be almost as many opinions as
there are fruits. But blessed is he who hath a relish
for Christ Jesus! Dear hearer, is He sweet to you?
Then He is yours. There never was a heart that did
relish Christ but what Christ belonged to that heart.
If thou hast been feeding on Him, and He is sweet to
thee, go on feasting, for He who gave thee a relish
gives thee Himself to satisfy thine appetite.

What are the fruits which come from Christ? Are
they not peace with God, renewal of heart, joy in the
Holy Ghost, love to the brethren? Are they not
regeneration, justification, sanctification, adoption, and
all the blessings of the covenant of grace? And are

they not each and all sweet to our taste? As we have fed upon them, have we not said, "Yes, these things are pleasant indeed. There is none like them. Let us live upon them evermore"? Now, sit down, sit down and feed. It seems a strange thing that we should have to persuade people to do that, but in the spiritual world things are very different from what they are in the natural. In the case of most men, if you put a joint of meat before them, and a knife and fork, they do not need many arguments to persuade them to fall to. But I will tell you when they will not do it, and that is when they are full: and I will also tell you when they will do it, and that is when they are hungry. Even so, if thy soul is weary after Christ the Saviour, thou wilt feed on Him; but if not, it is useless for me to preach to thee, or bid thee come. However, thou that art there, sitting under His shadow, thou mayest hear Him utter these words : " Eat, O friend : drink, yea, drink abundantly." Thou canst not have too much of these good things : the more of Christ, the better the Christian.

We know that the spouse feasted herself right heartily with this food from the tree of life, for *in after days she wanted more*. Will you kindly read on in the fourth verse? The verse which contains our text describes, as it were, her first love to her Lord, her country love, her rustic love. She went to the wood, and she found Him there like an apple tree, and she enjoyed Him as one relishes a ripe apple in the country. But she grew in grace, she learned more of her Lord, and she found that her Best-beloved was a King. I should not wonder but what she learned the doctrine of the Second Advent, for then she began to sing, "He brought me to the banqueting house." As much as to say,—He did not merely let me know Him out in the fields as the Christ in His humiliation, but He brought me into the royal palace; and, since He is a King, He brought forth a banner with His own brave escutcheon, and He waved it over me while I was sitting at the table, and the motto of that banneret was love.

She grew very full of this. It was such a grand thing to find a great Saviour, a triumphant Saviour, an exalted Saviour! But it was too much for her, and she became sick of soul with the excessive glory of what she had learned; and do you see what her heart craves for? She longs for her first simple joys, those countrified delights. "Comfort me with apples," she says. Nothing but the old joys will revive her. Did you ever feel like that? I have been satiated with delight in the love of Christ as a glorious exalted Saviour when I have seen Him riding on His white horse, and going forth conquering and to conquer; I have been overwhelmed when I have beheld Him in the midst of the throne, with all the brilliant assembly of angels and archangels adoring Him, and my thought has gone forward to the day when He shall descend with all the pomp of God, and make all kings and princes shrink into nothingness before the infinite majesty of His glory. Then I have felt as though, at the sight of Him, I must fall at His feet as dead; and I have wanted somebody to come and tell me over again "the old, old story" of how He died in order that I might be saved. His throne overpowers me, let me gather fruit from His cross. Bring me apples from "the tree" again. I am awe-struck while in the palace, let me get away to the woods again. Give me an apple plucked from the tree, such as I have given out to boys and girls in His family, such an apple as this, "Come unto Me all ye that labour and are heavy laden, and I will give you rest." Or this: "This man receiveth sinners." Give me a promise from the basket of the covenant. Give me the simplicity of Christ, let me be a child and feast on apples again, if Jesus be the apple tree. I would fain go back to Christ on the tree in my stead, Christ overshadowing me, Christ feeding me. This is the happiest state to live in. Lord, evermore give us these apples! You recollect the old story we told, years ago, of Jack the huckster who used to sing,—

> "I'm a poor sinner, and nothing at all,
>   But Jesus Christ is my all in all."

Those who knew him were astonished at his constant composure. They had a world of doubts and fears, and so they asked him why he never doubted. "Well," said he, "I can't doubt but what I am a poor sinner, and nothing at all, for I know that, and feel it every day. And why should I doubt that Jesus Christ is my all in all? for He says He is." "Oh!" said his questioner, "I have my ups and downs." "I don't," says Jack; "I can never go up, for I am a poor sinner, and nothing at all; and I cannot go down, for Jesus Christ is my all in all." He wanted to join the church, and they said he must tell his experience. He said, "All my experience is that I am a poor sinner, and nothing at all, and Jesus Christ is my all in all." "Well," they said, "when you come before the church-meeting, the minister may ask you questions." "I can't help it," said Jack, "all I know I will tell you ; and that is all I know,—

> "' I'm a poor sinner, and nothing at all,
>   But Jesus Christ is my all in all.' "

He was admitted into the church, and continued with the brethren, walking in holiness ; but that was still all his experience, and you could not get him beyond it. "Why," said one brother, "I sometimes feel so full of grace, I feel so advanced in sanctification, that I begin to be very happy." "I never do," said Jack ; "I am a poor sinner, and nothing at all." "But then," said the other, "I go down again, and think I am not saved, because I am not as sanctified as I used to be." "But I never doubt my salvation," said Jack, "because Jesus Christ is my all in all, and He never alters." That simple story is grandly instructive, for it sets forth a plain man's faith in a plain salvation ; it is the likeness of a soul under the apple tree, resting in the shade, and feasting on the fruit.

Now, at this time I want you to think of Jesus, not as a Prince, but as an apple tree ; and when this is done, I pray you to *sit down under His shadow.* It is not much to do. Any child, when it is hot, can sit down in a shadow. I want you next to feed on Jesus : any simpleton can eat apples when they are ripe upon the tree. Come and take Christ, then. You who never came before, come now. Come and welcome. You who have come often, and have entered into the palace, and are reclining at the banqueting table, you lords and peers of Christianity, come to the common wood and to the common apple tree where poor saints are shaded and fed. You had better come under the apple tree, like poor sinners such as I am, and be once more shaded with boughs and comforted with apples, for else you may faint beneath the palace glories. The best of saints are never better than when they eat their first fare, and are comforted with the apples which were their first gospel feast.

The Lord Himself bring forth His own sweet fruit to you! Amen.

OVER THE MOUNTAINS.

"My Beloved is mine, and I am His: He feedeth among the lilies. Until the day break, and the shadows flee away, turn, my Beloved, and be Thou like a roe or a young hart upon the mountains of Bether."—*Solomon's Song* ii. 16, 17.

OVER THE MOUNTAINS.

IT may be that there are saints who are always at
their best, and are happy enough never to lose
the light of their Father's countenance. I am not
sure that there are such persons, for those believers
with whom I have been most intimate have had a
varied experience; and those whom I have known,
who have boasted of their constant perfectness, have
not been the most reliable of individuals. I hope
there is a spiritual region attainable where there are
no clouds to hide the Sun of our soul; but I cannot
speak with positiveness, for I have not traversed that
happy land. Every year of my life has had a winter
as well as a summer, and every day its night. I have
hitherto seen clear shinings and heavy rains, and felt
warm breezes and fierce winds. Speaking for the
many of my brethren, I confess that though the
substance be in us, as in the teil-tree and the oak, yet
we do lose our leaves, and the sap within us does not
flow with equal vigour at all seasons. We have our
downs as well as our ups, our valleys as well as our
hills. We are not always rejoicing; we are sometimes in heaviness through manifold trials. Alas! we
are grieved to confess that our fellowship with the
Well-beloved is not always that of rapturous delight;
but we have at times to seek Him, and cry, "Oh, that
I knew where I might find Him!" This appears to

me to have been in a measure the condition of the
spouse when she cried, "Until the day break, and the
shadows flee away, turn, my Beloved."

I   These words teach us, first, that COMMUNION
MAY BE BROKEN. The spouse had lost the company
of her Bridegroom : conscious communion with Him
was gone, though she loved her Lord, and sighed for
Him. In her loneliness she was sorrowful ; but *she
had by no means ceased to love Him,* for she calls Him
her Beloved, and speaks as one who felt no doubt
upon that point. Love to the Lord Jesus may be
quite as true, and perhaps quite as strong, when we
sit in darkness as when we walk in the light. Nay,
she had not lost her assurance of His love to her, and of
their mutual interest in one another ; for she says,
"My Beloved is mine, and I am His ;" and yet she
adds, "Turn, my Beloved." The condition of our
graces does not always coincide with the state of our
joys. We may be rich in faith and love, and yet have
so low an esteem of ourselves as to be much depressed.

It is plain, from this Sacred Canticle, that the spouse
may love and be loved, may be confident in her Lord,
and be fully assured of her possession of Him, and
yet there may for the present be mountains between
her and Him. Yes, we may even be far advanced in
the divine life, and yet be exiled for a while from
conscious fellowship. There are nights for men as
well as babes, and the strong know that the sun is
hidden quite as well as do the ·sick and the feeble.
Do not, therefore, condemn yourself, my brother,
because a cloud is over you ; cast not away your
confidence ; but the rather let faith burn up in the
gloom, and let your love resolve to come at your

Lord again whatever be the barriers which divide you from Him.

When Jesus is absent from a true heir of heaven, sorrow will ensue. The healthier our condition, the sooner will that absence be perceived, and the more deeply will it be lamented. This sorrow is described in the text as darkness; this is implied in the expression, "*Until the day break.*" Till Christ appears, no day has dawned for us. We dwell in midnight darkness; the stars of the promises and the moon of experience yield no light of comfort till our Lord, like the sun, arises and ends the night. We must have Christ with us, or we are benighted : we grope like blind men for the wall, and wander in dismay.

The spouse also speaks of shadows. "Until the day break, *and the shadows flee away.*" Shadows are multiplied by the departure of the sun, and these are apt to distress the timid. We are not afraid of real enemies when Jesus is with us ; but when we miss Him, we tremble at a shade. How sweet is that song, "Yea, though I walk through the valley of the shadow of death, I will fear no evil : for Thou art with me ; Thy rod and Thy staff they comfort me ! " But we change our note when midnight is now come, and Jesus is not with us : then we people the night with terrors : spectres, demons, hobgoblins, and things that never existed save in fancy, are apt to swarm about us ; and we are in fear where no fear is.

The spouse's worst trouble was that *the back of her Beloved was turned to her*, and so she cried, "Turn, my Beloved." When His face is towards her, she suns herself in His love ; but if the light of His countenance is withdrawn, she is sorely troubled. Our Lord turns His face from His people though He never turns His heart from His people. He may even close His eyes in sleep when the vessel is tossed by the tempest, but His heart is awake all the while. Still, it is pain enough to have grieved Him in any degree : it cuts us to the quick to think that we have wounded His tender heart. He is jealous, but never without cause. If He turns His back upon us for a while, He has doubtless a more than sufficient reason. He would not walk contrary to us if we had not walked contrary to Him. Ah, it is sad work this! The presence of the Lord makes this life the preface to the life celestial ; but His absence leaves us pining and fainting, neither doth any comfort remain in the land of our banishment. The Scriptures and the ordinances, private devotion and public worship, are all as sun-dials,—most excellent when the sun shines, but of small avail in the dark. O Lord Jesus, nothing can compensate us for Thy loss! Draw near to Thy beloved yet again, for without Thee our night will never end.

> " See ! I repent, and vex my soul,
> That I should leave Thee so !
> Where will those vile affections roll
> That let my Saviour go ? "

When communion with Christ is broken, in all true hearts *there is a strong desire to win it back again.* The man who has known the joy of communion with Christ, if he loses it, will never be content until it is restored. Hast thou ever entertained the Prince Emmanuel ? Is He gone elsewhere ? Thy chamber will be dreary till He comes back again. "Give me

Christ or else I die," is the cry of every spirit that
has lost the dear companionship of Jesus. We do
not part with such heavenly delights without many a
pang. It is not with us a matter of " maybe He will
return, and we hope He will ; " but it must be, or we
faint and die. We cannot live without Him ; and this
is a cheering sign ; for the soul that cannot live
without Him shall not live without Him : He comes
speedily where life and death hang on His coming.
If you must have Christ you shall have Him. This is
just how the matter stands : we must drink of this
well or die of thirst ; we must feed upon Jesus or our
spirit will famish.

II. We will now advance a step, and say that
when communion with Christ is broken, THERE ARE
GREAT DIFFICULTIES IN THE WAY OF ITS RENEWAL.
It is much easier to go down hill than to climb to the
same height again. It is far easier to lose joy in God
than to find the lost jewel. The spouse speaks of
"mountains" dividing her from her Beloved : she
means that *the difficulties were great.* They were not
little hills, but mountains, that closed up her way.
Mountains of remembered sin, Alps of backsliding,
dread ranges of forgetfulness, ingratitude, worldliness,
coldness in prayer, frivolity, pride, unbelief. Ah me,
I cannot teach you all the dark geography of this
sad experience ! Giant walls rose before her like the
towering steeps of Lebanon. How could she come at
her Beloved ?

The dividing difficulties were many as well as great.
She does not speak of " a mountain", but of
"mountains" : Alps rose on Alps, wall after wall. She
was distressed to think that in so short a time so

much could come between her and Him of whom she sang just now, " His left hand is under my head, and His right hand doth embrace me." Alas, we multiply these mountains of Bether with a sad rapidity! Our Lord is jealous, and we give Him far too much reason for hiding His face. A fault, which seemed so small at the time we committed it, is seen in the light of its own consequences, and then it grows and swells till it towers aloft, and hides the face of the Beloved. Then has our sun gone down, and fear whispers, " Will His light ever return ? Will it ever be day-break ? Will the shadows ever flee away ?" It is easy to grieve away the heavenly sunlight, but ah, how hard to clear the skies, and regain the unclouded brightness !

Perhaps the worst thought of all to the spouse was the dread that *the dividing barrier might be permanent.* It was high, but it might dissolve ; the walls were many, but they might fall ; but, alas, they were mountains, and these stand fast for ages! She felt like the Psalmist, when he cried, " My sin is ever before me." The pain of our Lord's absence becomes intolerable when we fear that we are hopelessly shut out from Him. A night one can bear, hoping for the morning ; but what if the day should never break ? And you and I, if we have wandered away from Christ, and feel that there are ranges of immovable mountains between Him and us, will feel sick at heart. We try to pray, but devotion dies on our lips. We attempt to approach the Lord at the communion-table, but we feel more like Judas than John. At such times we have felt that we would give our eyes once more to behold the Bridegroom's face, and to know that He delights in us as in happier days. Still there stand the awful mountains, black, threatening, impassable ; and in the far-off land the Life of our life is away, and grieved.

So the spouse seems to have come to the conclusion that *the difficulties in her way were insurmountable by her own power.* She does not even think of herself going over the mountains to her Beloved, but she cries, " Until the day break, and the shadows flee away, turn, my Beloved, and be Thou like a roe or a young hart upon the mountains of Bether." She will not try to climb the mountains, she knows she cannot : if they had been less high, she might have attempted it ; but their summits reach to heaven. If they had been less craggy or difficult, she might have tried to scale them ; but these mountains are terrible, and no foot may stand upon their lone crags. Oh, the mercy of utter self-despair ! I love to see a soul driven into that close corner, and forced therefore to look to God alone. The end of the creature is the beginning of the Creator. Where the sinner ends the Saviour begins. If the mountains can be climbed, we shall have to climb them ; but if they are quite impassable, then the soul cries out with the prophet, " Oh, that Thou wouldest rend the heavens, that Thou wouldest come down, that the mountains might flow down at Thy presence. As when the melting fire burneth, the fire causeth the waters to boil, to make Thy name known to Thine adversaries, that the nations may tremble at Thy presence. When Thou didst terrible things which we looked not for, Thou camest down, the mountains flowed down at Thy presence." Our souls are lame, they cannot move to Christ, and lo !

we turn our strong desires to Him, and fix our hopes alone upon Him ; will He not remember us in love, and fly to us as He did to His servant of old when He rode upon a cherub, and did fly, yea, He did fly upon the wings of the wind ?

III. Here arises THAT PRAYER OF THE TEXT WHICH FULLY MEETS THE CASE. " Turn, my Beloved, and be Thou like a roe or a young hart upon the mountains of division." Jesus can come to us when we cannot go to Him. The roe and the young hart, or, as you may read it, the gazelle and the ibex, live among the crags of the mountains, and leap across the abyss with amazing agility. For swiftness and sure-footedness they are unrivalled. The sacred poet said, " He maketh my feet like hinds' feet, and setteth me upon my high places," alluding to the feet of those creatures which are so fitted to stand securely on the mountain's side. Our blessed Lord is called, in the title of the twenty-second Psalm, "the Hind of the morning " ; and the spouse in this golden Canticle sings, " My Beloved is like a roe or a young hart ; behold He cometh, leaping upon the mountains, skipping upon the hills."

Here I would remind you that this prayer is one that we may fairly offer, because *it is the way of Christ to come to us* when our coming to Him is out of the question. " How ? " say you. I answer that of old He did this ; for we remember " His great love wherewith He loved us even when we were dead in trespasses and in sins." His first coming into the world in human form, was it not because man could never come to God until God had come to him ? I hear of no tears, or prayers, or entreaties after God on the part of our first parents; but the offended Lord spontaneously gave the promise that the Seed of the woman should bruise the serpent's head. Our Lord's coming into the world was unbought, unsought, unthought of; he came altogether of His own free will, delighting to redeem.

> " With pitying eyes, the Prince of grace
>   Beheld our helpless grief ;
>   He saw, and (oh, amazing love !)
>   He ran to our relief."

His incarnation was a type of the way in which He comes to us by His Spirit. He saw us cast out, polluted, shameful, perishing; and as He passed by, His tender lips said, "Live!" In us is fulfilled that word, "I am found of them that sought Me not." We were too averse to holiness, too much in bondage to sin, ever to have returned to Him if He had not turned to us. What think you? Did He come to us when we were enemies, and will He not visit us now that we are friends? Did He come to us when we were dead sinners, and will He not hear us now that we are weeping saints? If Christ's coming to the earth was after this manner, and if His coming to each one of us was after this style, we may well hope that now He will come to us in like fashion, like the dew which refreshes the grass, and waiteth not for man, neither tarrieth for the sons of men. Besides, He is coming again in person, .in the latter-day, and mountains of sin, and error, and idolatry, and superstition, and oppression stand in the way of His kingdom ; but He will surely come and overturn, and overturn, till He shall reign over all. He will come in the latter-days, I say, though He shall leap the hills

to do it, and because of that I am sure we may
comfortably conclude that He will draw near to us
who mourn His absence so bitterly. Then let us bow
our heads a moment, and silently present to His most
excellent Majesty the petition of our text: " Turn,
my Beloved, and be Thou like a roe or a young hart
upon the mountains of division."

Our text gives us sweet assurance that *our Lord is
at home with those difficulties* which are quite
insurmountable by us. Just as the roe or the young
hart knows the passes of the mountains, and the
stepping-places among the rugged rocks, and is void
of all fear among the ravines and the precipices, so
does our Lord know the heights and depths, the
torrents and the caverns of our sin and sorrow. He
carried the whole of our transgression, and so became
aware of the tremendous load of our guilt. He is quite
at home with the infirmities of our nature ; He knew
temptation in the wilderness, heart-break in the
garden, desertion on the cross. He is quite at home
with pain and weakness, for " Himself took our
infirmities, and bare our sicknesses." He is at home
with despondency, for He was " a Man of sorrows, and
acquainted with grief." He is at home even with
death, for He gave up the ghost, and passed through
the sepulchre to resurrection. O yawning gulfs and
frowning steeps of woe, our Beloved, like hind or hart,
has traversed your glooms ! O my Lord, Thou
knowest all that divides me from Thee ; and Thou
knowest also that I am far too feeble to climb these
dividing mountains, so that I may come at Thee ;
therefore, I pray Thee, come Thou over the mountains
to meet my longing spirit ! Thou knowest each

yawning gulf and slippery steep, but none of these can stay Thee ; haste Thou to me, Thy servant, Thy beloved, and let me again live by Thy presence.

It is easy, too, for Christ to come over the mountains for our relief. It is easy for the gazelle to cross the mountains, it is made for that end ; so is it easy for Jesus, for to this purpose was He ordained from of old that He might come to man in his worst estate, and bring with Him the Father's love. What is it that separates us from Christ ? Is it a sense of sin ? You have been pardoned once, and Jesus can renew most vividly a sense of full forgiveness. But you say, " Alas ! I have sinned again : fresh guilt alarms me." He can remove it in an instant, for the fountain appointed for that purpose is opened, and is still full. It is easy for the dear lips of redeeming love to put away the child's offences, since He has already obtained pardon for the criminal's iniquities. If with His heart's blood He won our pardon from our Judge, he can easily enough bring us the forgiveness of our Father. Oh, yes, it is easy enough for Christ to say again, "Thy sins be forgiven " ! " But I feel so unfit, so unable to enjoy communion." He that healed all manner of bodily diseases can heal with a word your spiritual infirmities. Remember the man whose ankle-bones received strength, so that he ran and leaped ; and her who was sick of a fever, and was healed at once, and arose, and ministered unto her Lord. " My grace is sufficient for thee ; for My strength is made perfect in weakness." " But I have such afflictions, such troubles, such sorrows, that I am weighted down, and cannot rise into joyful fellow-ship." Yes, but Jesus can make every burden light,

and cause each yoke to be easy. Your trials can be
made to aid your heavenward course instead of
hindering it. I know all about those heavy weights,
and I perceive that you cannot lift them ; but skilful
engineers can adapt ropes and pulleys in such a way
that heavy weights lift other weights. The Lord
Jesus is great at gracious machinery, and He has the
art of causing a weight of tribulation to lift from us a
load of spiritual deadness, so that we ascend by that
which, like a millstone, threatened to sink us down.

What else doth hinder? I am sure that, if it were a
sheer impossibility, the Lord Jesus could remove it,
for things impossible with men are possible with God.
But someone objects, " I am so unworthy of Christ.
I can understand eminent saints and beloved
disciples being greatly indulged, but I am a worm,
and no man ; utterly below such condescension."
Say you so? Know you not that the worthiness of
Christ covers your unworthiness, and He is made of
God unto you wisdom, righteousness, sanctification,
and redemption? In Christ, the Father thinks not so
meanly of you as you think of yourself ; you are not
worthy to be called His child, but He does call you
so, and reckons you to be among His jewels. Listen,
and you shall hear Him say, " Since thou wast precious
in My sight, thou hast been honourable, and I have
loved thee. I gave Egypt for thy ransom ; Ethiopia
and Seba for thee." Thus, then, there remains
nothing which Jesus cannot overleap if He resolves to come to you, and re-establish your broken
fellowship.

To conclude, *our Lord can do all this directly*. As
in the twinkling of an eye the dead shall be raised

incorruptible, so in a moment can our dead affections
rise to fulness of delight. He can say to this
mountain, "Be thou removed hence, and be thou cast
into the midst of the sea," and it shall be done. In
the sacred emblems now upon this supper table, Jesus
is already among us. Faith cries, "He has come!"
Like John the Baptist, she gazes intently on Him, and
cries, "Behold the Lamb of God!" At this table
Jesus feeds us with His body and His blood. His
corporeal presence we have not, but His real spiritual
presence we perceive. We are like the disciples
when none of them durst ask Him, "Who art Thou?"
knowing that it was the Lord. He is come. He
looketh forth at these windows,—I mean this bread
and wine; showing Himself through the lattices of
this instructive and endearing ordinance. He speaks.
He saith, "The winter is past, the rain is over and
gone." And so it is; we feel it to be so: a heavenly
springtide warms our frozen hearts. Like the spouse,
we wonderingly cry, "Or ever I was aware, my soul
made me like the chariots of Ammi-nadib." Now in
happy fellowship we see the Beloved, and hear His
voice; our heart burns; our affections glow; we are
happy, restful, brimming over with delight. The
King has brought us into his banqueting-house, and
His banner over us is love. It is good to be here!

Friends, we must now go our ways. A voice saith,
"Arise, let us go hence." O Thou Lord of our hearts,
go with us! Home will not be home without Thee.
Life will not be life without Thee. Heaven itself
would not be heaven if Thou wert absent. Abide
with us. The world grows dark, the gloaming of time
draws on. Abide with us, for it is toward evening

Our years increase, and we near the night when dews fall cold and chill. A great future is all about us, the splendours of the last age are coming down; and while we wait in solemn, awe-struck expectation, our heart continually cries within herself, " Until the day break, and the shadows flee away, turn, my Beloved, and be Thou like a roe or a young hart upon the mountains of division."

> " Hasten, Lord ! the promised hour ;
> Come in glory and in power ;
> Still Thy foes are unsubdued ;
> Nature sighs to be renew'd.
> Time has nearly reach'd its sum,
> All things with Thy bride say ' Come ;'
> Jesus, whom all worlds adore,
> Come and reign for evermore ! "

FRAGRANT SPICES FROM THE MOUNTAINS OF MYRRH.

" Thou art all fair, My love ; there is no spot in thee."—*Solomon's Song* iv. 7.

FRAGRANT SPICES FROM THE MOUNTAINS OF MYRRH.

HOW marvellous are these words! "Thou art all fair, My love; there is no spot in thee." The glorious Bridegroom is charmed with His spouse, and sings soft canticles of admiration. When the bride extols her Lord there is no wonder, for He deserves it well, and in Him there is room for praise without possibility of flattery. But does He who is wiser than Solomon condescend to praise this sunburnt Shulamite? 'Tis even so, for these are His own words, and were uttered by His own sweet lips. Nay, doubt not, O young believer, for we have more wonders to reveal! There are greater depths in heavenly things than thou hast at present dared to hope. The Church not only *is* all fair in the eyes of her Beloved, but in one sense she always was so.

> "In God's decree, her form He view'd;
> All beauteous in His eyes she stood,
> Presented by Th' eternal name,
> Betroth'd in love, and free from blame.

> "Not as she stood in Adam's fall,
> When guilt and ruin cover'd all;
> But as she'll stand another day,
> Fairer than sun's meridian ray."

He delighted in her before she had either a natural or a spiritual being, and from the beginning could

He say, "My delights were with the sons of men."
(Prov. viii. 31.)   Having covenanted to be the Surety
of the elect, and having determined to fulfil every
stipulation of that covenant, He from all eternity
delighted to survey the purchase of His blood, and
rejoiced . to view His Church, in the purpose and
decree, as already by Him delivered from sin, and
exalted to glory and happiness.

> " Oh, glorious grace, mysterious plan
>   Too great for angel-mind to scan,
>   Our thoughts are lost, our numbers fail ;
>   All hail, redeeming love, all hail ! "

Now with joy and gladness let us approach the
subject of Christ's delight in His Church, as declared
by Him whom the Spirit has sealed in our hearts
as the faithful and true Witness.

Our first bundle of myrrh lies in the open hand
of the text.

I. CHRIST HAS A HIGH ESTEEM FOR HIS CHURCH.
He does not blindly admire her faults, or even conceal
them from Himself.   He is acquainted with her sin,
in all its heinousness of guilt, and desert of punishment.   That sin He does not shun to reprove.   His
own words are, "As many as I love, I rebuke and
chasten."   (Rev. iii. 19.)   He abhors sin in her as
much as in the ungodly world, nay even more, for
He sees in her an evil which is not to be found in the
transgressions of others,—sin against love and grace.
She is black in her own sight, how much more so in
the eyes of her Omniscient Lord !   Yet there it
stands, written by the inspiration of the Holy Spirit,
and flowing from the lips of the Bridegroom, " Thou
art all fair, My love ; there is no spot in thee."

How then is this? Is it a mere exaggeration of love, an enthusiastic canticle, which the sober hand of truth must strip of its glowing fables? Oh, no! The King is full of love, but He is not so overcome with it as to forget His reason. The words are true, and He means us to understand them as the honest expression of His unbiassed judgment, after having patiently examined her in every part. He would not have us diminish aught, but estimate the gold of His opinions by the bright glittering of His expressions; and, therefore, in order that there may be no mistake, *He states it positively* : " Thou art all fair, My love," *and confirms it by a negative:* "there is no spot in thee."

When He speaks *positively*, how complete is His admiration! She is " fair ", but that is not a full description ; He styles her " all fair." He views her in Himself, washed in His sin-atoning blood, and clothed in His meritorious righteousness, and He considers her to be full of comeliness and beauty. No wonder that such is the case, since it is but His own perfect excellences that He admires, seeing that the holiness, glory, and perfection of His Church are His own garments on the back of His own well-beloved spouse, and she is "bone of His bone, and flesh of His flesh." She is not simply pure, or well-proportioned ; she is positively lovely and fair ! She has actual merit ! Her deformities of sin are removed ; but more, she has through her Lord obtained a meritorious righteousness by which an actual beauty is conferred upon her. Believers have a positive righteousness given to them when they become " accepted in the Beloved." (Eph. i. 6.)

Nor is the Church barely lovely, she is *superlatively so.* Her Lord styles her, "Thou fairest among women." (Sol. Song i. 8.) She has a real worth and excellence which cannot be rivalled by all the nobility and royalty of the world. If Jesus could exchange His elect bride for all the queens and empresses of earth, or even for the angels in heaven, He would not, for He puts her first and foremost,— "fairest among women." Nor is this an opinion which He is ashamed of, for He invites all men to hear it. He puts a "behold" before it, a special note of exclamation, inviting and arresting attention. *"Behold*, thou art fair, My love ; *behold*, thou art fair." (Sol. Song iv. 1.) His opinion He publishes abroad even now, and one day from the throne of His glory He will avow the truth of it before the assembled universe. "Come, ye blessed of My Father" (Matt. xxv. 34), will be His solemn affirmation of the loveliness of His elect.

Let us mark well *the repeated sentences of His approbation.*

> "Lo, thou art fair ! lo, thou art fair !
>   Twice fair thou art, I say ;
> My righteousness and graces are
>   Thy double bright array.
>
> "But since thy faith can hardly own
>   My beauty put on thee ;
> Behold ! behold ! twice be it known
>   Thou art all fair to Me !"

He turns again to the subject, a second time looks into those doves' eyes of hers, and listens to her honey-dropping lips. It is not enough to say, "Behold, thou art fair, My love ;" He rings that golden bell again, and sings again, and again, "Behold, thou art fair."

After having surveyed her whole person with rapturous delight, He cannot be satisfied until He takes a second gaze, and afresh recounts her beauties. Making but little difference between His first description and the last, he adds extraordinary expressions of love to manifest His increased delight. "Thou art beautiful, O My love, as Tirzah, comely as Jerusalem, terrible as an army with banners. Turn away thine eyes from Me, for they have overcome Me : thy hair is as a flock of goats that appear from Gilead. Thy teeth are as a flock of sheep which go up from the washing, whereof every one beareth twins, and there is not one barren among them. As a piece of a pomegranate are thy temples within thy locks. . . . My dove, My undefiled is but one ; she is the only one of her mother, she is the choice one of her that bare her." (Sol. Song vi. 4—7, 9.)

The beauty which He admires is *universal,* He is as much enchanted with her temples as with her breasts. All her offices, all her pure devotions, all her earnest labours, all her constant sufferings, are precious to His heart. She is "all fair." Her ministry, her psalmody, her intercessions, her alms, her watching, all are admirable to Him, when performed in the Spirit. Her faith, her love, her patience, her zeal, are alike in His esteem as "rows of jewels" and "chains of gold." (Sol. Song i. 10.) He loves and admires her everywhere. In the house of bondage, or in the land of Canaan, she is ever fair. On the top of Lebanon His heart is ravished with one of her eyes, and in the fields and villages He joyfully

receives her loves. He values her above gold and
silver in the days of His gracious manifestations, but
He has an equal appreciation of her when He with-
draws Himself, for it is immediately after He had
said, "Until the day break, and the shadows flee
away, I will get Me to the mountain of myrrh, and
to the hill of frankincense," (Sol. Song iv. 6,) that He
exclaims, in the words of our text, "Thou art all fair,
My love."   At all seasons believers are very near
the heart of the Lord Jesus, they are always as the
apple of His eye, and the jewel of His crown. Our
name is still on His breastplate, and our persons are
still in His gracious remembrance. He never thinks
lightly of His people ; and certainly in all the
compass of His Word there is not one syllable which
looks like contempt of them. They are the choice
treasure and peculiar portion of the Lord of hosts ;
and what king will undervalue his own inheritance?
What loving husband will despise his own wife?
Let others call the Church what they may, Jesus
does not waver in His love to her, and does not differ
in His judgment of her, for He still exclaims, "How
fair and how pleasant art thou, O love, for delights!"
(Sol. Song vii. 6.)

Let us remember that He who pronounces the
Church and each individual believer to be "all fair"
is none other than the glorious Son of God, who is
"very God of very God."   Hence His declaration is
decisive, since infallibility has uttered it. There can
be no mistake where the all-seeing Jehovah is the
Judge. If He has pronounced her to be incomparably
fair, she is so, beyond a doubt ; and though hard for
our poor puny faith to receive, it is nevertheless as

divine a verity as any of the undoubted doctrines
of revelation.

Having thus pronounced her *positively* full of
beauty, He now confirms His praise by *a precious
negative:* " There is no spot in thee." As if the
thought occurred to the Bridegroom that the carping
world would insinuate that He had only mentioned
her comely parts, and had purposely omitted those
features which were deformed or defiled, He sums all
up by declaring her universally and entirely fair, and
utterly devoid of stain. A spot may soon be
removed, and is the very least thing that can
disfigure beauty, but even from this little blemish
the Church is delivered in her Lord's sight. If He
had said there is no hideous scar, no horrible
deformity, no filthy ulcer, we might even then
have marvelled; but when He testifies that she is
free from the slightest spot, all these things are
included, and the depth of wonder is increased.
If He had but promised to remove all spots, we
should have had eternal reason for joy; but when
He speaks of it as already done, who can restrain
the most intense emotions of satisfaction and delight?
O my soul, here is marrow and fatness for thee;
eat thy full, and be abundantly glad therein!

Christ Jesus has no quarrel with His spouse. She
often wanders from Him, and grieves His Holy
Spirit, but He does not allow her faults to affect
His love. He sometimes chides, but it is always
in the tenderest manner, with the kindest intentions;
—it is "My love" even then. There is no remembrance
of our follies, He does not cherish ill thoughts of us,
but He pardons, and loves as well after the offence

as before it. It is well for us it is so, for if Jesus
were as mindful of injuries as we are, how could He
commune with us? Many a time a believer will put
himself out of humour with the Lord for some slight
turn in providence, but our precious Husband knows
our silly hearts too well to take any offence at our
ill manners.

If He were as easily provoked as we are, who
among us could hope for a comfortable look or a
kind salutation? but He is "ready to pardon, ...
slow to anger." (Neh. ix. 17.) He is like Noah's
sons, He goes backward, and throws a cloak over our
nakedness; or we may compare Him to Apelles,
who, when he painted Alexander, put his finger over
the scar on the cheek, that it might not be seen in
the picture. "He hath not beheld iniquity in Jacob,
neither hath He seen perverseness in Israel" (Num.
xxiii. 21); and hence He is able to commune with
the erring sons of men.

But the question returns,—How is this? Can it be
explained, so as not to clash with the most evident
fact that sin remaineth even in the hearts of the
regenerate? Can our own daily bewailings of sin
allow of anything like perfection as a present attain-
ment? The Lord Jesus saith it, and therefore it
must be true; but in what sense is it to be understood? How are we "all fair" though we ourselves
feel that we are black, because the sun hath looked
upon us? (Sol. Song i. 6.) The answer is ready,
if we consider the analogy of faith.

1. In the matter of justification, the saints are
complete and without sin. As Durham says, these
words are spoken "in respect of the imputation of

Christ's righteousness wherewith they are adorned, and which they have put on, which makes them very glorious and lovely, so that they are beautiful beyond all others, through His comeliness put upon them."

And Dr. Gill excellently expresses the same idea, when he writes, "though all sin is seen by God, *in articulo providentiæ, in the matter of providence*, wherein nothing escapes His all-seeing eye; yet *in articulo iustificationis, in the matter of justification*, He sees no sin in His people, so as to reckon it to them, or condemn them for it; for they all stand 'holy and unblameable and unreproveable in His sight.'" (Col. i. 22.) The blood of Jesus removes all stain, and His righteousness confers perfect beauty; and, therefore, in the Beloved, the true believer is at this hour as much accepted and approved, in the sight of God, as He will be when He stands before the throne in heaven. The beauty of justification is at its fulness the moment a soul is by faith received into the Lord Jesus. This is righteousness so transcendent that no one can exaggerate its glorious merit. Since this righteousness is that of Jesus, the Son of God, it is therefore divine, and is, indeed, the holiness of God; and, hence, Kent was not too daring when, in a bold flight of rapture, he sang,—

> "In thy Surety thou art free,
>   His dear hands were pierced for thee;
>   With His spotless vesture on,
>   Holy as the Holy One.
>
> "Oh, the heights and depths of grace,
>   Shining with meridian blaze;
>   Here the sacred records show
>   Sinners black, but comely too!"

2. But perhaps it is best to understand this as

relating to the design of Christ concerning them.
It is His purpose to present them without "spot, or
wrinkle, or any such thing." (Eph. v. 27.) They shall
be holy and unblameable and unreproveable in the
sight of the Omniscient God. In prospect of this,
the Church is viewed as being virtually what she is
soon to be actually. Nor is this a frivolous antedating
of her excellence ; for be it ever remembered that
the Representative, in whom she is accepted, is actually
complete in all perfections and glories at this very
moment. As the Head of the body is already without
sin, being none other than the Lord from heaven, it is
but in keeping that the whole body should be pronounced comely and fair through the glory of the
Head. The fact of her future perfection is so certain
that it is spoken of as if it were already accomplished,
and indeed it is so in the mind of Him to whom a
thousand years are but as one day. "Christ often
expounds an honest believer, from His own heart-
purpose and design ; in which respect they get many
titles, otherwise unsuitable to their present condition."
(Durham.) Let us magnify the name of our Jesus,
who loves us so well that He will overleap the
dividing years of our pilgrimage, that He may give us
even now the praise which seems to be only fitted
for the perfection of Paradise. As Erskine sings,—

> " My love, thou seem'st a loathsome worm:
>   Yet such thy beauties be,
> I spoke but half thy comely form ;
>   Thou 'rt wholly fair to Me.
> " Whole justified, in perfect dress ;
>   Nor justice, nor the law
> Can in thy robe of righteousness
>   Discern the smallest flaw.

> "Yea, sanctified in ev'ry part,
>   Thou 'rt perfect in design :
> And I judge thee by what thou art
>   In thy intent and Mine.

> "Fair love, by grace complete in Me,
>   Beyond all beauteous brides ;
> Each spot that ever sullied thee
>   My purple vesture hides."

II. OUR LORD'S ADMIRATION IS SWEETENED BY
LOVE. He addresses the spouse as " My love." The
virgins called her " the fairest among women " ; they
saw and admired, but it was reserved for her Lord to
love her. Who can fully tell the excellence of His love ?
Oh, how His heart goeth forth after His redeemed ! As
for the love of David and Jonathan, it is far exceeded
in Christ. No tender husband was ever so fond as
He. No figures can completely set forth His heart's
affection, for it surpasses all the love that man or
woman hath heard or thought of. Our blessed Lord,
Himself, when He would declare the greatness of it,
was compelled to compare one inconceivable thing
with another, in order to express His own thoughts.
" As the Father hath loved Me, so have I loved you."
(John xv. 9.) All the eternity, fervency, immutability,
and infinity which are to be found in the love of
Jehovah the Father, towards Jehovah-Jesus the Son,
are copied to the letter in the love of the Lord Jesus
towards His chosen ones. Before the foundation of
the world He loved His people, in all their wanderings
He loved them, and unto the end He will abide in
His love. (John xiii. 1.) He has given them the
best proof of His affection, in that He gave Himself to
die for their sins, and hath revealed to them complete

pardon as the result of His death. The willing manner of His death is further confirmation of His boundless love. How Christ did delight in the work of our redemption! " Lo, I come: in the volume of the book it is written of Me, I delight to do Thy will, O my God." (Psalm xl. 7, 8.) When He came into the world to sacrifice His life for us, it was a freewill offering. "I have a baptism to be baptized with." (Luke xii. 50.) Christ was to be, as it were, baptized in His own blood, and how did He thirst for that time! "How am I straitened till it be accomplished." There was no hesitation, no desire to be quit of His engagement. He went to His crucifixion without once halting by the way to deliberate whether He should complete His sacrifice. The stupendous mass of our fearful debt He paid at once, asking neither delay nor diminution. From the moment when He said, "Not My will, but Thine, be done" (Luke xxii. 42), His course was swift and unswerving; as if He had been hastening to a crown rather than to a cross. The fulness of time was His only remembrancer; He was not driven by bailiffs to discharge the obligations of His Church, but joyously, even when full of sorrow, He met the law, answered its demands, and cried, "It is finished."

How hard it is to talk of love so as to convey our meaning with it! How often have our eyes been full of tears when we have realized the thought that Jesus loves us! How has our spirit been melted within us at the assurance that He thinks of us and bears us on His heart! But we cannot kindle the like emotion in others, nor can we give, by word of mouth, so much as a faint idea of the bliss which coucheth in that

exclamation, " Oh, how He loves !" Come, reader
canst thou say of thyself, " He loved me "? (Gal.
ii. 20.) Then look down into this sea of love, and
endeavour to guess its depth. Doth it not stagger
thy faith, that He should love *thee?* Or, if thou hast
strong confidence, say, does it not enfold thy spirit in
a flame of admiring and adoring gratitude? O ye
angels, such love as this ye never knew! Jesus doth
not bear your names upon His hands, or call you His
bride. No! this highest fellowship he reserves for
worms whose only return is tearful, hearty thanksgiving and love.

III. LET US NOTE THAT CHRIST DELIGHTS TO
THINK UPON HIS CHURCH, AND TO LOOK UPON
HER BEAUTY. As the bird returneth often to its
nest, and as the wayfarer hastens to his home, so doth
the mind continually pursue the object of its choice.
We cannot look too often upon that face which we
love ; we desire always to have our precious things in
our sight. It is even so with our Lord Jesus. From
all eternity, " His delights were with the sons of
men ;" His thoughts rolled onward to the time when
His elect should be born into the world ; He viewed
them in the mirror of His fore-knowledge. " In thy
book," He says, "all my members were written, which in
continuance were fashioned, when as yet there was
none of them." (Ps. cxxxix. 16.) When the world
was set upon its pillars, He was there, and He set the
bounds of the people according to the number of the
children of Israel. Many a time, before His incarnation, He descended to this earth in the similitude
of a man ; on the plains of Mamre (Gen. xviii.), by
the brook of Jabbok (Gen. xxxii. 24—30), beneath the

walls of Jericho (Josh. v. 13), and in the fiery furnace
of Babylon (Dan. iii. 19—25), the Son of man did
visit His people. Because His soul delighted in them,
He could not rest away from them, for His heart
longed after them. Never were they absent from His
heart, for He had written their names upon His hands,
and graven them upon His heart. As the breast-plate
containing the names of the tribes of Israel was the
most brilliant ornament worn by the high priest, so
the names of Christ's elect were His most precious
jewels, which He ever hung nearest His heart. We
may often forget to meditate upon the perfections of
our Lord, but He never ceases to remember us. He
cares not one half so much for any of His most glorious
works as He does for His children. Although His eye
seeth everything that hath beauty and excellence in
it, He never fixes His gaze anywhere with that admiration and delight which He spends upon His
purchased ones. He charges His angels concerning
them, and calls upon those holy beings to rejoice with
Him over His lost sheep. (Luke xv. 4—7.) He
talked of them to Himself, and even on the tree of
doom He did not cease to soliloquize concerning
them. He saw of the travail of His soul, and He was
abundantly satisfied.

> " That day acute of ignominious woe,
>   Was, notwithstanding, in a perfect sense,
> ' The day of His heart's gladness,' for the joy
> That His redeem'd should be brought home at last
> (Made ready as in robes of bridal white),
> Was set before Him vividly,—He look'd ;—
> And for that happiness anticipate,
> Endurance of all torture, all disgrace,
> Seem'd light infliction to His heart of love."

Like a fond mother, Christ Jesus, our thrice-blessed Lord, sees every dawning of excellence, and every bud of goodness in us, making much of our littles, and rejoicing over the beginnings of our graces. As He is to be our endless song, so we are His perpetual prayer. When He is absent He thinks of us, and in the black darkness He has a window through which He looks upon us. When the sun sets in one part of the earth, he rises in another place beyond our visible horizon; and even so Jesus, our Sun of Righteousness, is only pouring light upon His people in a different way, when to our apprehension He seems to have set in darkness. His eye is ever upon the vineyard, which is His Church: "I the Lord do keep it; I will water it every moment: lest any hurt it, I will keep it night and day." (Isa. xxvii. 3.) He will not trust to His angels to do it, for it is His delight to do all with His own hands. Zion is in the centre of His heart, and He cannot forget her, for every day His thoughts are set upon her. When the bride by her neglect of Him hath hidden herself from His sight, He cannot be quiet until again He looks upon her. He calls her forth with the most wooing words, "O My dove, that art in the clefts of the rock, in the secret places of the stairs, let Me see thy countenance, let Me hear thy voice; for sweet is thy voice, and thy countenance is comely." (Sol. Song ii. 14.) She thinks herself unmeet to keep company with such a Prince, but He entices her from her lurking-place, and inasmuch as she comes forth trembling, and bashfully hides her face with her veil, He bids her uncover her face, and let her Husband gaze upon her. She is ashamed to do so, for she is black in her own esteem, and therefore He urges that she is comely to Him.

Nor is He content with looking, He must feed His ears as well as His eyes, and therefore He commends her speech, and intreats her to let Him hear her voice. See how truly our Lord rejoiceth in us. Is not this unparalleled love! We have heard of princes who have been smitten by the beauty of a peasant's daughter, but what of that? Here is the Son of God doting upon a worm, looking with eyes of admiration upon a poor child of Adam, and listening with joy to the lispings of poor flesh and blood. Ought we not to be exceedingly charmed by such matchless condescension? And should not our hearts as much delight in Him as He doth in us? O surprising truth! Christ Jesus rejoices over His poor, tempted, tried, and erring people.

IV. IT IS NOT TO BE FORGOTTEN THAT SOMETIMES THE LORD JESUS TELLS HIS PEOPLE HIS LOVE THOUGHTS. "He does not think it enough behind her back to tell it, but in her very presence, He says, 'Thou art all fair, My love.' It is true, this is not His ordinary method; He is a wise lover, that knows when to keep back the intimation of love, and when to let it out; but there are times when He will make no secret of it; times when He will put it beyond all dispute in the souls of His people." *

The Holy Spirit is often pleased in a most gracious manner to witness with our spirits of the love of Jesus. He takes of the things of Christ, and reveals them unto us. No voice is heard from the clouds, and no vision is seen in the night, but we have a testimony

---

* R. Erskine's Sermons.

more sure than either of these. If an angel should fly from heaven, and inform the saint personally of the Saviour's love to him, the evidence would not be one whit more satisfactory than that which is borne in the heart by the Holy Ghost. Ask those of the Lord's people who have lived the nearest to the gates of heaven, and they will tell you that they have had seasons when the love of Christ towards them has been a fact so clear and sure, that they could no more doubt it than they could question their own existence.

Yes, beloved believer, you and I have had times of refreshing from the presence of the Lord, and then our faith has mounted to the topmost heights of assurance. We have had confidence to lean our heads upon the bosom of our Lord, and we have had no more question about our Master's affection than John had when in that blessed posture, nay, nor so much ; for the dark question, "Lord, is it I that shall betray Thee?" has been put far from us. He has kissed us with the kisses of His love, and killed our doubts by the closeness of His embrace. His love has been sweeter than wine to our souls. We felt that we could sing, "His left hand is under my head, and His right hand doth embrace me." (Sol. Song viii. 3.) Then all earthly troubles were light as the chaff of the threshing-floor, and the pleasures of the world as tasteless as the white of an egg. We would have welcomed death as the messenger who would introduce us to our Lord to whom we were in haste to be gone ; for His love had stirred us to desire more of Him, even His immediate and glorious presence. I have, sometimes, when the Lord has assured me of His love, felt as if I could not contain more joy and delight. My eyes ran down

with tears of gratitude. I fell upon my knees to bless
Him, but rose again in haste, feeling as if I had
nothing more to ask for, but must stand up and praise
Him; then have I lifted my hands to heaven, longing
to fill my arms with Him; panting to talk with Him,
as a man talketh with his friend, and to see Him in
His own person, that I might tell Him how happy He
had made His unworthy servant, and might fall on
my face, and kiss His feet in unutterable thankfulness
and love. Such a banquet have I had upon one word
of my Beloved,—"*thou art Mine,*"—that I wished, like
Peter, to build tabernacles in that mount, and dwell
for ever. But, alas, we have not, all of us, yet learned
how to preserve that blessed assurance. We stir up
our Beloved and awake Him, then He leaves our
unquiet chamber, and we grope after Him, and make
many a weary journey trying to find Him.

If we were wiser and more careful, we might
preserve the fragrance of Christ's words far longer;
for they are not like the ordinary manna which soon
rotted, but are comparable to that omer of it which
was put in the golden pot, and preserved for many
generations. The sweet Lord Jesus has been known
to write his love-thoughts on the heart of His people
in so clear and deep a manner, that they have for
months, and even for years, enjoyed an abiding sense of
His affection. A few doubts have flitted across their
minds like thin clouds before a summer's sun, but the
warmth of their assurance has remained the same for
many a gladsome day. Their path has been a smooth
one, they have fed in the green pastures beside the
still waters, for His rod and staff have comforted them,
and His right hand hath led them. I am inclined to

think that there is more of this in the Church than some men would allow. We have a goodly number who dwell upon the hills, and behold the light of the sun. There are giants in these days, though the times are not such as to allow them room to display their gigantic strength ; in many a humble cot, in many a crowded workshop, in many a village manse there are to be found men of the house of David, men after God's own heart, anointed with the holy oil. It is, however, a mournful truth, that whole ranks in the army of our Lord are composed of dwarfish Littlefaiths. The men of fearful mind and desponding heart are everywhere to be seen. Why is this ? Is it the Master's fault, or ours ? Surely *He* cannot be blamed. Is it not then a matter of enquiry in our own souls, Can I not grow stronger ? Must I be a mourner all my days ? How can I get rid of my doubts ? The answer must be : yes, you can be comforted, but only the mouth of the Lord can do it, for anything less than this will be unsatisfactory.

I doubt not that there are means, by the use of which those who are now weak and trembling may attain unto boldness in faith and confidence in hope ; but I see not how this can be done unless the Lord Jesus Christ manifest His love to them, and tell them of their union to Him. This He will do, if we seek it of Him. The importunate pleader shall not lack his reward. Haste thee to Him, O timid one, and tell Him that nothing will content thee but a smile from His own face, and a word from His own lips ! Speak to Him, and say, "O my Lord Jesus, I cannot rest unless I know that Thou lovest me ! I desire to have proof of Thy love under Thine own hand and seal.

I cannot live upon guesses and surmises; nothing but certainty will satisfy my trembling heart.   Lord, look upon me, if, indeed, Thou lovest me, and though I be less than the least of all saints, say unto my soul, ' I am thy salvation.' "   When this prayer is heard, the castle of despair must totter; there is not one stone of it which can remain upon another, if Christ whispers forth His love.   Even Despondency and Much-afraid will dance, and Ready-to-Halt leap upon his crutches.

Oh, for more of these Bethel visits, more frequent visitations from the God of Israel!   Oh, how sweet to hear Him say to us, as He did to Abraham, "Fear not, Abram, I am thy shield, and thy exceeding great reward." (Gen. xv. 1.)   To be addressed as Daniel was of old, "O man greatly beloved" (Dan. x. 19), is worth a thousand ages of this world's joy.   What more can a creature want this side of heaven to make him peaceful and happy than a plain avowal of love from his Lord's own lips?   Let me ever hear Thee, speak in mercy to my soul, and, O my Lord, I ask no more while here I dwell in the land of my pilgrimage!

Brethren, let us labour to obtain a confident assurance of the Lord's delight in us, for this, as it enables Him to commune with us, will be one of the readiest ways to produce a like feeling in our hearts towards Him.   Christ is well pleased with us; let us approach Him with holy familiarity; let us unbosom our thoughts to Him, for His delight in us will secure us an audience.   The child may stay away from the father, when he is conscious that he has aroused his father's displeasure, but why should we keep at a distance when Christ Jesus is smiling upon us?   No! since His smiles attract us, let us enter into His

courts, and touch His golden sceptre.   O Holy Spirit,
help us to live in happy fellowship with Him whose
soul is knit unto us!

"O Jesus ! let eternal blessings dwell
    On Thy transporting name.   *   *   *
      Let me be wholly Thine from this blest hour.
    Let Thy lov'd image be for ever present ;
    Of Thee be all my thoughts, and let my tongue
    Be sanctified with the celestial theme.
    Dwell on my lips, Thou dearest, sweetest name !
    Dwell on my lips, 'till the last parting breath !
    Then let me die, and bear the charming sound
    In triumph to the skies.   In other strains,
    In language all divine, I'll praise Thee then ;
    While all the Godhead opens in the view
    Of a Redeemer's love.   Here let me gaze,
    For ever gaze ; the bright variety
    Will endless joy and admiration yield.
      Let me be wholly Thine from this blest hour.
    Fly from my soul all images of sense,
    Leave me in silence to possess my Lord :
    My life, my pleasures, flow from Him alone,
    My strength, my great salvation, and my hope.
    Thy name is all my trust ; O name divine !
    Be Thou engraven on my inmost soul,
    And let me own Thee with my latest breath,
    Confess Thee in the face of ev'ry horror,
    That threat'ning death or envious hell can raise ;
    Till all their strength subdu'd, my parting soul
    Shall give a challenge to infernal rage,
    And sing salvation to the Lamb for ever."

THE WELL-BELOVED.

A COMMUNION ADDRESS AT MENTONE.

" Yea, He is altogether lovely."—*Solomon's Song* v. 16

THE WELL-BELOVED.

———

THE soul that is familiar with the Lord worships Him in the outer court of nature, wherein it admires His *works*, and is charmed by every thought of what HE must be who made them all. When that soul enters the nearer circle of inspiration, and reads the wonderful *words* of God, it is still more enraptured, and its admiration is heightened. In revelation, we see the same all-glorious Lord as in creation, but the vision is more clear, and the consequent love is more intense.

The Word is an inner court to the Creation; but there is yet an innermost sanctuary, and blessed are they who enter it, and have fellowship with the Lord HIMSELF. We come to Christ, and in coming to Him we come to God; for Jesus says, "He that hath seen Me hath seen the Father." When we know the Lord Jesus, we stand before the mercy-seat, where the glory of Jehovah shineth forth. I like to think of the text as belonging to those who are as priests unto God, and stand in the Holy of holies, while they say, "Yea, He is altogether lovely." His works are marvellous, His words are full of majesty, but He Himself is altogether lovely.

Can we come into this inner circle? All do not enter here. Alas! many are far off from Him, and are blind to His beauties. "He was despised and rejected of men," and He is so still. They do not see God in His works, but dream that these wonders were evolved, and not created by the Great Primal Cause. As for His words, they seem to them as idle tales, or, at best, as inspired only in the same sense as the language of Shakespeare or Spenser. They see not the Lord in the stately aisles of Holy Scripture ; and have no vision of *Himself.* May He, who openeth the eyes of the blind, have pity on them !

Certain others are in a somewhat happier position, for they are enquirers after Christ. They are like the persons who, in the ninth verse of the chapter, asked, " What is thy Beloved more than another beloved, O thou fairest among women ? What is thy Beloved more than another beloved, that thou dost so charge us ? " They want to know who this Jesus is. But they have not seen Him yet, and cannot join with the spouse in saying, " He is altogether lovely."

If we enter this sacred inner circle, we must become witnesses, as she does who speaks of Christ, " Yea, He is altogether lovely." She knows what He is, for she has seen Him. The verses which precede the text are a description of every feature of the heavenly Bride-groom ; all His members are there set forth with richness of Oriental imagery. The spouse speaks what she knows. Have we, also, seen the Lord ? Are we His familiar acquaintances ? If so, may the Lord help us to understand our text !

If we are to know the full joy of the text, we must come to our Lord as His intimates. He permits us this high honour, since, in this ordinance, He makes us His table-companions. He says, " Henceforth I call you not servants ; but I have called you friends."

He calls upon us to eat bread with Him; yea, to partake of Himself, by eating His flesh and drinking His blood. Oh, that we may pass beyond the outward signs into the closest intimacy with *Himself !* Perhaps, when you are at home, you will examine the spouse's description of her Lord. It is a wonderful piece of tapestry. She has wrought into its warp and woof all things charming, sweet, and precious. In Him she sees all lovely colours,—" My Beloved is white and ruddy." In comparison with Him all others fail, for He is "chief among ten thousand" chieftains. She cannot think of Him as comparable to anything less valuable than "fine gold." She sees, soaring in the air, birds of divers wing; and these must aid her, whether it be the raven or the dove. The rivers of waters, and the beds of spices and myrrh-dropping lilies, must come into the picture, with sweet flowers and goodly cedars. All kinds of treasured things are in Him; for He is like to gold rings set with the beryl, and bright ivory overlaid with sapphires, and pillars of marble set upon sockets of fine gold. She labours to describe His beauty and His excellency, and strains all comparisons to their utmost use, and somewhat more; and yet she is conscious of failure, and therefore sums up all with the pithy sentence, " Yea, He is altogether lovely."

If the Holy Spirit will help me, I should like to lift the veil, that we may, in sacred contemplation, look on our Beloved.

I. We would do so, first, WITH REVERENT EMOTIONS. In the words before us, " Yea, He is altogether lovely," two emotions are displayed, namely, admiration and affection.

It is *admiration* which speaks of Him as "altogether lovely" or beautiful. This admiration rises to the highest degree. The spouse would fain show that her Beloved is more than any other beloved ; therefore she cries, "He is altogether lovely." Surely no one else has reached that point. Many are lovely, but no one save Jesus is "altogether lovely." We see something that is lovely in one, and another point is lovely in another ; but all loveliness meets in Him. Our soul knows nothing which can rival Him : He is the gathering up of all sorts of loveliness to make up one perfect loveliness. He is the climax of beauty ; the crown of glory ; the uttermost of excellence.

Our admiration of Him, also, is unrestrained. The spouse dared to say, even in the presence of the daughters of Jerusalem, who were somewhat envious, "Yea, He is altogether lovely." They knew not, as yet, His perfections ; they even asked, "What is thy Beloved more than another beloved ?" But she was not to be blinded by their want of sympathy, neither did she withhold her testimony from fear of their criticism. To her, He was "altogether lovely", and she could say no less. Our admiration of Christ is such that we would tell the kings of the earth that they have no majesty in His presence ; and tell the wise men that He alone is wisdom ; and tell the great and mighty that He is the blessed and only Potentate, King of kings, and Lord of lords.

Our admiration of our Lord is inexpressible. We can never tell all we know of our Lord ; yet all our knowledge is little. All that we know is, that His love passeth knowledge, that His excellence baffles understanding, that His glory is unutterable. We can embrace Him by our love, but we can scarcely touch Him with our intellect, He is so high, so glorious. As to describing Him, we cry, with Mr. Berridge,—

> " Then my tongue would fain express
> All His love and loveliness ;
> But I lisp, and falter forth
> Broken words, not half His worth.

> " Vex'd, I try and try again,
> Still my efforts all are vain :
> Living tongues are dumb at best,
> We must die to speak of Christ."

" He is altogether lovely." Do we not feel an inexpressible admiration for Him ? There is none like unto Thee, O Son of God !

Still, our paramount emotion is not admiration, but *affection*. " He is altogether "—not beautiful, nor admirable,—but " lovely." All His beauties are loving beauties towards us, and beauties which draw our hearts towards Him in humble love. He charms us, not by a cold comeliness, but by a living loveliness, which wins our hearts. His is an approachable beauty, which not only overpowers us with its glory, but holds us captive by its charms. We love Him : we cannot do otherwise, for " He is altogether lovely." He has within Himself an unquenchable flame of love, which sets our soul on fire. He is all love, and all the love in the world is less than His. Put together all the loves of husbands, wives, parents, children, brothers, sisters, and they only make a drop compared with His great deeps of love, unexplored and unexplorable. This love of His has a wonderful power to beget love in unlovely hearts, and to nourish it into a mighty force. It is a torrent which sweeps all before it when its founts break forth within the soul. It is a Gulf Stream in which all icebergs melt. When our heart is full of love to Jesus, His loveliness becomes the passion of the soul, and sin and self are swept away. May we feel it now!

There He stands: we know Him by the thorn-crown, and the wounds, and the visage more marred than that of any man! He suffered all this for us. O Son of man! O Son of God! With the spouse, we feel, in the inmost depths of our soul, that Thou art "altogether lovely."

II. Now would I lift the veil a second time, with deep solemnity, not so much to suggest emotions as to secure your intelligent assurance of the fact that " He is altogether lovely." We say this WITH ABSOLUTE CERTAINTY. The spouse places a " *Yea* " before her enthusiastic declaration, because she is sure of it. She sees her Beloved, and sees Him to be altogether lovely. This is no fiction, no dream, no freak of imagination, no outburst of partiality. The highest love to Christ does not make us speak more than the truth; we are as reasonable when we are filled with love to Him as ever we were in our lives; nay, never are we more reasonable than when we are carried clean away by a clear perception of His superlative excellence.

Let us meditate upon the proof of our assertion.

" He is altogether lovely " in *His person.* He is God. The glory of Godhead I must leave in lowly silence. Yet is our Jesus also man, more emphatically man than any one here present this afternoon, for we are English, American, French, German, Dutch,

Russian; but Christ is *man*, the second Adam, the
Head of the race : as truly as He is very God of
very God, so is He man, of the substance of His
mother. What a marvellous union! The miracle of
miracles! In His incomparable personality He is
altogether lovely; for in Him we see how God comes
down to man in condescension, and how man goes up
to God in close relationship. There is no other such
as He, in all respects, even in heaven itself : in His
personality He must ever stand alone, in the eyes of
both God and man, "altogether lovely."

As for *His character*, time would fail us to enter
upon that vast subject; but the more we know of the
character of our Lord, and the more we grow like
Him, the more lovely will it appear to us. In all
aspects, it is lovely; in all its minutiæ and details, it
is perfect; and as a whole, it is perfection's model.
Take any one action of His, look into its mode, its
spirit, its motive, and all else that can be revealed by
a microscopic examination, and it is "altogether
lovely." Consider His life, as a whole, in reference to
God, to man, to His friends, to His foes, to those
around Him, and to the ages yet to be, and you shall
find it absolutely perfect. More than that : there is
such a thing as a cold perfection, with which one can
find no fault, and yet it commands no love ; but in
Christ, our Well-beloved, every part of His character
attracts. To a true heart, the life of Christ is as
much an object of love as of reverence : "He is
altogether lovely." We must *love* that which we see
in Him : admiration is not the word. When cold
critics commend Him, their praise is half an insult :
what know these frozen hearts of our Beloved ? As

for a word against Him, it wounds us to the soul.
Even an omission of His praise is a torture to us.   If
we hear a sermon which has no Christ in it, we
weary of it.   If we read a book that contains a
slighting syllable of Him, we abhor it.   He, Himself, has become everything to us now, and only in
the atmosphere of fervent love to Him can we feel
at home.

Passing from His character to *His sacrifice ;* there
especially " He is altogether lovely."   You may have
read " Rutherford's Letters " ; I hope you have.   How
wondrously he writes, when he describes his Lord in
garments red from His sweat of blood, and with
hands bejewelled with His wounds !   When we view
His body taken down from the cross, all pale and
deathly, and wrapped in the cerements of the grave,
we see a strange beauty in Him.   He is to us never
more lovely than when we read in our Beloved's white
and red that His sacrifice is accomplished, and He
has been obedient unto death for us.   In Him, as the
sacrifice once offered, we see our pardon, our life, our
heaven, our all.   So lovely is Christ in His sacrifice,
that He is for ever most pleasing to the great Judge
of all, ay, so lovely to His Father, that He makes us
also lovely to God the Father, and we are " accepted
in the Beloved."   His sacrifice has such merit and
beauty in the sight of heaven, that in Him God is
well pleased, and guilty men become in Him pleasant
unto the Lord.   Is not His sacrifice most sweet to
us ?   Here our guilty conscience finds peace ; here we
see ourselves made comely in His comeliness.   We
cannot stand at Calvary, and see the Saviour die, and
hear Him cry, " It is finished," without feeling that

"He is altogether lovely." Forgive me that I speak so coolly! I dare not enter fully into a theme which would pull up the sluices of my heart.

Remember what He was when He rose from the grave on the third day. Oh, to have seen Him in the freshness of *His resurrection beauty!* And what will He be in *His glory*, when He comes again the second time, and all His holy angels with Him, when He shall sit upon the throne of His glory, and heaven and earth shall flee away before His face? To His people He will then be "altogether lovely." Angels will adore Him, saints made perfect will fall on their faces before Him; and we ourselves shall feel that, at last, our heaven is complete. We shall see Him, and being like Him, we shall be satisfied.

Every feature of our Lord is lovely. You cannot think of anything that has to do with Him which is unworthy of our praise. All over glorious is our Lord. The spouse speaks of His head, His locks, His eyes, His cheeks, His lips, His hands, His legs, His countenance, His mouth; and when she has mentioned them all, she sums up with reference to all by saying, "Yea, He is altogether lovely."

There is *nothing unlovely about Him*. Certain persons would be beautiful were it not for a wound or a bruise, but our Beloved is all the more lovely for His wounds; the marring of His countenance has enhanced its charms. His scars are, for glory and for beauty, the jewels of our King. To us He is lovely even from that side which others dread: His very frown has comfort in it to His saints, since He only frowns on evil. Even His feet, which are "like unto fine brass, as if they burned in a furnace," are lovely to us for His sake ; these are His poor saints, who are sorely tried, but are able to endure the fire. Everything of Christ, everything that partakes of Christ, everything that hath a flavour or savour of Christ, is lovely to us.

There is *nothing lacking about His loveliness.* Some would be very lovely were there a brightness in their eyes, or a colour in their countenances : but something s away. The absence of a tooth or of an eyebrow may spoil a countenance, but in Christ Jesus there is no omission of excellence. Everything that should be in Him is in Him ; everything that is conceivable in perfection is present to perfection in Him.

In Him is nothing excessive. Many a face has one feature in it which is overdone; but in our Lord's character everything is balanced and proportionate. You never find His kindness lessening His holiness, nor His holiness eclipsing His wisdom, nor His wisdom abating His courage, nor His courage injuring His meekness. Everything is in our Lord that should be there, and everything in due measure. Like rare spices, mixed after the manner of the apothecary, our Lord's whole person, and character, and sacrifice, are as incense sweet unto the Lord.

Neither is there anything in our Lord which is incongruous with the rest. In each one of us there is, at least, a little that is out of place. We could not be fully described without the use of a "but." If we could all look within, and see ourselves as God sees us, we should note a thousand matters, which we now permit, which we should never allow again. But in the Well-beloved all is of a piece, all is lovely ; and when the sum of the whole is added up, it comes to an absolute perfection of loveliness: " Yea, He is altogether lovely."

We are sure that the Lord Jesus must be Himself exceedingly lovely, since *He gives loveliness to His people.* Many saints are lovely in their lives; one reads biographies of good men and women which make us wish to grow like them; yet all the loveliness of all the most holy among men has come from Jesus their Lord, and is a copy of His perfect beauty. Those who write well do so because He sets the copy.

What is stranger and more wonderful still, *our Lord Jesus makes sinners lovely.* In their natural state, men are deformed and hideous to the eye of God; and as they have no love to God, so He has no delight in them. He is weary of them, and is grieved that He made men upon the earth. The Lord is angry with the wicked every day. Yet, when our Lord Jesus comes in, and covers these sinful ones with His righteousness, and, at the same time, infuses into them His life, the Lord is well pleased with them for His Son's sake. Even in heaven, the infinite Jehovah sees nothing which pleases Him like His Son. The Father from eternity loved His Only-begotten, and again and again He hath said of Him, " This is My beloved Son, in whom I am well pleased." What higher encomium can be passed upon Him?

If we had time to think over this subject, we should say of our Lord that *He is lovely in every office.* He is the most admirable Priest, and King, and Prophet that ever yet exercised the office. He is a lovely Shepherd of a chosen flock, a lovely Friend, a lovely Husband, a lovely Brother : He is admirable in every position that He occupies for our sakes.

Our Lord's loveliness appears in every condition : in the manger, or in the temple ; by the well, or on the sea ; in the garden, or on the cross ; in the tomb, or in the resurrection ; in His first, or in His second coming. He is not as the herb, which flowers only at one season ; or as the tree, which loses its leaves in winter ; or as the moon, which waxes and wanes ; or as the sea, which ebbs and flows. In every condition, and at every time, " He is altogether lovely."

He is lovely, whichever way we look at Him. If we view Him as in the past, entering into a covenant of peace on our behalf ; or, in the present, yielding Himself to us as Intercessor, Representative, and Forerunner ; or, in the future, coming, reigning, and glorifying His people ; " He is altogether lovely." Behold Him from heaven, view Him from the gates of hell, regard Him as he goes before, look up to Him as He sits above ; He is as beautiful from one point of view as from another ; " Yea, He is altogether lovely." Wherever we may be, He is the same in His perfection. How lovely He was to my eyes when I was sinking in despair ! To see Him suffering for my sin upon the tree, was as the opening of the gates of the morning to my darkened soul. How lovely He is to us when we are sick, and the hours of night seem lengthened into days ! " He giveth songs in the night." How lovely has . He been to us when the world has frowned, and friends have forsaken, and worldly goods have been scant ! To see " the King in His beauty " is a sight sufficient, even if we never saw another ray of comfort. How blessed, when we

lie dying, to hear Him say, "I am the resurrection
and the life"! Mark that word; He says not, "I will
give you resurrection and life," but, "*I am* the resurrection and the life." Blessed are the eyes which can
see that in Jesus which is really in Him. When we
think of seeing Him as He is, and being like Him,
how heaven approaches us! We shall soon behold
the beatific vision, of which He will be the centre and
the sun. At the thought thereof our soul takes wing,
and our imagination soars aloft, while our faith, with
eagle eye, beholds the glory. As we think of that
glad period, when we shall be with our Beloved for
ever, we are ready to swoon away with delight. It is
near, far nearer than we think.

III. The little time which we can give to this
meditation has run out, and therefore I hasten to a
close. I have bidden you look at our Lord as "altogether lovely" with reverent emotions, and with
absolute certainty. Now, to conclude, think of
Him WITH PRACTICAL RESULTS. "He is altogether
lovely." What shall we do for this chief among ten
thousand?

First, *we will tell others of Him*. For that cause
was our text spoken. The daughters of Jerusalem
asked the spouse, "What is thy Beloved more than
another beloved?" Her answer is here: "He is
altogether lovely." It is a great joy to praise our
Lord to enquiring minds. We, who are preachers,
have a glorious time of it when we extol our Lord.
If we had nothing to do but to preach Christ, and
had no discipline to administer, no sin to battle with,
no doubts to drive away, we should have a heavenly
service. For my part, I wish I could be bound over

to play only upon this one string. Paul did well when he turned ignoramus, and determined to know nothing among the Corinthians save Jesus Christ, and Him crucified. As the harp of Anacreon would resound love alone, so would I have but one sole subject for my ministry,—the love and loveliness of my Lord. Then to speak would be its own reward; and to study and prepare discourses would be only a phase of rest. Fain would I make my whole ministry to speak of Christ and His surpassing loveliness.

You who are not preachers cannot do better than speak much of Jesus, as opportunity offers. Make *Him* the theme of conversation. People talk about ministers; but we beg you to talk of our Master. Our undecided neighbours are always talking of hypocrites and inconsistent professors; but we would say to them, "Never mind about His followers: talk about the Master Himself." His followers, by themselves considered, never were worth your words; but what a theme is this,—"He is altogether lovely"! Our Lord's people are far worthier than the world thinks them to be; for my part, I rejoice in the many gracious and beautiful characters with which I meet, but even if all the ill reports we hear were true, this would not detract from the loveliness of our Lord, who is infinitely beyond all praise.

The next practical result of viewing the loveliness of our blessed Lord is, that *we appropriate Him to ourselves*, grasping Him with our two hands of faith and love, and making the rest of the verse to be our own: "This is my Beloved, and this is my Friend, O daughters of Jerusalem!" Since He is so amiable, He must be "my Beloved"; my heart clings to Him.

Since He is admirable, I rejoice that He is "my
Friend"; my soul trusts in Him. The heart that
most appreciates Jesus is the most eager to appropriate
Him. He who beholds Jesus as "altogether lovely"
will never rest till he is altogether sure that Jesus is
altogether his own. I think I may also add that
appreciation is in great measure the seal of appropria-
tion, for the soul that values Christ most is the soul
that hath most surely taken possession of Christ.
Sometimes a heart prizes the Lord very highly, and
tremblingly longs for Him; but it is my conviction
that the very fact of prizing Him argues a measure of
possession of Him. Jesus never wins a heart to which
He refuses His love. If thou lovest Him, He loves
thee: be sure of that. No soul ever cries, "Yea, He
is altogether lovely," without sooner or later adding,
"This is my Beloved, and this is my Friend."

Rest not, any one of you, till you know of a surety
that Jesus is yours. Do not be content with a hope,
struggle after the full assurance of faith. This is to
be had, and you ought not to be content without it.
It may be your lifelong song, "My Beloved is mine,
and I am His." You need not pine in the shade:
the sun is shining, "walk in the light." Away with
the idea that we cannot know whether we are condemned or forgiven, in Christ or out of Him! We
may know, we must know; and, as we appreciate our
Lord, we shall know. Either Jesus is ours, or He is
not. If He is, let us rejoice in the priceless possession.
If He is not ours, let us at once lay hold upon Him
by faith; for, the moment we trust Him, He is ours.
The enjoyment of religion lies in assurance: a mere
hope is scant diet.

Once more, it is a fair fruit of our delight in our Lord that *our valuation of Him becomes a bond of union between us and others.* The spouse cries, " This is my Beloved, and this is my Friend, O daughters of Jerusalem!" and they reply, " Whither is thy Beloved gone, O thou fairest among women? Whither is thy Beloved turned aside, that we may seek Him with thee?" Thus, you see, they institute a companionship through the Well-beloved. Few of us, in this room, would ever have known each other, had it not been for our common admiration of the Lord Jesus. We should have gone on walking past each other by the sea to this day, and we should have missed much cheering fellowship. Our Lord has become our centre; we meet in Him, and feel that in Him we are partakers of one life. We seek our Well-beloved together, and around His table we find Him together; and finding HIM, we have found one another, and the lost jewel of Christian love glitters on every bosom. We have differing views on certain parts of divine truth; and I do not know that it is wrong for us to differ where the Holy Spirit has left truth without rigidly defining it. We are bound each one devoutly to use his judgment in the interpretation of the Sacred Word; but we all agree in this one clear judgment: " Yea, He is altogether lovely." This is the point of union. Those who enthusiastically. love the same person are on the way to loving each other. This is growingly our case; and it is the same with all spiritual people. Professors quarrel, but possessors are at one. We hear much discourse upon " the Unity of the Church" as a thing to be desired, and we may heartily agree with it; but it would be well also to remember that in the true Church of Christ real union already exists. Our Lord prayed for those whom the Father had given Him, that they might be one, and the Father granted the prayer: the Lord's own people are one. In this room we have an example of how closely we are united in Christ. Some of you are more at home in this assembly, taken out of all churches, than you are in the churches to which you nominally belong. Our union in one body as Episcopalians, Baptists, Presbyterians, or Independents, is not the thing which our Lord prayed for; but our union *in Himself*. *That* union we do at this moment enjoy; and therefore do we eat of one bread, and drink of one cup, and are baptized into one Spirit, at His feet who is to each one of us, and so to all of us, ALTOGETHER LOVELY.

> " White and ruddy is my Belovèd,
>   All His heavenly beauties shine ;
> Nature can't produce an object,
>   Nor so glorious, so divine ;
>   He hath wholly
>   Won my soul to realms above.

> " Farewell, all ye meaner creatures,
>   For in Him is every store ;
> Wealth, or friends, or darling beauty,
>   Shall not draw me any more ;
>   In my Saviour
>   I have found a glorious whole."

THE SPICED WINE OF MY POMEGRANATE;

OR, THE COMMUNION OF COMMUNICATION.

"I would cause Thee to drink of spiced wine of the juice of my pomegranate."—*Solomon's Song* viii. 2.

"And of His fulness have all we received, and grace for grace." *John* i. 16.

THE SPICED WINE OF MY POMEGRANATE.

THE immovable basis of communion having been laid of old in the eternal union which subsisted between Christ and His elect, it only needed a fitting occasion to manifest itself in active development. The Lord Jesus had for ever delighted Himself with the sons of men, and he ever stood prepared to reveal and communicate that delight to His people; but they were incapable of returning His affection or enjoying His fellowship, having fallen into a state so base and degraded, that they were dead to Him, and careless concerning Him. It was therefore needful that something should be done for them, and in them, before they could hold converse with Jesus, or feel concord with Him. This preparation being a work of grace and a result of previous union, Jesus determined that, even in the preparation for communion, there should be communion. If they must be washed before they could fully converse with Him, He would commune with them in the washing; and if they must be enriched by gifts before they could have full access to Him, He would commune with them in the giving. He has therefore established a fellowship in imparting His grace, and in partaking of it.

This order of fellowship we have called "The Communion of Communication," and we think that a few remarks will prove that we are not running beyond the warranty of Scripture.

The word κοινωνια, or communion, is frequently employed by inspired writers in the sense of communication or contribution. When, in our English version, we read, " For it hath pleased them of Macedonia and Achaia to make *a certain contribution* for the poor saints which are at Jerusalem " (Romans xv. 26), it is interesting to know that the word κοινωνιαν is used, as if to show that the generous gifts of the Church in Achaia to its sister Church at Jerusalem was a communion. Calvin would have us notice this, because, saith he, " The word here employed well expresses the feeling by which it behoves us to succour the wants of our brethren, even because there is to be a common and mutual regard on account of the union of the body." He would not have strained the text if he had said that there was in the contribution the very essence of communion. Gill, in his commentary upon the above verse, most pertinently remarks, "Contribution, or communion, as the word signifies, it being one part of the communion of churches and of saints to relieve their poor by communicating to them." The same word is employed in Hebrews xiii. 16, and is there translated by the word *"communicate."* " But to do good, and to communicate, forget not : for with such sacrifices God is well pleased." It occurs again in 2 Corinthians ix. 13, "And for your liberal *distribution* unto them, and unto all men ; " and in numerous other passages the careful student will observe the word in various forms, representing the ministering of the saints to one another as an act of fellowship. Indeed, at the Lord's supper, which is the embodiment of communion, we have ever been wont to make a special contribution for the poor of the flock, and we believe that in the collection there is as true and real an element of communion as in the partaking of the bread and wine. The giver holds fellowship with the receiver when he bestows his benefaction for the Lord's sake, and because of the brotherhood existing between him and his needy friends. The teacher holds communion with the young disciple when he labours to instruct him in the faith, being moved thereto by a spirit of Christian love. He who intercedes for a saint because he desires his well-being as a member of the one family, enters into fellowship with his brother in the offering of prayer. The loving and mutual service of church-members is fellowship of a high degree. And let us remember that the recipient communes with the benefactor: the communion is not confined to the giver, but the heart overflowing with liberality is met by the heart brimming with gratitude, and the love manifested in the bestowal is reciprocated in the acceptance. When the hand feeds the mouth or supports the head, the divers members feel their union, and sympathize with one another; and so is it with the various portions of the body of Christ, for they commune in mutual acts of love.

Now, this meaning of the word communion furnishes us with much instruction, since it indicates the manner in which recognized fellowship with Jesus is commenced and maintained, namely, by giving and receiving, by *communication* and reception. The Lord's supper is the divinely-ordained exhibition of communion, and therefore in it there is the breaking of bread and the pouring forth of wine, to picture the free gift of the Saviour's body and blood to us; and

there is also the eating of the one and the drinking of
the other, to represent the reception of these priceless
gifts by us. As without bread and wine there could
be no Lord's supper, so without the gracious bequests
of Jesus to us there would have been no communion
between Him and our souls: and as participation is
necessary before the elements truly represent the
meaning of the Lord's ordinance, so is it needful that
we should receive His bounties, and feed upon His
person, before we can commune with Him.

It is one branch of this mutual communication
which we have selected as the subject of this address.
" Looking unto Jesus," who hath delivered us from
our state of enmity, and brought us into fellowship
with Himself, we pray for the rich assistance of the
Holy Spirit, that we may be refreshed in spirit, and
encouraged to draw more largely from the covenant
storehouse of Christ Jesus the Lord.

We shall take a text, and proceed at once to our
delightful task. "*And of His fulness have all we
received, and grace for grace.*" (John i. 16.)

As the life of grace is first begotten in us by the
Lord Jesus, so is it constantly sustained by Him.
We are always drawing from this sacred fountain,
always deriving sap from this divine root; and as
Jesus communes with us in the bestowing of mercies,
it is our privilege to hold fellowship with Him in the
receiving of them.

There is this difference between Christ and ourselves,
He never gives without manifesting fellowship, but we
often receive in so ill a manner that communion is
not reciprocated, and we therefore miss the heavenly
opportunity of its enjoyment. We frequently receive

grace insensibly, that is to say, the sacred oil runs through the pipe, and maintains our lamp, while we are unmindful of the secret influence. We may also be the partakers of many mercies which, through our dulness, we do not perceive to be mercies at all; and at other times well-known blessings are recognized as such, but we are backward in tracing them to their source in the covenant made with Christ Jesus.

Following out the suggestion of our explanatory preface, we can well believe that when the poor saints received the contribution of their brethren, many of them did in earnest acknowledge the fellow-ship which was illustrated in the generous offering, but it is probable that some of them merely looked upon the material of the gift, and failed to see the spirit moving in it. Sensual thoughts in some of the receivers might possibly, at the season when the contribution was distributed, have mischievously injured the exercise of spirituality, for it is possible that, after a period of poverty, they would be apt to give greater prominence to the fact that their need was removed than to the sentiment of fellowship with their sympathizing brethren. They would rather rejoice over famine averted than concerning fellowship manifested. We doubt not that, in many instances, the mutual benefactions of the Church fail to reveal our fellowship to our poor brethren, and produce in them no feelings of communion with the givers.

Now this sad fact is an illustration of the yet more lamentable statement which we have made. We again assert that, as many of the partakers of the alms of the Church are not alive to the communion contained therein, so the Lord's people are never

sufficiently attentive to fellowship with Jesus in
receiving His gifts, but many of them are entirely
forgetful of their privilege, and all of them are too
little aware of it. Nay, worse than this, how often
doth the believer pervert the gifts of Jesus into food
for his own sin and wantonness! We are not free
from the fickleness of ancient Israel, and well might
our Lord address us in the same language: " Now
when I passed by thee, and looked upon thee, behold,
thy time was the time of love ; and I spread My
skirt over thee, and covered thy nakedness: yea, I
sware unto thee, and entered into a covenant with
thee, saith the Lord God, and thou becamest Mine.
Then washed I thee with water ; yea, I throughly
washed away thy blood from thee, and I anointed thee
with oil. I clothed thee also with broidered work, and
shod thee with badgers' skin, and I girded thee
about with fine linen, and I covered thee with silk.
I decked thee also with ornaments, and I put bracelets
upon thy hands, and a chain on thy neck. And I put
a jewel on thy forehead, and earrings in thine ears,
and a beautiful crown upon thine head. Thus wast
thou decked with gold and silver ; and thy raiment was
of fine linen, and silk, and broidered work ; thou didst
eat fine flour, and honey, and oil: and thou wast exceeding beautiful, and thou didst prosper into a kingdom.
And thy renown went forth among the heathen for
thy beauty : for it was perfect through My comeliness,
which I had put upon thee, saith the Lord God. But
thou didst trust in thine own beauty, and playedst the
harlot because of thy renown." (Ezek. xvi. 8—16.)

Ought not the mass of professors to confess the
truth of this accusation ? Have not the bulk of us

most sadly departed from the purity of our love? We rejoice, however, to observe a remnant of choice spirits, who live near the Lord, and know the sweetness of fellowship. These receive the promise and the blessing, and so digest them that they become good blood in their veins, and so do they feed on their Lord that they grow up into Him. Let us imitate those elevated minds, and obtain their high delights. There is no reason why the meanest of us should not be as David, and David as the servant of the Lord. We may now be dwarfs, but growth is possible; let us therefore aim at a higher stature. Let the succeeding advice be followed, and, the Holy Spirit helping us, we shall have attained thereto.

Make every time of need a time of embracing thy Lord. Do not leave the mercy-seat until thou hast clasped Him in thine arms. In every time of need He has promised to give thee grace to help, and what withholdeth thee from obtaining sweet fellowship as a precious addition to the promised assistance? Be not as the beggar who is content with the alms, however grudgingly it may be cast to him; but, since thou art a near kinsman, seek a smile and a kiss with every benison He gives thee. Is He not better than His mercies? What are they without Him? Cry aloud unto Him, and let thy petition reach His ears, "O my Lord, it is not enough to be a partaker of Thy bounties, I must have Thyself also; if Thou dost not give me Thyself with Thy favours, they are but of little use to me! O smile on me, when Thou blessest me, for else I am still unblest! Thou puttest perfume into all the flowers of Thy garden, and fragrance into Thy spices; if Thou withdrawest Thyself, they are no more

pleasant to me. Come, then, my Lord, and give me
Thy love with Thy grace." Take good heed, Christian, that thine own heart is in right tune, that when
the fingers of mercy touch the strings, they may
resound with full notes of communion. How sad is it
to partake of favour without rejoicing in it! Yet such
is often the believer's case. The Lord casts His lavish
bounties at our doors, and we, like churls, scarcely
look out to thank Him. Our ungrateful hearts and
unthankful tongues mar our fellowship, by causing us
to miss a thousand opportunities for exercising it.

If thou wouldst enjoy communion with the Lord
Jesus in the reception of His grace, *endeavour to be
always sensibly drawing supplies from Him*. Make
thy needs public in the streets of thine heart, and
when the supply is granted, let all the powers of thy
soul be present at the reception of it. Let no mercy
come into thine house unsung. Note in thy memory
the list of thy Master's benefits. Wherefore should
the Lord's bounties be hurried away in the dark, or
buried in forgetfulness? Keep the gates of thy soul
ever open, and sit thou by the wayside to watch the
treasures of grace which God the Spirit hourly conveys
into thy heart from Jehovah-Jesus, thy Lord.

Never let an hour pass without drawing upon the
bank of heaven. If all thy wants seem satisfied, look
steadfastly until the next moment brings another need,
and then delay not, but with this warrant of necessity,
hasten to thy treasury again. Thy necessities are so
numerous that thou wilt never lack a reason for
applying to the fulness of Jesus; but if ever such an
occasion should arise, enlarge thine heart, and then
there will be need of more love to fill the wider space.

But do not allow any supposititious riches of thine own to suspend thy daily receivings from the Lord Jesus. You have constant need of Him. You need His intercession, His upholding, His sanctification ; you need that He should work all your works in you, and that He should preserve you unto the day of His appearing. There is not one moment of your life in which you can do without Christ. Therefore be always at His door, and the wants which you bemoan shall be remembrances to turn your heart unto your Saviour. Thirst makes the heart pant for the water-brooks, and pain reminds man of the physician. Let your wants conduct you to Jesus, and may the blessed Spirit reveal Him unto you while He lovingly affords you the rich supplies of His love ! Go, poor saint, let thy poverty be the cord to draw thee to thy rich Brother. Rejoice in the infirmity which makes room for grace to rest upon thee, and be glad that thou hast constant needs which compel thee perpetually to hold fellowship with thine adorable Redeemer.

Study thyself, seek out thy necessities, as the housewife searches for chambers where she may bestow her summer fruits. Regard thy wants as rooms to be filled with more of the grace of Jesus, and suffer no corner to be unoccupied. Pant after more of Jesus. Be covetous after Him. Let all the past incite thee to seek greater things. Sing the song of the enlarged heart,—

> " All this is not enough : methinks I grow
> More greedy by fruition ; what I get
>   Serves but to set
> An edge upon my appetite ;
> And all Thy gifts invite
>   My pray'rs for more."

Cry out to the Lord Jesus to fill the dry beds of thy
rivers until they overflow, and then empty thou the
channels which have hitherto been filled with thine
own self-sufficiency, and beseech Him to fill these also
with His superabundant grace. If thy heavy trials
sink thee deeper in the flood of His consolations, be
glad of them ; and if thy vessel shall be sunken up to
its very bulwarks, be not afraid. I would be glad to
feel the mast-head of my soul twenty fathoms beneath
the surface of such an ocean ; for, as Rutherford said,
" Oh, to be over the ears in this well ! I would not have
Christ's love entering into me, but I would enter into
it, and be swallowed up of that love." Cultivate an
insatiable hunger and a quenchless thirst for this
communion with Jesus through His communications.
Let thine heart cry for ever, " Give, give," until it is
filled in Paradise.

> " O'ercome with Jesu's condescending love,
>   Brought into fellowship with Him and His,
>   And feasting with Him in His house of wine,
>   I'm sick of love,—and yet I pant for more
>   Communications from my loving Lord.
>   Stay me with flagons full of choicest wine,
>   Press'd from His heart upon Mount Calvary,
>   To cheer and comfort my love-conquer'd soul.
>   *   *   *   Thyself I crave !
>   Thy presence is my life, my joy, my heav'n,
>   And all, without Thyself, is dead to me.
>   Stay me with flagons, Saviour, hear my cry,
>   Let promises, like apples, comfort me ;
>   Apply atoning blood, and cov'nant love,
>   Until I see Thy face among the guests
>   Who in Thy Father's kingdom feast."
>   (*Nymphas,* by JOSEPH IRONS.)

This is the only covetousness which is allowable : but

this is not merely beyond rebuke, it is worthy of commendation. O saints, be not straitened in your own bowels, but enlarge your desires, and so receive more of your Saviour's measureless fulness! I charge thee, my soul, thus to hold continual fellowship with thy Lord, since He invites and commands thee thus to partake of His riches.

Rejoice thyself in benefits received. Let the satisfaction of thy spirit overflow in streams of joy. When the believer reposes all his confidence in Christ, and delights himself in Him, there is an exercise of communion. If he forgetteth his psalm-book, and instead of singing is found lamenting, the mercies of the day will bring no communion. Awake, O music! stir up thyself, O my soul, be glad in the Lord, and exceedingly rejoice! Behold His favours, rich, free, and continual; shall they be buried in unthankfulness? Shall they be covered with a winding-sheet of ingratitude? No! I will praise Him. I must extol Him. Sweet Lord Jesus, let me kiss the dust of Thy feet, let me lose myself in thankfulness, for Thy thoughts unto me are precious, how great is the sum of them! Lo, I embrace Thee in the arms of joy and gratitude, and herein I find my soul drawn unto Thee!

This is a blessed method of fellowship. It is kissing the divine lip of benediction with the sanctified lip of affection. Oh, for more rejoicing grace, more of the songs of the heart, more of the melody of the soul!

Seek to recognize the source of thy mercies as lying alone in Him who is our Head. Imitate the chicken, which, every time it drinketh of the brook, lifts up its head to heaven, as if it would return thanks for every drop. If we have anything that is commendable and gracious, it must come from the Holy Spirit, and that Spirit is first bestowed on Jesus, and then through Him on us. The oil was first poured on the head of Aaron, and thence it ran down upon his garments. Look on the drops of grace, and remember that they distil from the Head, Christ Jesus. All thy rays are begotten by this Sun of Righteousness, all thy showers are poured from this heaven, all thy fountains spring from this great and immeasurable depth. Oh, for grace to see the hand of Jesus on every favour! So will communion be constantly and firmly in exercise. May the great Teacher perpetually direct us to Jesus by making the mercies of the covenant the handposts on the road which leadeth to Him. Happy is the believer who knows how to find the secret abode of his Beloved by tracking the footsteps of His loving providence: herein is wisdom which the casual observer of mere second causes can never reach. Labour, O Christian, to follow up every clue which thy Master's grace affords thee!

Labour to maintain a sense of thine entire dependence upon His good will and pleasure for the continuance of thy richest enjoyments. Never try to live on the old manna, nor seek to find help in Egypt. All must come from Jesus, or thou art undone for ever. Old anointings will not suffice to impart unction to our spirit; thine head must have fresh oil poured upon it from the golden horn of the sanctuary, or it will cease from its glory. To-day thou mayest be upon the summit of the mount of God; but He who has put thee there must keep thee there, or thou wilt sink far more speedily than thou dreamest. Thy mountain only stands firm when He settles it in its place; if He hide His face, thou wilt soon be troubled. If the Saviour should see fit, there is not a window through which thou seest the light of heaven which he could not darken in an instant. Joshua bade the sun stand still, but Jesus can shroud it in total darkness. He can withdraw the joy of thine heart, the light of thine eyes, and the strength of thy life ; in His hand thy comforts lie, and at His will they can depart from thee. Oh ! how rich the grace which supplies us so continually, and doth not refrain itself because of our ingratitude ! O Lord Jesus, we would bow at Thy feet, conscious of our utter inability to do aught without Thee, and in every favour which we are privileged to receive, we would adore Thy blessed name, and acknowledge Thine unexhausted love !

When thou hast received much, admire the all-sufficiency which still remaineth undiminished, thus shall you commune with Christ, not only in what you obtain from Him, but also in the superabundance which remains treasured up in Him. Let us ever remember that giving does not impoverish our Lord. When the clouds, those wandering cisterns of the skies, have poured floods upon the dry ground, there remains an abundance in the storehouse of the rain : so in Christ there is ever an unbounded supply, though the most liberal showers of grace have fallen ever since the foundation of the earth. The sun is as bright as ever after all his shining, and the sea is quite as full after all the clouds have been drawn from it : so is our Lord Jesus ever the same overflowing fountain of fulness. All this is ours, and we may make it the subject of rejoicing fellowship. Come, believer, walk through the length and breadth of the land, for as far as the eye can reach, the land is thine, and far beyond the utmost range of thine observation it is thine also, the gracious gift of thy gracious Redeemer and Friend.   Is there not ample space for fellowship *here?*

Regard every spiritual mercy as an assurance of the Lord's communion with thee.   When the young man gives jewels to the virgin to whom he is affianced, she regards them as tokens of his delight in her.   Believer, do the same with the precious presents of thy Lord. The common bounties of providence are shared in by all men, for the good Householder provides water for His swine as well as for His children : such things, therefore, are no proof of divine complacency.   But thou hast richer food to eat ; " the children's bread " is in thy wallet, and the heritage of the righteous is reserved for thee.   Look, then, on every motion of grace in thine heart as a pledge and sign of the moving of thy Saviour's heart towards thee.   There is His whole heart in the bowels of every mercy which He sends thee.   He has impressed a kiss of love upon each gift, and He would have thee believe that every jewel of mercy is a token of His boundless love. Look on thine adoption, justification, and preservation, as sweet enticements to fellowship.   Let every note of the promise sound in thine ears like the ringing of the bells of the house of thy Lord, inviting thee to come to the banquets of His love.   Joseph sent to his father asses laden with the good things of Egypt, and good old Jacob doubtless regarded them as pledges of the love of his son's heart : be sure not to think less of the kindnesses of Jesus.

Study to know the value of His favours.   They are

no ordinary things, no paste jewels, no mosaic gold : they are every one of them so costly, that, had all heaven been drained of treasure, apart from the precious offering of the Redeemer, it could not have purchased so much as the least of His benefits. When thou seest thy pardon, consider how great a boon is contained in it ! Bethink thee that hell had been thine eternal portion unless Christ had plucked thee from the burning ! When thou art enabled to see thyself as clothed in the imputed righteousness of Jesus, admire the profusion of precious things of which thy robe is made. Think how many times the Man of sorrows wearied Himself at that loom of obedience in which He wove that matchless garment ; and reckon, if thou canst, how many worlds of merit were cast into the fabric at every throw of the shuttle ! Remember that all the angels in heaven could not have afforded Him a single thread which would have been rich enough to weave into the texture of His perfect righteousness. Consider the cost of thy maintenance for an hour ; remember that thy wants are so large, that all the granaries of grace that all the saints could fill, could not feed thee for a moment.

What an expensive dependent thou art ! King Solomon made marvellous provision for his household (1 Kings iv. 22), but all his beeves and fine flour would be as the drop of the bucket compared with thy daily wants. Rivers of oil, and ten thousand rams or fed beasts, would not provide enough to supply the necessities of thy hungering soul. Thy least spiritual want demands infinity to satisfy it, and what must be the amazing aggregate of thy perpetually-repeated draughts upon thy Lord ! Arise, then, and bless thy loving Immanuel for the invaluable riches with which He has endowed thee. See what a dowry thy Bridegroom has brought to His poor, penniless spouse. He knows the value of the blessings which He brings thee, for He has paid for them out of His heart's richest blood ; be not thou so ungenerous as to pass them over as if they were but of little worth. Poor men know more of the value of money than those who have always revelled in abundance of wealth. Ought not thy former poverty to teach thee the preciousness of the grace which Jesus gives thee ? For remember, there was a time when thou wouldst have given a thousand worlds, if they had been thine, in order to procure the very least of His abundant mercies.

Remember how impossible it would have been for thee to receive a single spiritual blessing unless thou hadst been in Jesus. On none of Adam's race can the love of God be fixed, unless they are seen to be in union with His Son. No exception has ever been made to the universal curse on those of the first Adam's seed who have no interest in the second Adam. Christ is the only Zoar in which God's Lots can find a shelter from the destruction of Sodom. Out of Him, the withering blast of the fiery furnace of God's wrath consumes every green herb, and it is only in Him that the soul can live. As when the prairie is on fire, men see the heavens wrapped in sheets of flame, and in hot haste they fly before the devouring element. They have but one hope. There is in the distance a lake of water. They reach it, they plunge into it, and are safe. Although the skies are molten with the heat, the sun darkened with the smoke, and the earth

utterly consumed in the fire, they know that they are
secure while the cooling flood embraces them.   Christ
Jesus is the only escape for a sinner pursued by the
fiery wrath of God, and we would have the believer
remember this.   Our own works could never shelter
us, for they have proved but refuges of lies.   Had
they been a thousand times more and better, they
would have been but as the spider's web, too frail to
hang eternal interests upon.   There was but one name,
one sacrifice, one blood, by which we could escape.
All other attempts at salvation were a grievous failure.
For, "though a man could scourge out of his body
rivers of blood, and in neglect of himself could outfast
Moses or Elias ; though he could wear out his knees
with prayer, and had his eyes nailed on heaven ;
though he could build hospitals for all the poor on
earth, and exhaust the mines of India in alms ; though
he could walk like an angel of light, and with the
glittering of an outward holiness dazzle the eyes of all
beholders ; nay (if it were possible to be conceived)
though he should live for a thousand years in a perfect
and perpetual observation of the whole law of God, if
the only exception to his perfection were the very
least deviation from the law, yet such a man as this
could no more appear before the tribunal of God's
justice, than stubble before a consuming fire." *   How,
then, with thine innumerable sins, couldst thou
escape the damnation of hell, much less become the
recipient of bounties so rich and large ?   Blessed
window of heaven, sweet Lord Jesus, let Thy Church
for ever adore Thee, as the only channel by which

---

* Reynolds on the Life of Christ.

mercies can flow to her. My soul, give Him continual praise, for without Him thou hadst been poorer than a beggar. Be thou mindful, O heir of heaven, that thou couldst not have had one ray of hope, or one word of comfort, if thou hadst not been in union with Christ Jesus! The crumbs which fall from thy table are more than grace itself would have given thee, hadst thou not been in Jesus beloved and approved.

All thou hast, thou hast in Him : in Him chosen, in Him redeemed, in Him justified, in Him accepted. Thou art risen in Him, but without Him thou hadst died the second death. Thou art in Him raised up to the heavenly places, but out of Him thou wouldst have been damned eternally. Bless Him, then. Ask the angels to bless Him. Rouse all ages to a harmony of praise for His condescending love in taking poor guilty nothings into oneness with His all-adorable person. This is a blessed means of promoting communion, if the sacred Comforter is pleased to take of the things of Christ, and reveal them to us as ours, but only ours as we are in Him. Thrice-blessed Jesus, let us never forget that we are members of Thy mystical body, and that it is for this reason that we are blessed and preserved.

Meditate upon the gracious acts which procured thy blessings. Consider the ponderous labours which thy Lord endured for thee, and the stupendous sufferings by which He purchased the mercies which He bestows. What human tongue can speak forth the unutterable misery of His heart, or describe so much as one of the agonies which crowded upon His soul? How much less shall any finite comprehension arrive at an idea of the vast total of His woe! But all His sorrows were necessary for thy benefit, and without them not one of thine unnumbered mercies could have been bestowed. Be not unmindful that—

> " There's ne'er a gift His hand bestows,
> But cost His heart a groan."

Look upon the frozen ground of Gethsemane, and behold the bloody sweat which stained the soil! Turn to the hall of Gabbatha, and see the victim of justice pursued by His clamorous foes! Enter the guard-room of the Prætorians, and view the spitting, and the plucking of the hair! and then conclude your review upon Golgotha, the mount of doom, where death consummated His tortures; and if, by divine assistance thou art enabled to enter, in some humble measure, into the depths of thy Lord's sufferings, thou wilt be the better prepared to hold fellowship with Him when next thou receivest His priceless gifts. In proportion to thy sense of their costliness will be thy capacity for enjoying the love which is centred in them.

Above all, and chief of all, never forget that Christ is thine. Amid the profusion of His gifts, never forget that the chief gift is Himself, and do not forget that, after all, His gifts are but Himself. He clothes thee, but it is with Himself, with His own spotless righteousness and character. He washes thee, but His innermost self, His own heart's blood, is the stream with which the fountain overflows. He feeds thee with the bread of heaven, but be not unmindful that the bread is Himself, His own body which He gives to be the food of souls. Never be satisfied with a less communication than a whole Christ. A wife will not be put off with maintenance, jewels, and attire, all these will be nothing to her unless she can call her husband's heart and person her own. It was the Paschal lamb upon which the ancient Israelite did feast on that night that was never to be forgotten. So do thou feast on Jesus, and on nothing less than Jesus, for less than this will be food too light for thy soul's satisfaction. Oh, be careful to eat His flesh and drink His blood, and so receive Him into thyself in a real and spiritual manner, for nothing short of this will be an evidence of eternal life in thy soul!

What more shall we add to the rules which we have here delivered? There remains but one great exhortation, which must not be omitted. *Seek the abundant assistance of the Holy Spirit* to enable you to put into practice the things which we have said, for without His aid, all that we have spoken will but be tantalizing the lame with rules to walk, or the dying with regulations for the preservation of health. O thou Divine Spirit, while we enjoy the grace of Jesus, lead us into the secret abode of our Lord, that we may sup with Him, and He with us, and grant unto us hourly grace that we may continue in the company of our Lord from the rising to the setting of the sun! Amen.

THE WELL-BELOVED'S VINEYARD.

AN ADDRESS TO A LITTLE COMPANY OF BELIEVERS,
IN MR. SPURGEON'S OWN ROOM AT MENTONE.

"My Well-beloved hath a vineyard in a very fruitful hill."—*Isaiah* v. 1.

THE WELL-BELOVED'S VINEYARD.

———

WE recognize at once that Jesus is here. Who but He can be meant by "My Well-beloved"? Here is a word of possession and a word of affection, —He is mine, and my Well-beloved. He is loveliness itself, the most loving and lovable of beings; and we personally love Him with all our heart, and mind, and soul, and strength: He is ours, our Beloved, our Well-beloved, we can say no less.

The delightful relationship of our Lord to us is accompanied by words which remind us of our relationship to Him, "My Well-beloved hath a vineyard," and what vineyard is that but our heart, our nature, our life? We are His : and we are His for the same reason that any other vineyard belongs to its owner. He made us a vineyard. Thorns and briars were all our growth naturally, but He bought us with a price, He hedged us about, and set us apart for Himself, and then He planted and cultivated us. All within us that can bring forth good fruit is of His creating, His tending, and His preserving; so that if we be vineyards at all we must be *His* vineyards. We gladly agree that it shall be so. I pray that I may not have a hair on my head that does not belong to Christ, and you all pray that your every pulse and breath may be the Lord's.

This happy afternoon I want you to note that this

vineyard is said to be upon "a very fruitful hill."
I have been thinking of the advantages of my own
position towards the Lord, and lamenting with great
shamefacedness that I am not bringing forth such
fruit to Him as my position demands. Considering
our privileges, advantages, and opportunities, I fear
that many of us have need to feel great searchings of
heart. Perhaps to such the text may be helpful, and
it will not be without profit to any one of us, if the
Lord will bless our meditation upon it.

I. Our first thought, in considering these words, is
that OUR POSITION AS THE LORD'S VINEYARD IS A
VERY FAVOURABLE ONE: "My Well-beloved hath a
vineyard in a very fruitful hill." No people could be
better placed for serving Christ than we are. I hardly
think that any man is better situated for glorifying
God than I am. I do not think that any women
could be in better positions for serving Christ than
some of you, dear sisters, now occupy. Our heavenly
Father has placed us just where He can do the most
for us, and where we can do the most for Him. Infinite
wisdom has occupied itself with carefully selecting the
soil, and site, and aspect of every tree in the vineyard.
We differ greatly, and need differing situations in
order to fruitfulness: the place which would suit one
might be too trying for another. Friend, the Lord
has planted you in the right spot: your station may
not be the best in itself, but it is the best for you.
We are in the best possible position for some present
service at this moment; the providence of God has
put us on a vantage ground for our immediate duty:
"My Well-beloved hath a vineyard in a very fruitful
hill."

Let us think of *the times in which we live* as calling upon us to be very fruitful when we compare them with the years gone by. Time was when we could not have met thus happily in our own room : if we had been taken in the act of breaking bread, or reading God's Word, we should have been haled off to prison, and perhaps put to death. Our forefathers scarcely dared to lift up their voices in a psalm of praise, lest the enemy should be upon them. Truly, the lines have fallen unto us in pleasant places ; yea, we have a goodly heritage, in a very fruitful hill.

We do not even live in times when error is so rampant as to be paramount. There is too much of it abroad ; but taking a broad view of things, I venture to say that there never was a time when the truth had a wider sway than it has now, or when the gospel was more fully preached, or when there was more spiritual activity. Black clouds of error hover over us ; but at the same time we rejoice that, from John o' Groat's House to the Land's End, Christ is preached by ten thousand voices, and even in the dark parts of the earth the name of Jesus is shining like a candle in the house. If we had the pick of the ages in which to live, we could not have selected a better time for fruit-bearing than that which is now occurrent : this age is " a very fruitful hill."

That this is the case some of us know positively, *because we have been fruitful*. Look back, brothers and sisters, upon times when your hearts were warm, and your zeal was fervent, and you served the Lord with gladness. I join with you in those happy memories. Then we could run with the swiftest, we could fight with the bravest, we could work with the strongest;

we could suffer with the most patient. The grace of God has been upon certain of us in such an unmistakable manner that we have brought forth all the fruits of the Spirit. Perhaps to-day we look back with deep regret because we are not so fruitful as we once were: if it be so, it is well that our regrets should multiply, but we must change each one of them into a hopeful prayer. Remember, the vine may have changed, but the soil is the same. We have still the same motives for being fruitful, and even more than we used to have. Why are we not more useful? Has some spiritual phylloxera taken possession of the vines, or have we become frost-bitten, or sun-burnt? What is it that withholds the vintage? Certainly, if we were fruitful once, we ought to be more fruitful now. The fruitful hill is not exhausted; what aileth us that our grapes are so few?

We are planted on a fruitful hill, *for we are called to work which of all others is the most fruitful.* Blessed and happy is the man who is called to the Christian ministry; for this service has brought more glory to Christ than any other. You, beloved friends, are not called to be rulers of nations, nor inventors of engines, nor teachers of sciences, nor slayers of men; but we are soul-winners, our work is to lead men to Jesus. Ours is, of all the employments in the world, the most fruitful in benefits to men and glory to God. If we are not serving God in the gospel of His Son with all our might and ability, then we have a heavy responsibility resting upon us. "Our Well-beloved hath a vineyard in a very fruitful hill:" there is not a richer bit of soil outside Immanuel's land than the holy ministry for souls. Certain of us are teachers, and gather the young about us while we speak of Jesus. This also is choice soil. Many teachers have gathered a grand vintage from among the little ones, and have not been a whit behind pastors and evangelists in the glory of soul-winning. Dear teachers, your vines are planted in a very fruitful hill. But I do not confine myself to preachers and teachers; for all of us, as we have opportunities of speaking for the Lord Jesus Christ, and privately talking to individuals, have also a fertile soil to grow in. If we do not glorify God by soul-winning, we shall be greatly blamable, since of all forms of service it is most prolific in praise of God.

And what is more, *the very circumstances with which we are surrounded* all tend to make our position exceedingly favourable for fruit-bearing. In this little company we have not one friend who is extremely poor; but if such were among us, I should say the same thing. Christ has gathered some of His choicest clusters from the valley of poverty. Many eminent saints have never owned a foot of land, but lived upon their weekly wage, and found scant fare at that. Yes, by the grace of God, the vale of poverty has blossomed as the rose. It so happens, however, that the most of us here have a competence, we have all that we need, and something over to give to the poor and to the cause of God. Surely we ought to be fruitful in alms-giving, in caring for the sick, and in all manner of sweet and fragrant influences. "Give me neither poverty nor riches," is a prayer that has been answered for most of us; and if we do not now give honour unto God, what excuse can we make for our barren-ness? I am speaking to some who are singularly healthy, who are never hindered by aches and pains;

and to others who have been prospered in business for twenty years at a stretch : yours is great indebtedness to your Lord : in your case, " My Well-beloved hath a vineyard in a very fruitful hill." Give God your strength and your wealth, my brother, while they last : see that all His care of thee is not thrown away. Others of us seldom know many months together of health, but have often had to suffer sorely in body ; this ought to make us fruitful, for there is much increase from the tillage of affliction. Has not the Master obtained the richest of all fruit from bleeding vines ? Do not His heaviest bunches come from vines which have been sharply cut and pruned down to the ground ? Choice flavours, dainty juices, and delicious aromas come mostly from the use of the keen-edged knife of trial. Some of us are at our best for fruit-bearing when in other respects we are at our worst. Thus I might truly say that, whatever our circumstances may be, whether we are poor or rich, in health or in affliction, each one of our cases has its advantages, and we are planted " in a very fruitful hill."

Furthermore, when I look at *our spiritual condition*, I must say for myself, and I think for you also, " My Well-beloved hath a vineyard in a very fruitful hill " For what has God done for us ? To change the question,—what has God *not* done for us ? What more could He say than to us He hath said ? What more could He do than to us He hath done ? He hath dealt with us like a God. He has loved us up from the pit, He has loved us up to the cross, and up to the gates of heaven ; He has quickened us, forgiven us, and renewed us ; He dwells in us, comforts us, instructs us, upholds us, preserves us, guides us, leads us, and He will surely perfect us. If we are not fruitful, to His praise, how shall we excuse ourselves? Where shall we hide our guilty heads? Shall yonder sea suffice to lend us briny tears wherewith to weep over our ingratitude?

II. I go a step further, by your leave, and say that OUR POSITION, as the Lord's vineyard, IS FAVOURABLE TO THE PRODUCTION OF THE FRUIT WHICH HE LOVES BEST. I believe that my own position is the most favourable for the production of the fruit that the Lord loves best in me, and that your position is the same. What is this fruit?

First, it is *faith*. Our Lord is very delighted to see faith in His people. The trust which clings to Him with childlike confidence is pleasant to His loving heart. Our position is such that faith ought to be the easiest thing in the world to us. Look at the promises He has given us in His Word : can we not believe them? Look at what the Father has done for us in the gift of His dear Son : can we not trust Him after that? Our daily experience all goes to strengthen our confidence in God. Every mercy asks, " Will you not trust Him?" Every want that is supplied cries, " Can you not trust Him?" Every sorrow sent by the great Father tests our faith, and drives us to Him on whom we repose, and so strengthens and confirms our confidence in God. Mercies and miseries alike operate for the growth of faith. Some of us have been called upon to trust God on a large scale, and that necessity has been a great help towards fruit-bearing. The more troubles we have, the more is our vine digged about, and the more nourishment is laid to its roots. If faith does not ripen under trial, when will it ripen? Our afflictions fertilize the soil wherein faith may grow.

Another choice fruit is *love*. Jesus delights in love. His tender heart delights to see its love returned. Am I not of all men most bound to love the Lord? I speak for each brother and sister here, is not that your language? Do you not all say, "Lives there a person beneath yon blue sky who ought to love Jesus more than I should do?" Each sister soliloquizes, "Sat there ever a woman in her chamber who had more reason for loving God than I have?" No, the sin which has been forgiven us should make us love our Saviour exceeding much. The sin which has been prevented in other cases should make us love our Preserver much. The help which God has sent us in hours of need, the guidance which He has given in times of difficulty, the joy which He has poured into us in days of fellowship, and the quiet He has breathed upon us in seasons of trial,—all ought to make us love Him. Along our life-road, reasons for loving God are more numerous than the leaves upon the olives. He has hedged us about with His goodness, even as the mountains and the sea are round our present resting-place. Look backward as far as time endures, and then look far beyond that, into the eternity which has been, and you will see the Lord's great love set upon us : all through time and eternity reasons have been accumulating which constrain us to love our Lord. Now turn sharply round, and gaze before you, and all along the future faith can see reasons for loving God, golden milestones on the way that is yet to be traversed, all calling for our loving delight in God.

Christ is also very pleased with the fruit of *hope*, and we are so circumstanced that we ought to produce much of it. The aged ought to look forward, for they cannot expect to see much more on earth. Time is short, and eternity is near ; how precious is a good hope through grace! We who are not yet old ought to be exceedingly hopeful ; and the younger folk, who are just beginning the spiritual life, should abound in hope most fresh and bright. If any man has expectations greater than I have, I should like to see him. We have the greatest of expectations. Have you never felt like Mercy in her dream, when she laughed, and when Christiana asked her what made her laugh, she said that she had had a vision of things yet to be revealed?

Select any fruit of the Spirit you choose, and I maintain that we are favourably circumstanced for producing it ; we are planted upon a very fruitful hill. What a fruitful hill we are living in as regards *labour for Christ!* Each one of us may find work for the Master ; there are capital opportunities around us. There never was an age in which a man, consecrated to God, might do so much as he can at this time. There is nothing to restrain the most ardent zeal. We live in such happy times that, if we plunge into a sea of work, we may swim, and none can hinder us. Then, too, our labour is made, by God's grace, to be so pleasant to us. No true servant of Christ is weary *of* the work, though he may be weary *in* the work : it is not the work that he ever wearies of, for he wishes that he could do ten times more. Then our Lord makes our work to be successful. We bring one soul to Jesus, and that one brings a hundred. Sometimes,

when we are fishing for Jesus, there may be few fish,
but, blessed be His name, most of them enter the net ;
and we have to live praising and blessing God for all
the favour with which He regards our labour of love.
I do think I am right in saying that, for the bearing of
the fruit which Jesus loves best, our position is
exceedingly favourable.

III. And now, this afternoon, at this table, OUR
POSITION HERE IS FAVOURABLE EVEN NOW TO OUR
PRODUCING IMMEDIATELY, and upon the spot, the
richest, ripest, rarest fruit for our Well-beloved. Here,
at the communion-table, we are at the centre of the
truth, and at the well-head of consolation. Now we
enter the holy of holies, and come to the most sacred
meeting-place between our souls and God.

Viewed from this table, *the vineyard slopes to the
south*, for everything looks towards Christ, our Sun.
This bread, this wine, all set our souls aslope towards
Jesus Christ, and He shines full upon our hearts, and
minds, and souls, to make us bring forth much fruit.
Are we not planted on a very fruitful hill ?

As we think of His passion for our sake, we feel
that *a wall is set about us to the north*, to keep back
every sharp blast that might destroy the tender grapes.
No wrath is dreaded now, for Jesus has borne it for
us ; behold the tokens of His all-sufficient sacrifice !
No anger of the Lord shall come to our restful spirits,
for the Lord saith, " I have sworn that I will not be
wroth with thee, nor rebuke thee." Here, on this
table, are the pledges of His love unspeakable, and
these, like a high wall, keep out the rough winds.
Surely, we are planted on a very fruitful hill.

Moreover, *the Well-beloved Himself is among us.*

He has not let us out to husbandmen, but He Himself doth undertake to care for us; and that He is
here we are sure, for here is His flesh, and here is His
blood. You see the outward tokens, may you feel
the unseen reality.; for we believe in His real presence,
though not in the gross corporeal sense with which
worldly spirits blind themselves. The King has come
into His garden : let us entertain Him with our fruits.
He who for this vineyard poured out a bloody sweat,
is now surveying the vines; shall they not at this
instant give forth a goodly smell? The presence of our
Lord makes this assembly a very fruitful hill : where
He sets His feet, all good things flourish.

Around this table, *we are in a place where others have
fruited well*. Our literature contains no words more
precious than those which have been spoken at the
time of communion. Perhaps you know and appreciate the discourses of Willison, delivered on sacra-
mental occasions. Rutherford's communion sermons
have a sacred unction upon them. The poems of
George Herbert, I should think, were most of them
inspired by the sight of Christ in this ordinance.
Think of the canticles of holy Bernard, how they flame
with devotion. Saints and martyrs have been nourished
at this table of blessing. This hallowed ordinance,
I am sure, is a spot where hopes grow bright, and
hearts grow warm, resolves become firm, and lives
become fruitful, and all the clusters of our soul's fruit
ripen for the Lord.

Blessed be God, *we are where we have ourselves often
grown*. We have enjoyed our best times when cele-
brating this sacred Eucharist. God grant it may be so
again! Let us, in calm meditation and inward thought,

now produce from our hearts sweet fruits of love, and zeal, and hope, and patience; let us yield great clusters like those of Eshcol, all for Jesus, and for Jesus only. Even now, let us give ourselves up to meditation, gratitude, adoration, communion, rapture; and let us spend the rest of our lives in glorifying and magnifying the ever-blessed name of our Well-beloved whose vineyard we are.

> " While such a scene of sacred joys
>   Our raptured eyes and souls employs,
>   Here we could sit, and gaze away
>   A long, an everlasting day.

> " Well, we shall quickly pass the night,
>   To the fair coasts of perfect light ;
>   Then shall our joyful senses rove
>   O'er the dear object of our love.

> " There shall we drink full draughts of bliss,
>   And pluck new life from heavenly trees :
>   Yet now and then, dear Lord, bestow
>   A drop of heaven on worms below."

REDEEMED SOULS FREED FROM FEAR.

A TALK WITH A FEW FRIENDS AT MENTONE.

"Fear not : for I have redeemed thee."—*Isaiah* xliii. 1.

REDEEMED SOULS FREED FROM FEAR.

I WAS lamenting this morning my unfitness for my work, and especially for the warfare to which I am called. A sense of heaviness came over me, but relief came very speedily, for which I thank the Lord. Indeed, I was greatly burdened, but the Lord succoured me. The first verse read at the Sabbath morning service exactly met my case. It is in Isaiah xliii. 1 : " But now thus saith the Lord that created thee, O Jacob, and He that formed thee, O Israel, Fear not." I said to myself, " I am what God created me, and I am what He formed me, and therefore I must, after all, be the right man for the place wherein He has put me." We may not blame our Creator, nor suspect that He has missed His mark in forming an instrument for His work. Thus new comfort comes to us. Not only do the operations of grace in the spiritual world yield us consolation, but we are even comforted by what the Lord has done in creation. We are told to cease from our fears ; and we do so, since we perceive that it is the Lord that made us, and not we ourselves, and He will justify His own creating skill by accomplishing through us the purposes of His love. Pray, I beseech you, for me, the weakest of my Lord's servants, that I may be equal to the overwhelming task imposed upon me.

The next sentence of the chapter is usually most

comforting to my soul, although on this one occasion
the first sentence was a specially reviving cordial to
me.   The verse goes on to say,—

> "*Fear not: for I have redeemed thee.*"

Let us think for a few minutes of the wonderful
depth of consolation which lies in this fact.   We have
been redeemed by the Lord Himself, and this is a
grand reason why we should never again be subject to
fear.   Oh, that the logic of this fact could be turned
into practice, so that we henceforth rejoiced, or at
least felt the peace of God!

These words may be spoken, first of all, of those
frequent occasions in which the Lord has redeemed
His people out of *trouble*.   Many a time and oft might
our Lord say to each one of us, "I have redeemed
thee."   Out of six, yea, six thousand trials He has
brought us forth by the right hand of His power.   He
has released us from our afflictions, and brought us
forth into a wealthy place.   In the remembrance of
all these redemptions the Lord seems to say to us,
"What I have done before, I will do again.   I have
redeemed thee, and I will still redeem thee.   I have
brought thee from under the hand of the oppressor;
I have delivered thee from the tongue of the slanderer;
I have borne thee up under the load of poverty, and
sustained thee under the pains of sickness; and I am
able still to do the same: wherefore, then, dost thou
fear?   Why shouldst thou be afraid, since already I
have again and again redeemed thee?   Take heart,
and be confident; for even to old age and to death
itself I will continue to be thy strong Redeemer."

I suppose there would be a reference here to the

great redemption out of Egypt. This word is addressed to the people of God under captivity in Babylon, and we know that the Lord referred to the Egyptian redemption ; for He says in the third verse, " I gave Egypt for thy ransom." Egypt was a great country, and a rich country, for we read of " all the treasures of Egypt", but God gave them for His chosen : He would give all the nations of the earth for His Israel. This was a wonderful stay to the people of God : they constantly referred to Egypt and the Red Sea, and made their national song out of it. In all Israel's times of disaster, and calamity, and trial, they joyfully remembered that the Lord had redeemed them when they were a company of slaves, helpless and hopeless, under a tyrant who cast their firstborn children into the Nile, a tyrant whose power was so tremendous that all the armies of the world could not have wrought their deliverance from his iron hand. The very nod of Pharaoh seemed to the inhabitants of Egypt to be omnipotent; he was a builder of pyramids, a master of all the sciences of peace and the arts of war. What could the Israelites have done against him ? Jehovah came to their relief in their dire extremity. His plagues followed each other in quick succession. The dread volleys of the Lord's artillery confounded His foes. At last He smote all the firstborn of Egypt, the chief of all their strength. Then was Egypt glad that Israel departed, and the Lord brought forth His people with silver and gold. All the chivalry of Egypt was overthrown and destroyed at the Red Sea, and the timbrels of the daughters of Israel sounded joyously upon its shores. This redemption out of Egypt is so remarkable that it is remembered even in heaven. The Old Testament song is woven into that of the New Covenant; for there they "sing the song of Moses the servant of God, and the song of the Lamb." The first redemption was so wonderful a type and prophecy of the other that it is no alloy to the golden hymn of eternal glory, but readily melts into the same celestial chant. Other types may cease to be remembered, but this was so much a fact as well as a type that it shall be had in memory for ever and ever. Every Israelite ought to have had confidence in God after what He had done for the people in redeeming them out of Egypt. To every one of the seed of Jacob it was a grand argument to enforce the precept, " Fear not."

But I take it that the chief reference of these words is to that redemption which has been wrought out for us by Him who loved us, and washed us from our sins in His own blood. Let us think of it for a minute or two before we break the bread and drink of the cup of communion.

The remembrance of this transcendent redemption ought to comfort us in all times of *perplexity*. When we cannot see our way, or cannot make out what to do, we need not be at all troubled concerning it ; for the Lord Jehovah can see a way out of every intricacy. There never was a problem so hard to solve as that which is answered in redemption. Herein was the tremendous difficulty—How can God be just, and yet be the Saviour of sinners? How can He fulfil His threatenings, and yet forgive sin? If that problem had been left to angels and men, they could never have worked it out throughout eternity ; but God has

solved it through freely delivering up His own Son.
In the glorious sacrifice of Jesus we see the justice of
God magnified ; for He laid sin on the blessed Lord,
who had become one with His chosen. Jesus
identified Himself with His people, and therefore their
sin was laid upon Him, and the sword of the Lord
awoke against Him. He was not taken arbitrarily to
be a victim, but He was a voluntary Sufferer. His
relationship amounted to covenant oneness with His
people, and "it behoved Christ to suffer." Herein is a
wisdom which must be more than equal to all minor
perplexities. Hear this, then, O poor soul in suspense !
The Lord says, "I have redeemed thee. I have
already brought thee out of the labyrinth in which
thou wast lost by sin, and therefore I will take thee
out of the meshes of the net of temptation, and lead
thee through the maze of trial ; I will bring the blind
by a way that they know not, and lead them in paths
which they have not known. I will bring again from
Bashan, I will bring up My people from the depths of
the sea." Let us commit our way unto the Lord.
Mine is a peculiarly difficult one, but I know that
my Redeemer liveth, and He will lead me by a right
way. He will be our Guide even unto death ; and
after death He will guide us through those tracks unknown of the mysterious region, and cause us to rest
with Him for ever.

So also, if at any time we are in great *poverty*, or in
great straitness of means for the Lord's work, and we
are, therefore, afraid that we shall never get our needs
supplied, let us cast off such fears as we listen to the
music of these words : "Fear not: for I have redeemed
thee." God Himself looked down from heaven, and

saw that there was no man who could give to Him a ransom for his brother, and each man on his own part was hopelessly bankrupt; and then, despite our spiritual beggary, He found the means of our redemption. What then? Let us hear the use which the Holy Spirit makes of this fact: " He that spared not His own Son, but delivered Him up for us all, how shall He not with Him also freely give us all things?" We cannot have a want which the Lord will not supply. Since God has given us Jesus, He will give us, not some things, but " all things." Indeed, all things are ours in Christ Jesus. No necessity of this life can for a single moment be compared to that dread necessity which the Lord has already supplied. The infinite gift of God's own Son is a far greater one than all that can be included in the term "all things": wherefore, it is a grand argument to the poor and needy, " Fear not: for I have redeemed thee." Perplexity and poverty are thus effectually met.

We are at times troubled by a sense of our personal *insignificance*. It seems too much to hope that God's infinite mind should enter into our mean affairs. Though David said, " I am poor and needy, yet the Lord thinketh upon me," we are not always quite prepared to say the same. We make our sorrows great under the vain idea that they are too small for the Lord to notice. I believe that our greatest miseries spring from those little worries which we hesitate to bring to our heavenly Father. Our gracious God puts an end to all such thoughts as these by saying, " Fear not: for I have redeemed thee." You are not of such small account as you suppose. The Lord would never be wasteful of His sacred expenditure.

He bought you with a price, and therefore He sets great store by you. Listen to what the Lord says : " Since thou wast precious in My sight, thou hast been honourable, and I have loved thee : therefore will I give men for thee, and people for thy life." It is amazing that the Lord should think so much of us as to give Jesus for us. " What is man that Thou art mindful of him ? " Yet God's mind is filled with thoughts of love towards man. Know ye not that His only-begotten Son entered this world, and became a man ? The man Christ Jesus has a name at which every knee shall bow, and He is so dear to the Father that, for His sake, His chosen ones are accepted, and are made to enjoy the freest access to Him. We sing truly,—

> " So near, so very near to God,
>   Nearer we cannot be,
> For in the person of His Son
>   We are as near as He."

And now the very hairs of our head are all numbered, and the least burden we may roll upon the Lord. Those cares which we ought not to have may well cease, for " He careth for us." He that redeemed us never forgets us : His wounds have graven us upon the palms of His hands, and written our names deep in His side. Jesus stoops to our level, for He stooped to bear the cross to redeem us. Do not, therefore, be again afraid because of your insignificance. " Why sayest thou, O Jacob, and speakest, O Israel, My way is hid from the Lord, and my judgment is passed over from my God ? Hast thou not known ? Hast thou not heard, that the everlasting God, the Lord, the Creator of the ends of the earth, fainteth not, neither is weary? There is no searching of His understanding. He giveth power to the faint; and to them that have no might He increaseth strength." The Lord's memory is toward the little in Israel. He carrieth the lambs in His bosom.

We are liable to fret a little when we think of our *changeableness*. If you are at all like me, you are very far from being always alike; I am sometimes lifted up to the very heavens, and then I go down to the deeps; I am at one time bright with joy and confidence, and at another time dark as midnight with doubts and fears. Even Elijah, who was so brave, had his fainting fits. We are to be blamed for this, and yet the fact remains: our experience is as an April day, when shower and sunshine take their turns. Amid our mournful changes we rejoice to hear the Lord's own voice, saying, "Fear not: for I have redeemed thee." Everything is not changeful wave; there is rock somewhere. Redemption is a fact accomplished.

"The Cross, it standeth fast. Hallelujah!"

The price is paid, the ransom accepted. This is done, and can never be undone. Jesus says, "I have redeemed thee." Change of feeling within does not alter the fact that the believer has been bought with a price, and made the Lord's own by the precious blood of Jesus. The Lord God has already done so much for us that our salvation is sure in Christ Jesus. Will He begin to build, and fail to finish? Will He lay the foundation in the everlasting covenant? Will He dedicate the walls with the infinite sacrifice of the Lamb of God? Will He give up the choicest treasure He ever had, the chosen of God and precious, to be the corner-stone, and then not finish the work He has begun? It is impossible. If He has redeemed us, He has, in that act, given us the pledge of all things.

See how the gifts of God are bound to this redemption. "I have redeemed thee. I have called thee." "For whom He did foreknow, He also did predestinate to be conformed to the image of His Son, that He might be the firstborn among many brethren. Moreover whom He did predestinate, them He also called: and whom He called, them He also justified: and whom He justified, them He also glorified." Here is a chain in which each link is joined to all the rest, so that it cannot be separated. If God had only gone so far as to make a promise, He would not have drawn back from it; if God had gone as far as to swear an oath by Himself, He would not have failed to keep it; but when He went beyond promise and oath, and in very deed the sacrifice was slain, and the covenant was ratified: why, then it would be blasphemous to imagine that He would afterwards disannul it, and turn from His solemn pledge. There is no going back on the part of God, and consequently His redemption will redeem, and in redeeming it will secure us all things. "Who shall separate us from the love of Christ?" With the blood-mark upon us we may well cease to fear. How can we perish? How can we be deserted in the hour of need? We have been bought with too great a price for our Redeemer to let us slip. Therefore, let us march on with confidence, hearing our Redeemer say to us, "When thou passest through the waters, I will be with thee; and through the rivers, they shall not overflow thee: when thou walkest through the fire, thou shalt not be burned; neither shall the flame kindle upon thee." Concerning His redeemed, the Lord will say to the enemy, "Touch not Mine anointed, and do My prophets no harm." The stars in their courses fight for the ransomed of the Lord. If their eyes were opened, they would see the mountain full of horses of fire and chariots of fire round about them. Oh, how my weary heart prizes redeeming love! If it were not for this, I would lay me down, and die. Friends forsake me, foes surround me, I am filled with contempt, and tortured with the subtlety which I cannot baffle; but as the Lord of all brought again from the dead our Lord Jesus, that great Shepherd of the sheep, by the blood of the everlasting covenant, so by the blood of His covenant doth He loose His prisoners, and sustain the hearts of those who tremble at His Word. "O my soul, thou hast trodden down strength," for the Lord hath said unto thee, "Fear not: for I have redeemed thee."

JESUS, THE GREAT OBJECT OF ASTONISHMENT.

A COMMUNION ADDRESS AT MENTONE.

"Behold, My Servant shall deal prudently, He shall be exalted and extolled, and be very high. As many were astonied at Thee; His visage was so marred more than any man, and His form more than the sons of men; so shall He sprinkle many nations; the kings shall shut their mouths at Him: for that which had not been told them shall they see; and that which they had not heard shall they consider."

Isaiah lii. 13—15

JESUS, THE GREAT OBJECT OF ASTONISHMENT.

———

OUR Lord Jesus Christ bore from of old the name of "WONDERFUL", and the word seems all too poor to set forth His marvellous person and character. He says of Himself, in the language of the prophet,—" Behold, I and the children whom the Lord hath given Me are for signs and for wonders." He is a fountain of astonishment to all who know Him, and the more they know of Him, the more are they "astonied" at Him. It is an astonishing thing that there should have been a Christ at all: the Incarnation is the miracle of miracles; that He who is the Infinite should become an infant, that He who made the worlds should be wrapt in swaddling-bands, remains a fact out of which, as from a hive, new wonders continually fly forth. In His complex nature He is so mysterious, and yet so manifest, that doubtless all the angels of heaven were and are astonished at Him. O Son of God, and Son of man, when Thou, the Word, wast made flesh, and dwelt among us, and Thy saints beheld Thy glory, it was but natural that many should be astonished at Thee!

Our text seems to say that our Lord was, first, *a great wonder in His griefs;* and, secondly, that He was *a great wonder in His glory.*

I. HE WAS A GREAT WONDER IN HIS GRIEFS: "As many were astonied at Thee; His visage was so

marred more than any man, and His form more than
the sons of men."

His visage was marred : no doubt His countenance
bore the signs of a matchless grief.　There were
ploughings on His brow as well as upon His back ;
suffering, and brokenness of spirit, and agony of heart,
had told upon that lovely face, till its beauty, though
never to be destroyed, was "so" marred that never
was any other so spoiled with sorrow.　But it was not
His face only, His whole form was marred more than
the sons of men.　The contour of His bodily manhood showed marks of singular assaults of sorrow,
such as had never bowed another form so low.　I do
not know whether His gait was stooping, or whether
His knees tottered, and His walk was feeble ; but
there was evidently a something about Him which
gave Him the appearance of premature age, since to
the Jews He looked older than He was, for when He
was little more than thirty they said unto Him, "Thou
art not yet fifty years old."　I cannot conceive that
He was deformed or ungainly ; but despite His
natural dignity, His worn and emaciated appearance
marked Him out as "the Man of sorrows", and to
the carnal eye His whole natural and spiritual form
had in it nothing which evoked admiration ; even as
the prophet said, "When we shall see Him, there is
no beauty that we should desire Him."　The marring
was not of that lovely face alone, but of the whole
fabric of His wondrous manhood, so that many were
astonied at Him.

Our astonishment, when in contemplation we
behold our suffering Lord, will arise from the con-
sideration of what His natural beauty must have

been, enshrined as He was from the first within a
perfect body. Conceived without sin, and so born of
a pure virgin without taint of hereditary sin, I doubt
not that He was the flower and glory of manhood as
to His form, and from His early youth He must
have been a joy to His mother's eye. Great masters
of the olden time expended all their skill upon the
holy child Jesus, but it is not for the colours of earth
to depict the Lord from heaven. That "holy thing"
which was born of Mary was "seen of angels," and it
charmed their eyes. Must such loveliness be marred?
His every look was pure, His every thought was holy,
and therefore the expression of His face must have
been heavenly, and yet it must be marred. Poverty
must mark it; hunger, and thirst, and weariness,
must plough it; heart-griefs must seam and scar it;
spittle must distain it; tears must scald it; smiting
must bruise it; death must make it pale and
bloodless. Well does Bernard sing,—

> "O sacred Head, once wounded,
> With grief and pain weigh'd down,
> How scornfully surrounded
> With thorns, Thine only crown;
> How pale art Thou with anguish,
> With sore abuse and scorn!
> How does that visage languish,
> Which once was bright as morn!"

The second astonishment to us must be that he
could be so marred who had nothing in His character
to mar His countenance. Sin is a sad disfigurement
to faces which in early childhood were surpassingly
attractive. Passion, if it be indulged in, soon sets a
seal of deformity upon the countenance. Men that

plunge into vice bear upon their features the traces of their hearts' volcanic fires. We most of us know some withered beings, whose beauty has been burned up by the fierce fires of excess, till they are a horror to look upon, as if the mark of Cain were set upon them. Every sin makes its line on a fair face. But there was no sin in the blessed Jesus, no evil thought to mar His natural perfectness. No redness of eyes ever came to Him by tarrying long at the wine ; no unhallowed anger ever flushed His cheek ; no covetousness gave to His eye a wolfish glance ; no selfish care lent to His features a sharp and anxious cast. Such an unselfish, holy life as His ought to have rendered Him, if it had been possible, more beautiful every day. Indulging such benevolence, abiding in such communion with God, surely the face of Christ must, in the natural order of things, have more and more astonished all sympathetic observers with its transcendent charms. But sorrow came to engrave her name where sin had never made a stroke, and she did her work so effectually that His visage was more marred than that of any man, although the God of mercy knows there have been other visages that have been worn with pain and anguish past all recognition. I need not repeat even one of the many stories of human woe : that of our Lord surpasses all.

Remember that the face of our Well-beloved, as well as all His form, must have been an accurate index of His soul. Physiognomy is a science with much truth in it when it deals with men of truth. Men weaned from simplicity know how to control their countenances; the crafty will appear to be honest, the hardened will seem to sympathize with the distressed, the revengeful will mimic good-will. There are some who continually use their countenance as they do their speech, to conceal their feelings ; and it is almost a point of politeness with them never to show themselves, but always to go masked among their fellows.

But the Christ had learned no such arts. He was so sincere, so transparent, so child-like and true, that whatever stirred within Him was apparent to those about Him, so far as they were capable of understanding His great soul. We read of Him that He was "moved with compassion." The Greek word means that He experienced a wonderful emotion of His whole nature, He was thrilled with it, and His disciples saw how deeply He felt for the people, who were as sheep without a shepherd. Though He did not commit Himself to men, He did not conceal Himself, but wore His heart upon His sleeve, and all could see what He was, and knew that He was full of grace and truth. We are, therefore, not surprised, when we devoutly consider our Lord's character, that His visage and form should indicate the inward agonies of His tender spirit ; it could not be that His face should be untrue to His heart. The ploughers made deep furrows upon His soul as well as upon His back, and His heart was rent with inward convulsions, which could not but affect His whole appearance. Those eyes saw what those around Him could not see; those shoulders bore a constant burden which others could not know ; and, therefore, His countenance and form betrayed the fact. O dear, dear Saviour, when we think of Thee, and of Thy majesty and purity, we are again astonished that woes should come upon Thee so grievously as to mar Thy visage and Thy form !

Now think, dear friends, what were the causes of this marring. It was not old age that had wrinkled His brow, for He was still in the prime of life, neither was it a personal sickness which had caused decay ; much less was it any congenital weakness and disease, which at length betrayed itself, for in His flesh there was no possibility of impurity, which would, in death, have led to corruption. It was occasioned, first, by His constant sympathy with the suffering. There was a heavy wear and tear occasioned by the extraordinary compassion of His soul. In three years it had told upon Him most manifestly, till His visage was marred more than that of any other man. To Him there was a kind of sucking up into Himself of all the suffering of those whom He blessed. He always bore upon Him the burden of mortal woe. We read of Christ healing all that were sick, "that it might be fulfilled which was spoken by Esaias the prophet, saying, Himself took our infirmities, and bare our sicknesses." Yes, He took those infirmities and sicknesses in some mystical way to Himself, just as I have heard of certain trees, which scatter health, because they themselves imbibe the miasma, and draw up into themselves those noxious vapours which otherwise would poison mankind. Thus, without being themselves polluted, they disinfect the atmosphere around them. This, our Saviour did, but the cost was great to Him. You can imagine, living as He did in the midst of one vast hospital, how constantly He must have seen sights that grieved and pained Him. Moreover, with a nature so pure and loving, He must have been daily tortured with the sin, and hypocrisy, and oppression which so abounded in His day. In a certain sense, He was always laying down His life for men, for He was spent in their service, tortured by their sin, and oppressed with their sorrow. The more we look into that marred visage, the more shall we be astonished at the anguish which it indicated.

Do not wonder that He was more marred than any man, for He was more sensitive than other men. No part of Him was callous, He had no seared conscience, no blunted sensibility, no drugged and deadened nerve. His manhood was in its glory, in the perfection in which Adam was when God made him in His own image, and therefore He was ill-housed in such a fallen world. We read of Christ that He was "grieved for the hardness of their hearts," "He marvelled because of their unbelief," "He sighed deeply in His spirit," "He groaned in the spirit, and was troubled." This, however, was only the beginning of the marring.

His deepest griefs and most grievous marring came of *His substitutionary work,* while bearing the penalty of our sin. One word recalls much of His woe : it is, "Gethsemane." Betrayed by Judas, His trusted friend, that the Scripture might be fulfilled, "He that eateth bread with Me hath lifted up his heel against Me ;" deserted even by John, for all the disciples forsook Him and fled ; not one of all the loved ones with Him : He was left alone. He had washed their feet, but they could not watch with Him one hour ; and in that garden He wrestled with our deadly foe, till His sweat was as it were great drops of blood falling down to the ground, and as Hart puts it, He—

"Bore all Incarnate God could bear,
    With strength enough, but none to spare."

I do verily believe that verse to be true. Herein you see what marred His countenance, and His form, even while in life. The whole of His manhood felt that dreadful shock, when He and the prince of darkness, in awful duel, fought it out amidst the gloom of the olives on that cold midnight when our redemption began to be fully accomplished.

The whole of His passion marred His countenance and His form with its unknown sufferings. I restrain myself, lest this meditation should grow too painful. They bound Him, they scourged Him, they mocked Him, they plucked off the hair from His face, they spat upon Him, and at last they nailed Him to the tree, and there He hung. His physical pain alone must have been very great, but all the while there was within His soul an inward torment which added immeasurably to His sufferings. His God forsook Him. "Eloi, Eloi, lama, sabachthani?" is a voice enough to rend the rocks, and assuredly it makes us all astonished when, in the returning light, we look upon His visage, and are sure that never face of any man was so marred before, and never form of any son of man so grievously disfigured. Weeping and wondering, astonied and adoring, we leave the griefs of our own dear Lord, and with loving interest turn to the brighter portion of His unrivalled story.

> "Behold your King! Though the moonlight steals
>   Through the silvery sprays of the olive tree,
> No star-gemmed sceptre or crown it reveals,
>   In the solemn shade of Gethsemane.
>   Only a form of prostrate grief,
>   Fallen, crushed, like a broken leaf!
> Oh, think of His sorrow, that we may know
> The depth of love in the depth of woe!

"Behold your King, with His sorrow crowned,
  Alone, alone in the valley is He!
The shadows of death are gathering round,
  And the cross must follow Gethsemane.
    Darker and darker the gloom must fall,
    Filled is the cup, He must drink it all!
Oh, think of His sorrow, that we may know
His wondrous love in His wondrous woe!"

II. There is AN EQUAL ASTONISHMENT AT HIS
GLORIES. I doubt not, if we could see Him now, as
He appeared to John in Patmos, we should feel that
we must do exactly as the beloved disciple did, for
He deliberately wrote, "When I saw Him, I fell at
His feet as dead." His astonishment was so
great that he could not endure the sight. He had
doubtless longed often to behold that glorified face
and form, but the privilege was too much for him.
While we are encumbered with these frail bodies, it is
not fit for us to behold our Lord, for we should die
with excess of delight if we were suddenly to behold
that vision of splendour. Oh, for those glorious days
when we shall lie for ever at His feet, and see our
exalted Lord!

"*Behold, My servant shall deal prudently, He shall be
exalted and extolled, and be very high.*" Observe the
three words, "exalted and extolled, and be very
high;" language pants for expression. Our Lord is
now *exalted* in being lifted up from the grave, lifted
up above all angels, and principalities, and powers.
The Man Christ Jesus is the nearest to the eternal
throne, ay, the Lamb is before the throne. "And I
beheld, and, lo, in the midst of the throne and of the
four beasts, and in the midst of the elders, stood a
Lamb as it had been slain." He is in His own state

and person exalted, and then by the praise rendered Him he is *extolled*, for he is worshipped and adored by the whole universe. All praise goes up before Him now, so that men extol Him, while " God also hath highly exalted Him, and given Him a name, which is above every name ; that at the name of Jesus every knee should bow, of things in heaven, and things in earth, and things under the earth ; and that every tongue should confess that Jesus Christ is Lord, to the glory of God the Father." Deep were His sorrows, but as high are His joys. It is said that, around many of the lochs in Scotland, the mountains are as high as the water is deep ; and so our Lord's glories are as immeasurable as were His woes. What a meditation is furnished by these two-fold and incalculable heights and depths ! Our text says that He shall " *be very high.*" It cannot tell us how high. It is inconceivable how great and glorious in all respects the Lord Jesus Christ is at this moment. Oh, that He may be very high in our esteem ! He is not yet exalted and extolled in any of our hearts as He deserves to be. I would we loved Him a thousand times as much as we do, but our whole heart goeth after Him, does it not ? Would we not die for Him ? Would we not set Him on a throne as high as seven heavens, and then think that we had not done enough for Him, who is now our all in all, and more than all ?

You notice what is said, concerning the Christ, as the most astonishing thing of all : " *So shall He sprinkle many nations.*" Now is it the glory of our risen Lord, at this moment, that His precious blood is to save many nations. Before the throne, men of all nations shall sing, "Thou wast slain, and hast redeemed us unto God by Thy blood." Not the English nation alone shall be purified by His atoning blood, but many nations shall He sprinkle with His reconciling blood, even as Israel of old was sprinkled with the blood of sacrifice. We read in the tenth chapter of the Epistle to the Hebrews, at the twenty-second verse, of "having our hearts sprinkled from an evil conscience," and this is effected by that precious blood by which we have been once purged so effectually that we have no more consciousness of sins, but enter into perfect peace. The blood of bulls and of goats, and the ashes of an heifer, sprinkling the unclean, sanctified to the purifying of the flesh, and much more doth the blood of Christ purge our conscience from dead works, to serve the living God.

The sprinkling of the blood was meant also to confirm the covenant: thus Moses "sprinkled both the book and all the people, saying, This is the blood of the testament which God hath enjoined unto you." Our Lord Himself said, "This is My blood of the new covenant, which is shed for many for the remission of sins." But is it not a wonderful thing that He should die as a malefactor on the tree, amid scorn and ridicule, and yet that He is this day bringing nations into covenant with God ? Once so despised, and now so mighty ! God has given Him "for a covenant of the people, for a light of the Gentiles." Many nations shall by Him be joined in covenant with the God of the whole earth. Do not fall into the erroneous idea that this world is like a great ship-wrecked vessel, soon to go to pieces on an iron-bound coast ; but rather let us expect the conversion of the world to the

Lord Jesus. As a reward for the travail of His soul, He shall cause many nations to " exult with joy ", for so some read the passage ; the peoples of the earth shall not only be astonished at His griefs, but they shall admire His glories, adore His perfections, and be filled with an amazement of joy at His coming and kingdom. I can conceive nothing in the future too great and glorious to result from the passion and death of our Divine Lord.

Listen to this, "*Kings shall shut their mouths at Him.*" They shall see such a King as they themselves have never been ; they speak freely to their brother-kings, but they shall not dare to speak to Him, and as for speaking against Him, that will be altogether out of the question.

> " Kings shall fall down before Him,
> And gold and incense bring."

" *For that which had not been told them shall they see.*" Kings are often out of the reach of the gospel, they do not hear it, it is not told to them. They would despise the lowly preacher, and little gatherings of believers meeting together for worship ; they would only listen to stately discourses, which do not touch the heart and conscience. The great ones of the earth are usually the least likely to know the things of God, for while the poor have the gospel preached unto them, princes are more likely to hear soft flatteries and fair speeches. The time shall come, however, when Cæsar shall bow before a real Imperator, and monarchs shall behold the Prince of the kings of the earth. "For the Lord Himself shall descend from heaven with a shout, with the voice of the archangel, and with the trump of God." They shall see His majesty, of which they had not even been told.

"*That which they had not heard shall they consider.*" They shall be obliged, even on their thrones, to think about the kingdom of the King of kings, and they shall retire to their closets to confess their sins, and to put on sackcloth and ashes, and to give heed to the words of wisdom. "Be wise now, therefore, O ye kings : be instructed, ye judges of the earth." To-day, the humble listen to Christ, but by-and-by the mightiest of the mighty shall turn all their thoughts towards Him. He shall gather sheaves of sceptres beneath His arm, and crowns shall be strewn at His feet ; and "He shall reign for ever and ever," and "of the increase of His government and peace there shall be no end." If we were astonished at the marring of His face, we shall be much more astonished at the magnificence of His glory. Upon His throne none shall question His supremacy, none shall doubt His loveliness ; but His enemies shall weep and wail because of Him whom they pierced ; while He shall be admired in all them that believe. Adorable Lord, we long for Thy glorious appearing ! We beseech Thee, tarry not !

> " Come, and begin Thy reign
>   Of everlasting peace ;
> Come, take the kingdom to Thyself,
>   Great King of Righteousness ! "

BANDS OF LOVE; OR, UNION TO CHRIST.

"I drew them with cords of a man, with bands of love : and I was to them as they that take off the yoke on their jaws, and I laid meat unto them."—*Hosea* xi. 4.

BANDS OF LOVE; OR, UNION TO CHRIST.

———

SYSTEMATIC theologians have usually regarded union to Christ under three aspects, *natural*, *mystical* and *federal*, and it may be that these three terms are comprehensive enough to embrace the whole subject, but as our aim is simplicity, let us be pardoned if we appear diffuse when we follow a less concise method.

1. The saints were from the beginning joined to Christ by bands of *everlasting love*. Before He took on Him their nature, or brought them into a conscious enjoyment of Himself, His heart was set upon their persons, and His soul delighted in them. Long ere the worlds were made, His prescient eye beheld His chosen, and viewed them with delight. Strong were the indissoluble bands of love which then united Jesus to the souls whom He determined to redeem. Not bars of brass, or triple steel, could have been more real and effectual bonds. True love, of all things in the universe, has the greatest cementing force, and will bear the greatest strain, and endure the heaviest pressure : who shall tell what trials the Saviour's love has borne, and how well it has sustained them ? Never union was more true than this. As the soul of Jonathan was knit to the soul of David so that he loved David as his own soul, so was our glorious Lord united and joined to us by the ties of fervent, faithful love. Love has a most potent power in effecting and

sustaining union, but never does it display its force so
well as when we see it bringing the Creator into
oneness with the creature, the divine into alliance
with the human.   This, then, is to be regarded as the
day-spring of union—the love of Christ embracing in
its folds the whole of the elected family.

2. There is, moreover, a *union of purpose* as well as
of love.   By the first, we have seen that the elect are
made one with Jesus by the act and will of the Son;
by the second, they are joined to Him by the ordina-
tion and decree of the Father.   These divine acts are
co-eternal.   The Son loved and chose His people to
be His own bride, the Father made the same choice,
and decreed the chosen ones for ever one with His
all-glorious Son.   The Son loved them, and the Father
decreed them His portion and inheritance ;   the
Father ordained them to be what the Son Himself did
make them.

In God's purpose they have been eternally associated
as parts of one design.   Salvation was the fore-ordained
scheme whereby God would magnify Himself, and a
Saviour was in that scheme from necessity associated
with the persons chosen to be saved.   The scope of
the dispensation of grace included both ;   the circle of
wisdom comprehended Redeemer and redeemed in its
one circumference.   They could not be dissociated in
the mind and will of the all-planning Jehovah.

> "' Christ be My first elect,' He said,
>   Then chose our souls in Christ, our Head."

The same Book which contains the names of the heirs
of life contains the name of their Redeemer.   He
could not be a Redeemer unless souls had been given

Him to redeem, nor could they have been called the ransomed of the Lord, if He had not engaged to purchase them. Redemption, when determined upon by the God of heaven, included in it both Christ and His people; and hence, in the decree which fixed it, they were brought into a near and intimate alliance.

The foresight of the Fall led the divine mind to provide for the catastrophe in which the elect would have perished, had not their ruin been prevented by gracious interposition. Hence followed as part of the divine arrangement other forms of union, which, besides their immediate object in salvation, had doubtless a further design of illustrating the condescending alliance which Jesus had formed with His chosen. The next and following points are of this character.

3. *Jesus is one with His elect federally.* As every heir of flesh and blood has a personal interest in Adam, because he is the covenant head and representative of the race as considered under the law of works; so, under the law of grace, every redeemed soul is one with the Lord from heaven, since He is the Second Adam, the Sponsor and Substitute of the elect in the new covenant of love. The apostle Paul declares that Levi was in the loins of Abraham when Melchizedek met him: it is equally true that the believer was in the loins of Jesus Christ, the Mediator, when in old eternity the covenant settlements of grace were decreed, ratified, and made sure for ever. Thus, whatever Christ hath done, He hath wrought for the whole body of His Church. We were crucified in Him, and buried with Him (read Col. ii. 10—13), and to make it still more wonderful, we are risen with Him, and

have even ascended with Him to the seats on high
(Eph. ii. 6). It is thus that the Church has fulfilled
the law, and is " accepted *in the Beloved.*" It is thus
that she is regarded with complacency by the just
Jehovah, for He views her in Jesus, and does not look
upon her as separate from her covenant Head. As the
anointed Redeemer of Israel, Christ Jesus has nothing
distinct from His Church, but all that He has He
holds for her. Adam's righteousness was ours as long as
ɪɪe maintained it, and his sin was ours the moment that
he committed it; and, in the same manner, all that the
Second Adam is, or does, is ours as well as His, seeing
that He is our Representative. Here is the foundation
of the covenant of grace. This gracious system of
representation and substitution, which moved Justin
Martyr to cry out, " O blessed change ! O sweet
permutation !" this, I say, is the very groundwork of
the gospel of our salvation, and is to be received with
strong faith and rapturous joy. In every place the
saints are perfectly one with Jesus.

> " One in the tomb, one when He rose,
>   One when He triumph'd o'er His foes,
>   One when in heaven He took His seat,
>   While seraphs sang all hell's defeat.

> " This sacred tie forbids their fears,
>   For all He is or has is theirs ;
>   With Him, their Head, they stand or fall,
>   Their life, their Surety, and their all."

4. For the accomplishment of the great works of
atonement and perfect obedience, it was needful that
the Lord Jesus should take upon Him " the likeness of
sinful flesh." Thus, *He became one with us in our
nature,* for in Holy Scripture all partakers of flesh and

blood are regarded as of one family. By the fact of common descent from Adam, all men are of one race, seeing that "God hath made of one blood all nations that dwell upon the face of the earth." Hence, in the Bible, man is spoken of universally as "thy brother" (Lev. xix. 17 ; Job xxii. 6 ; Matt. v. 23, 24 ; Luke xvii. 3 ; Rom. xiv. 10, &c., &c.) ; and "thy neighbour" (Exod. xx. 16 ; Lev. xix. 13—18 ; Matt. v. 43 ; Rom. xiii. 9 ; James ii. 8) ; to whom, on account of nature and descent, we are required to render kindness and goodwill. Now, although our great Melchizedek in His divinity is without father, without mother, without descent, having neither beginning of days nor end of life, and is both in essence and rank at an infinite remove from fallen manhood ; yet as to His manhood He is to be reckoned as one of ourselves. He was born of a woman, He hung upon her breasts, and was dandled upon her knee ; He grew from infancy to youth and thence to manhood, and in every stage He was a true and real partaker of our humanity. He is as certainly of the race of Adam as He is divine. He is God without fiction or metaphor, and He is man beyond doubt or dispute. The Godhead was not humanized, and so diluted ; and the manhood was not transformed into divinity, and so rendered more than human. Never was any man more a portion of His kind than was the Son of man, the Man of sorrows and the Acquaintance of grief. He is man's Brother for He bore the whole nature of man. "The Word was made flesh, and dwelt among us." He who wa very God of very God made Himself a little lower th the angels, and took upon Him the form of a servant and was made in the likeness of men.

This was done with the most excellent design with regard to our redemption, inasmuch as it was necessary that, as *man* had sinned, *man* should suffer; but doubtless it had a further motive, the honouring of the Church, and the enabling of her Lord to sympathize with her. The apostle most sweetly remarks, " Forasmuch then as the children are partakers of flesh and blood, He also Himself likewise took part of the same ; that through death He might destroy him that had the power of death, that is, the devil ; and deliver them who through fear of death were all their lifetime subject to bondage " (Heb. ii. 14, 15); and again, "For we have not an high priest which cannot be touched with the feeling of our infirmities ; but was in all points tempted like as we are, yet without sin " (Heb. iv. 15). Thus, in ties of blood, Jesus, the Son of man, is one with all the heirs of heaven : " For which cause He is not ashamed to call them brethren " (Heb. ii. 11). What reason we have here for the strongest consolation and delight, seeing that, " Both He that sanctifieth and they who are sanctified are all of one." We can say of our Lord as poor Naomi said of bounteous Boaz, "The man is near of kin unto us, one of our next kinsmen." Overwhelmed by the liberality of our blessed Lord, we are often led to cry with Ruth, "Why have I found grace in thine eyes, that thou shouldest take knowledge of me, seeing I am a stranger ? " and are we not ready to die with wonder when, in answer to such a question, He tells us that He is our Brother, bone of our bone, and flesh of our flesh ?

If, in all our straits and distresses, we would always treasure in our minds the remembrance of our

Redeemer's manhood, we should never bemoan the absence of a sympathizing heart, since we should always have His abundant compassion for our consolation. He is no stranger, He is able to enter into the heart's bitterness, for He has Himself tasted the wormwood and the gall. Let us never doubt His power to sympathize with us in our infirmities and sorrows.

There is one aspect of this subject of our natural union to Christ which it were improper to pass over in silence, for it is very precious to the believer. While the Lord Jesus takes upon Himself our nature (2 Peter i. 4), He restores in us that image of God (Gen. i. 27) which was blotted and defaced by the fall of Adam. He raises us from the degradation of sin to the dignity of perfection. So that, in a two-fold sense, the Head and members are of one nature, and not like that monstrous image which Nebuchadnezzar saw in his dream. The head was of fine gold, but the belly and the thighs were of brass, the legs of iron, and the feet, part of iron and part of clay. Christ's mystical body is no absurd combination of opposites; the Head is immortal, and the body is immortal, too, for thus the record stands, "Because I live, ye shall live also." "As is the heavenly, such are they also that are heavenly." " As we have borne the image of the earthy, we shall also bear the image of the heavenly:" and this shall in a few more years be more fully manifest to us, for "this corruptible must put on incorruption, and this mortal must put on immortality." Such as is the Head, such is the body, and every member in particular ;—a chosen Head, and chosen members ; an accepted Head, and accepted members ;

a living Head, and living members. If the Head be of pure gold, all the parts of the body are of pure gold also. Thus is there a double union of nature as a basis for the closest communion.

Pause here, and see if thou canst, without ecstatic amazement, contemplate the infinite condescension of the Son of God in exalting thy wretchedness into blessed union with His glory. Thou art so mean that, in remembrance of thy mortality, thou mayest say to corruption, "Thou art my father," and to the worm, "Thou art my sister;" and yet, in Christ, thou art so honoured that thou canst say to the Almighty, "Abba, Father," and to the Incarnate God, "Thou art my Brother and my Husband." Surely, if relationships to ancient and noble families make men think highly of themselves, *we* have whereof to glory over the heads of them all. Lay hold upon this privilege; let not a senseless indolence make thee negligent to trace this pedigree, and suffer no foolish attachment to present vanities to occupy thy thoughts to the exclusion of this glorious privilege, this heavenly honour of union with Christ.

We must now retrace our steps to the ancient mountains, and contemplate this union in one of its earliest forms.

5. *Christ Jesus is also joined unto His people in a mystical union.* Borrowing once more from the story of Ruth, we remark that Boaz, although one with Ruth by kinship, did not rest until he had entered into a nearer union still, namely, that of marriage; and in the same manner there is, superadded to the natural union of Christ with His people, a mystical union by which He assumes the position of Husband,

while the Church is owned as His bride. In love He espoused her to Himself, as a chaste virgin, long before she fell under the yoke of bondage. Full of burning affection, He toiled like Jacob for Rachel, until the whole of her purchase-money had been paid, and now, having sought her by His Spirit, and brought her to know and love Him, He awaits the glorious hour when their mutual bliss shall be consummated at the marriage-supper of the Lamb. Not yet hath the glorious Bridegroom presented His betrothèd, perfected and complete, before the Majesty of heaven; not yet hath she actually entered upon the enjoyment of her dignities as His wife and queen; she is as yet a wanderer in a world of woe, a dweller in the tents of Kedar; but she is even now the bride, the spouse of Jesus, dear to His heart, precious in His sight, and united with His person. In love and tenderness, He says to her,—

> "Forget thee I will not, I cannot, thy name
> Engraved on My heart doth for ever remain:
> The palms of My hands whilst I look on I see
> The wounds I received when suffering for thee."

He exercises towards her all the affectionate offices of Husband. He makes rich provision for her wants, pays all her debts, allows her to assume His name, and to share in all His wealth. Nor will He ever act otherwise to her. The word divorce He will never mention, for "He hateth putting away." Death must sever the conjugal tie between the most loving mortals, but it cannot divide the links of this immortal marriage. In heaven they marry not, but are as the angels of God; yet is there this one marvellous exception to the rule, for in heaven Christ and His

Church shall celebrate their joyous nuptials. And this affinity, as it is more lasting, so is it more near than earthly wedlock. Let the love of husband be never so pure and fervent, it is but a faint picture of the flame that burns in the heart of Jesus. Passing all human union is that mystical cleaving unto the Church, for which Christ did leave His Father, and become one flesh with her.

If this be the union which subsists between our souls and the person of our Lord, how deep and broad is the channel of our communion! This is no narrow pipe through which a thread-like stream may wind its way, it is a channel of amazing depth and breadth, along whose breadth and length a ponderous volume of living water may roll its strength. Behold, He hath set before us an open door; let us not be slow to enter. This city of communion hath many pearly gates, every several gate is of one pearl, and each gate is thrown open to the uttermost that we may enter, assured of welcome. If there were but one small loophole through which to talk with Jesus, it would be a high privilege to thrust a word of fellowship through the narrow door ; how much we are blessed in having so large an entrance! Had the Lord Jesus been far away from us, with many a stormy sea between, we should have longed to send a messenger to Him to carry Him our love, and bring us tidings from His Father's house ; but see His kindness, He has built His house next door to ours, nay, more, He takes lodgings with us, and tabernacles in poor humble hearts, that so He may have perpetual intercourse with us. Oh, how foolish must we be, if we do not live in habitual communion with Him! When the road is long, and dangerous, and difficult, we need not wonder that friends seldom meet each other; but when they live together, shall Jonathan forget his David? A wife may, when her husband is upon a journey, abide many days without holding converse with him; but she could never endure to be separated from him if she knew him to be in one of the chambers of their own house. Seek thy Lord, for He is near; embrace Him, for He is thy Brother; hold Him fast, for He is thine Husband; press Him to thine heart, for He is of thine own flesh.

6. As yet we have only considered the acts of Christ for us, whereby He effects and proves His union to us; we must now come to *more personal and sensible forms of this great truth.*

Those who are set apart for the Lord are in due time severed from the impure mass of fallen humanity, and are by sovereign grace engrafted into the person of the Lord Jesus. This, which we call *vital union,* is rather a matter of experience than of doctrine; it must be learned in the heart, and not by the head. Like every other work of the Spirit, the actual implantation of the soul into Christ Jesus is a mysterious and secret operation, and is no more to be understood by carnal reason than is the new birth of which it is an attendant. Nevertheless, the spiritual man discerns it as a most essential thing in the salvation of the soul, and he clearly sees how a living union to Christ is the sure consequence of the quickening influence of the Holy Spirit, and is indeed, in some respects, identical with it.

When the Lord in mercy passed by and saw us in our blood, He first of all said, "Live"; and this He did *first*, because, without life, there can be no spiritual knowledge, feeling, or motion. Life is one of the absolutely essential things in spiritual matters; and until it be bestowed, we are incapable of partaking in the things of the kingdom. Now, the life which grace confers upon the saints at the moment of their quickening is none other than the life of Christ, which, like the sap from the stem, runs into us, the branches, and establishes a living connection between our souls and Jesus. Faith is the grace which perceives this union, and proceeds from it as its firstfruit. It is, to use a metaphor from the Canticles, the neck which joins the body of the Church to its all-glorious Head.

> " *O Faith !*. thou bond of union with the Lord,
> Is not this office thine? and thy fit name,
> In the economy of gospel types,
> And symbols apposite—the Church's *neck ;*
> Identifying her in will and work
> With Him ascended?"

Faith lays hold upon the Lord Jesus with a firm and determined grasp. She knows His excellence and worth, and no temptation can induce her to repose her trust elsewhere; and Christ Jesus is so delighted with this heavenly grace, that He never ceases to strengthen and sustain her by the loving embrace and all-sufficient support of His eternal arms. Here, then, is established a living, sensible, and delightful union, which casts forth streams of love, confidence, sympathy, complacency, and joy, whereof both the bride and Bridegroom love to drink. When the eye is clear, and the soul can evidently perceive this oneness between itself and Christ, the pulse may be felt as beating for both, and the one blood may be known as flowing through the veins of each. Then is the heart made exceedingly glad, it is as near heaven as it ever can be on earth, and is prepared for the enjoyment of the most sublime and spiritual kind of fellowship. This union may be quite as true when we are troubled with doubts concerning it, but it cannot afford consolation to the soul unless it be indisputably proven and assuredly felt; then is it indeed a honeycomb dropping with sweetness, a precious jewel sparkling with light. Look well to this matter, ye saints of the Most High!

"I WILL GIVE YOU REST."

A COMMUNION ADDRESS AT MENTONE.

"I will give you rest."—*Matthew* xi. 28.

"I WILL GIVE YOU REST."

WE have a thousand times considered these words as an encouragement to the labouring and the laden; and we may, therefore, have failed to read them as a promise to ourselves. But, beloved friends, we *have* come to Jesus, and therefore He stands engaged to fulfil this priceless pledge to us. We may now enjoy the promise; for we have obeyed the precept. The faithful and true Witness, whose word is truth, promised us rest if we would come to Him; and, therefore, since we have come to Him, and are always coming to Him, we may boldly say, " O Thou, who art our Peace, make good Thy word to us wherein Thou hast said, ' I will give you rest.' "

By faith, I see our Lord standing in our midst, and I hear Him say, with voice of sweetest music, first to all of us together, and then to each one individually, " I will give you rest." May the Holy Spirit bring to each of us the fulness of the rest and peace of God! For a few minutes only shall I need your attention; and we will begin by asking the question,—

I. WHAT MUST THESE WORDS MEAN?

A dear friend prayed this morning that, while studying the Scriptures, we might be enabled to read between the lines, and beneath the letter of the Word. May we have holy insight thus to read our Lord's most gracious language!

This promise must mean rest to all parts of our spiritual nature. Our bodies cannot rest if the head is aching, or the feet are full of pain ; if one member is disturbed, the whole frame is unable to rest ; and so the higher nature is one, and such intimate sympathies bind together all its faculties and powers, that every one of them must rest, or none can be at ease. Jesus gives real, and, consequently, universal rest to every part of our spiritual being.

The heart is by nature restless as old ocean's waves ; it seeks an object for its affection ; and when it finds one beneath the stars, it is doomed to sorrow. Either the beloved changes, and there is disappointment ; or death comes in, and there is bereavement. The more tender the heart, the greater its unrest. Those in whom the heart is simply one of the largest valves are undisturbed, because they are callous ; but the sensitive, the generous, the unselfish, are often found seeking rest and finding none. To such, the Lord Jesus says, " Come unto Me, and I will give you rest." Look hither, ye loving ones, for here is a refuge for your wounded love ! You may delight yourselves in the Well-beloved, and never fear that He will fail or forget you. Love will not be wasted, however much it may be lavished upon Jesus. He deserves it all, and he requites it all. In loving Him, the heart finds a delicious content. When the head lies in His bosom, it enjoys an ease which no pillow of down could bestow. How Madame Guyon rested amid severe persecutions, because her great love to Jesus filled her soul to the brim ! O aching heart, O breaking heart, come hither, for Jesus saith, " I will give you rest."

The conscience, when it is at all alive and awake, is

much disturbed because the holy law of God has been broken by sin. Now, conscience once aroused is not easily quieted. Neither unbelief nor superstition can avail to lull it to sleep; it defies these opiates of falsehood, and frets the soul with perpetual annoyance. Like the troubled sea, it cannot rest; but constantly casts up upon the shore of memory the mire and dirt of past transgressions and iniquities. Is this your case? Then Jesus says, "I will give you rest." If, at any time, fears and apprehensions arise from an awakened conscience, they can only be safely and surely quieted by our flying to the Crucified. In the blessed truth of a substitution, accepted of God, and fully made by the Lord Jesus, our mind finds peace. Justice is honoured, and law is vindicated, in the sacrifice of Christ. Since God is satisfied, I may well be so. Since the Father has raised Jesus from the dead, and set Him at His own right hand, there can be no question as to His acceptance; and, consequently, all who are in Him are accepted also. We are under no apprehension now as to our being condemned; Jesus gives us rest, by enabling us to utter the challenge, "Who is he that condemneth?" and to give the reassuring answer, "Christ hath died."

The intellect is another source of unrest; and in these times it operates with special energy towards labour and travail of mind. Doubts, stinging like mosquitoes, are suggested by almost every page of the literature of the day. Most men are drifting, like vessels which have no anchors, and these come into collision with us. How can we rest? This scheme of philosophy eats up the other; this new fashion of heresy devours the last. Is there any foundation? Is anything true?

Or is it all romance, and are we doomed to be the
victims of an ever-changing lie? O soul, seek not a
settlement by learning of men; but come and learn of
Jesus, and thou shalt find rest! Believe Jesus, and
let all the Rabbis contradict. The Son of God was
made flesh, He lived, He died, He rose again, He lives,
He loves; this is true, and all that He teaches in His
Word is assured verity; the rest may blow away, like
chaff before the wind. A mind in pursuit of truth is
a dove without a proper resting-place for the sole
of its foot, till it finds its rest in Jesus, the true Noah.

Next, *these words mean rest about all things.* He
who is uneasy about anything has not found rest. A
thousand thorns and briars grow on the soil of this
earth, and no man can happily tread life's ways unless
his feet are shod with that preparation of the gospel of
peace which Jesus gives. In Christ, we are at rest
as to our duties; for He instructs and helps us in
them. In Him, we are at rest about our trials;
for He sympathizes with us in them. With His
love, we are restful as to the movements of
Providence; for His Father loves us, and will
not suffer anything to harm us. Concerning the
past, we rest in His forgiving love; as to the present,
it is bright with His loving fellowship; as to the future,
it is brilliant with His expected Advent. This is true
of the little as well as of the great. He who saves us
from the battle-axe of Satanic temptation, also extracts
the thorn of a domestic trial. We may rest in Jesus
as to our sick child, as to our business trouble, or as to
grief of any kind. He is our Comforter in all things,
our Sympathizer in every form of temptation. Have
you such all-covering rest? If not, why not? Jesus

gives it ; why do you not partake of it ? Have you something which you could not bring to Him ? Then, fly from it ; for it is no fit thing for a believer to possess. A disciple should know neither grief nor joy which he could not reveal to his Lord.

This rest, we may conclude, *must be a very wonderful one*, since Jesus gives it. His hands give not by penny-worths and ounces ; he gives golden gifts, in quantity immeasurable. It is Jesus who gives the peace of God which passeth all understanding. It is written, "Great peace have they which love Thy law ; " what peace must they have who love God's Son! There are periods when Jesus gives us a heavenly Elysium of rest ; we cannot describe the divine repose of our hearts at such times. We read, in the Gospels, that when Jesus hushed the storm, "there was a great calm," not simply "a calm", but a great calm, unusual, absolute, perfect, memorable. It reminds us of the stillness which John describes in the Revelation : "I saw four angels standing on the four corners of the earth, holding the four winds of the earth, that the wind should not blow on the earth, nor on the sea, nor on any tree ; " not a ripple stirred the waters, not a leaf moved on the trees.

Assuredly, our Lord has given a blessed rest to those who trust Him, and follow Him. They are often unable to inform others as to their deep peace, and the reasons upon which it is founded ; but they know it, and it brings them an inward wealth compared with which the fortune of an ungodly millionaire is poverty itself. May we all know to the full, by happy, personal experience, the meaning of our Saviour's promise, "I will give you rest"!

II. But now, in the second place, let us ask,—
WHY SHOULD WE HAVE THIS REST?

The first answer is in our text. We should enjoy
this rest *because Jesus gives it*. As He gives it, we
ought to take it. Because He gives it, we *may* take it.
I have known some Christians who have thought that
it would be presumption on their part to take this rest;
so they have kept fluttering about, like frightened birds,
weary with their long flights, but not daring to fold
their tired wings, and rest. If there is any presumption
in the case, let us not be so presumptuous as to think
that we know better than our Lord. He gives us rest:
for that reason, if for no other, let us take it, promptly
and gratefully. " Rest in the Lord, and wait patiently
for Him." Say with David, " My heart is fixed, O
God, my heart is fixed: I will sing and give praise."

> " Now rest, my long-divided heart;
>   Fix'd on this blissful centre, rest."

Next, we should take the rest that Jesus gives,
because it will refresh us. We are often weary; sometimes we are weary *in* God's work, though I trust we
are never weary *of* it. There are many things to cause
us weariness: sin, sorrow, the worldliness of professors,
the prevalence of error in the Church, and so on.
Often, we are like a tired child, who can hold up his
little head no longer. What does he do? Why, he
just goes to sleep in his mother's arms! Let us be as
wise as the little one; and let us rest in our loving
Saviour's embrace. The poet speaks of—

> " Tired nature's sweet restorer, balmy sleep ; "

and so it is. Sometimes, the very best thing a Christian
man can do is, literally, to go to sleep. When he

wakes, he will be so refreshed, that he will seem to be
in a new world. But spiritually, there is no refreshing
like that which comes from the rest which Christ gives.
As Isaiah said, "This is the rest wherewith ye may
cause the weary to rest : and this is the refreshing."
Dr. Bonar's sweet hymn, which is so suitable for a
sinner coming to Christ for the first time, is just as
appropriate for a weary saint returning to his Saviour's
arms ; for he, too, can sing,—

> "I heard the voice of Jesus say,
>   'Come unto Me, and rest ;
> Lay down, thou weary one, lay down
>   Thy head upon My breast.'
> I came to Jesus as I was,
>   Weary, and worn, and sad :
> I found in Him a resting-place,
>   And He has made me glad."

Another reason why we should have this rest is, that
it will enable us to concentrate all our faculties. Many,
who might be strong servants of the Lord, are very
weak, because their energies are not concentrated upon
one object. They do not say with Paul, "This one
thing I do." We are such poor creatures that we
cannot occupy our minds with more than one subject
at a time. Why, even the buzzing of a fly, or the
trumpeting of a mosquito, would be quite sufficient to
take our thoughts away from our present holy service !
As long as we have any burden resting on our shoulders,
we cannot enjoy perfect rest ; and as long as there is
any burden on our conscience or heart, we cannot
have rest of soul. How are we to be freed from these
burdens ? Only by yielding ourselves wholly to the
Great Burden-Bearer, who says, "Come unto Me, and

I will give you rest." Possessing this rest, all our faculties will be centred and focussed upon one object, and with undivided hearts we shall seek God's glory.

Having obtained this rest, *we shall be able to testify for our Lord.* I remember, when I first began to teach in a Sunday-school, that I was speaking one day to my class upon the words, " He that believeth on Me hath everlasting life." I was rather taken by surprise when one of the boys said to me, " Teacher, have *you* got everlasting life ? " I replied, " I hope so." The scholar was not satisfied with my answer, so he asked another question, " But, teacher, don't you *know ?* " The boy was right ; there can be no true testimony except that which springs from assured conviction of our own safety and joy in the Lord. We speak that we do know ; we believe, and therefore speak. Rest of heart, through coming to Christ, enables us to invite others to Him with great confidence, for we can tell them what heavenly peace He has given to us. This will enable us to put the gospel very attractively, for the evidence of our own experience will help others to trust the Lord for themselves. With the beloved apostle John, we shall be able to say to our hearers, " That which was from the beginning, which we have heard, which we have seen with our eyes, which we have looked upon, and our hands have handled, of the Word of life ; (for the life was manifested, and we have seen it, and bear witness, and shew unto you that eternal life, which was with the Father, and was manifested unto us ;) that which we have seen and heard declare we unto you, that ye also may have fellowship with us : and truly our fellowship is with the Father, and with His Son Jesus Christ."

Once more, *this rest is necessary to our growth.* The lily in the garden is not taken up and transplanted two or three times a day; that would be the way to prevent all growth. But it is kept in one place, and tenderly nurtured. It is by keeping it quite still that the gardener helps it to attain to perfection. A child of God would grow much more rapidly if he would but rest in one place instead of being always on the move. "In returning and rest shall ye be saved; in quietness and in confidence shall be your strength." Martha was cumbered about much serving; but Mary sat at Jesus' feet. It is not difficult to tell which of them would be the more likely to grow in the grace and knowledge of our Lord Jesus Christ.

This is a tempting theme, but I must not linger over it, as we must come to the communion. I will give only one more answer to the question, "Why should we have this rest?" *It will prepare us for heaven.* I was reading a book, the other day, in which I met with this expression,—" The streets of heaven begin on earth." That is true; heaven is not so far away as some people think. Heaven is the place of perfect holiness, the place of sinless service, the place of eternal glory; and there is nothing that will prepare us for heaven like this rest that Jesus gives. Heaven must be in us before we are in heaven; and he who has this rest has heaven begun below. Enoch was virtually in heaven while he walked with God on the earth, and he had only to continue that holy walk to find himself actually in heaven. This world is part of our Lord's great house, of which heaven is the upper story. Some of us may hear the Master's call, "Come up higher," sooner than we think; and then, with we rest *in* Christ, there we shall rest *with* Christ. The more we have of this blessed rest now, the better shall we be prepared for the rest that remaineth to the people of God, that eternal " keeping of a Sabbath " in the Paradise above.

III. I have left myself only a minute for the answers to my third question,—HOW CAN WE OBTAIN THIS REST ?

First, by *coming to Christ.* He says, " Come unto Me, ... and I will give you rest." I trust that all in this little company have come to Christ by faith ; now let us come to Him in blessed fellowship and communion at His table. Let us keep on coming to Him, as the apostle says, " to whom coming," continually coming, and never going away. When we wake in the morning, let us come to Christ in the act of renewed communion with Him ; all the day long, let us keep on coming to Him even while we are occupied with the affairs of this life ; and at night, let our last waking moments be spent in coming to Jesus. Let us come to Christ by searching the Scriptures, for we shall find Him there on almost every page. Let us come to Christ in our thoughts, desires, aspirations wishes ; so shall the promise of the text be fulfilled to us, " I wili give you rest."

Next, we obtain rest by *yielding to Christ.* " Take My yoke upon you, ... and ye shall find rest unto your souls." Christ bids us wear *His* yoke, not make one for ourselves. He wants us to share the yoke with Him, to be His true yoke-fellow. It is wonderful that He should be willing to be yoked with us ; the only greater wonder is that we should be so unwilling to be yoked with Him. In taking His yoke upon us

what joy we shall enter upon our eternal rest! Here
we find rest unto our souls; a further rest beyond that
which He gives us when we come to Him. We first
rest in Jesus by faith, and then we rest in Him by
obedience. The first rest He gives through His death;
the further rest we find through copying His life.

Lastly, we secure this rest by *learning of Christ.*
" Learn of Me, for I am meek and lowly in heart: and
ye shall find rest unto your souls." We are to be
workers with Christ, taking His yoke upon us; and,
at the same time, we are to be scholars in Christ's
school, learning of Him. We are to learn *of* Christ,
and to learn *Christ;* He is both Teacher and lesson.
His gentleness of heart fits Him to teach, and makes
Him the best illustration of His own teaching. If
we can become as He is, we shall rest as He does.
The lowly in heart will be restful of heart. Now, as
we come to the table of communion, may we find to
the full that rest of which we have been speaking, for
the Great Rest-Giver's sake! Amen.

THE MEMORABLE HYMN.

" And when they had sung an hymn, they went out into the mount of Olives."—*Matthew* xxvi. 30.

THE MEMORABLE HYMN.

THE occasion on which these words were spoken was the last meal of which Jesus partook in company with His disciples before He went from them to His shameful trial and His ignominious death. It was His farewell supper before a bitter parting, and yet they needs must sing. He was on the brink of that great depth of misery into which He was about to plunge, and yet He would have them sing "an hymn." It is wonderful that HE sang, and in a second degree it is remarkable that THEY sang. We will consider both singular facts.

I. Let us dwell a while on THE FACT THAT JESUS SANG AT SUCH A TIME AS THIS. What does He teach us by it? Does He not say to each of us, His followers, "*My religion is one of happiness and joy; I, your Master, by My example would instruct you to sing even when the last solemn hour is come, and all the glooms of death are gathering around you?* Here, at the table, I am your Singing-master, and set you lessons in music, in which My dying voice shall lead you: notwithstanding all the griefs which overwhelm My heart, I will be to you the Chief Musician, and the Sweet Singer of Israel"? If ever there was a time when it would have been natural and consistent with the solemnities of the occasion for the Saviour to have bowed His head upon the table, bursting into a

flood of tears ; or, if ever there was a season when He
might have fittingly retired from all company, and
have bewailed His coming conflict in sighs and groans,
it was just then.   But no ; that brave heart will sing
"an hymn."   Our glorious Jesus plays the man
beyond all other men.   Boldest of the sons of men,
He quails not in the hour of battle, but tunes His
voice to loftiest psalmody.   The genius of that
Christianity of which Jesus is the Head and Founder,
its object, spirit, and design, are happiness and joy,
and they who receive it are able to sing in the very
jaws of death.

This remark, however, is quite a secondary one to
the next : *our Lord's complete fulfilment of the law is
even more worthy of our attention.*   It was customary,
when the Passover was held, to sing, and this is
the main reason why the Saviour did so.   During
the Passover, it was usual to sing the hundred and
thirteenth, and five following Psalms, which were called
the "*Hallel.*"   The first commences, you will observe, in
our version, with "Praise ye the Lord!" or, "Halle-
lujah!"   The hundred and fifteenth, and the three
following, were usually sung as the closing song of the
Passover.   Now, our Saviour would not diminish the
splendour of the great Jewish rite, although it was the
last time that He would celebrate it.   No ; there shall
be the holy beauty and delight of psalmody ; none of
it shall be stinted ; the "Hallel" shall be full and
complete.   We may safely believe that the Saviour
sang through, or probably chanted, the whole of these
six Psalms; and my heart tells me that there was no
one at the table who sang more devoutly or more
cheerfully than did our blessed Lord.   There are some

parts of the hundred and eighteenth Psalm, especially, which strike us as having sounded singularly grand, as they flowed from His blessed lips. Note verses 22, 23, 24. Particularly observe those words, near the end of the Psalm, and think you hear the Lord Himself singing them, " God is the Lord, which hath shewed us light: bind the sacrifice with cords, even unto the horns of the altar. Thou art my God, and I will praise Thee: Thou art my God, I will exalt Thee. O give thanks unto the Lord ; for He is good : for His mercy endureth for ever."

Because, then, it was the settled custom of Israel to recite or sing these Psalms, our Lord Jesus Christ did the same ; for He would leave nothing unfinished. Just as, when He went down into the waters of baptism, He said, " Thus it becometh us to fulfil all righteousness," so He seemed to say, when sitting at the table, " Thus it becometh us to fulfil all righteousness ; therefore let us sing unto the Lord, as God's people in past ages have done." Beloved, let us view with holy wonder the strictness of the Saviour's obedience to His Father's will, and let us endeavour to follow in His steps, in all things, seeking to be obedient to the Lord's Word in the little matters as well as in the great ones.

May we not venture to suggest another and deeper reason ? Did not the singing of " an hymn " at the supper show *the holy absorption of the Saviour's soul in His Father's will ?* If, beloved, you knew that at —say ten o'clock to-night—you would be led away to be mocked, and despised, and scourged, and that to-morrow's sun would see you falsely accused, hanging, a convicted criminal, to die upon a cross, do you think that you could sing to-night, after your last meal? I am sure you could not, unless with more than earth-born courage and resignation your soul could say, "Bind the sacrifice with cords, even unto the horns of the altar." You would sing if your spirit were like the Saviour's spirit; if, like Him, you could exclaim, "Not as I will, but as Thou wilt;" but if there should remain in you any selfishness, any desire to be spared the bitterness of death, you would not be able to chant the "Hallel" with the Master. Blessed Jesus, how wholly wert Thou given up! how perfectly consecrated! so that, whereas other men sing when they are marching to their joys, Thou didst sing on the way to death; whereas other men lift up their cheerful voices when honour awaits them, Thou hadst a brave and holy sonnet on Thy lips when shame, and spitting, and death were to be Thy portion.

This singing of the Saviour also teaches us *the whole-heartedness of the Master in the work which He was about to do.* The patriot-warrior sings as he hastens to battle; to the strains of martial music he advances to meet the foeman; and even thus the heart of our all-glorious Champion supplies Him with song even in the dreadful hour of His solitary agony. He views the battle, but He dreads it not; though in the contest His soul will be "exceeding sorrowful even unto death," yet before it, He is like Job's war-horse, "he saith among the trumpets, Ha, ha; and he smelleth the battle afar off." He has a baptism to be baptized with, and He is straitened until it be accomplished. The Master does not go forth to the agony in the garden with a cowed and trembling spirit, all bowed and crushed in the dust, but He advances to the conflict like a man who has his full strength about him—taken out to be a victim (if I may use such a figure), not as a worn-out ox that has long borne the yoke, but as the firstling of the bullock, in the fulness of His strength. He goes forth to the slaughter, with His glorious undaunted spirit fast and firm within Him, glad to suffer for His people's sake. and for His Father's glory.

> " For as at first Thine all-pervading look
>   Saw from Thy Father's bosom to th' abyss,
>   Measuring in calm presage
>   The infinite descent ;
>   So to the end, though now of mortal pangs
>   Made heir, and emptied of Thy glory a while,
>   With unaverted eye
>   Thou meetest all the storm."

Let us, O fellow-heirs of salvation, learn to sing when our suffering time comes, when our season for stern labour approaches ; ay, let us pour forth a canticle of deep, mysterious, melody of bliss, when our dying hour is near at hand ! Courage, brother ! The waters are chilly ; but fear will not by any means diminish the terrors of the river. Courage, brother ! Death is solemn work ; but playing the coward will not make it less so. Bring out the silver trumpet ; let thy lips remember the long-loved music, and let the notes be clear and shrill as thou dippest thy feet in the Jordan : " Yea, though I walk through the valley of the shadow of death, I will fear no evil : for Thou art with me ; Thy rod and Thy staff they comfort me." Dear friends, let the remembrance of the melodies of that upper room go with you to-morrow into business ; and if you expect a great trial, and are afraid you will not be able to sing after it, then sing before it comes. Get your holy praise-work done before affliction mars the tune. Fill the air with music while you can. While yet there is bread upon the table, sing, though famine may threaten ; while yet the child runs laughing about the house, while yet the flush of health is in your own cheek, while yet your goods are spared, while yet your heart is whole and sound, lift up your song of praise to the Most High God ; and let your Master, the singing Saviour, be in this your goodly and comfortable example.

There is much more that might be said concerning our Lord's sweet swan-song, but there is no need to crowd one thought out with another ; your leisure will be well spent in meditation upon so fruitful a theme.

II. We will now consider THE SINGING OF THE DISCIPLES. *They* united in the " Hallel "—like true Jews, they joined in the national song. Israel had good cause to sing at the Passover, for God had wrought for His people what He had done for no other nation on the face of the earth. Every Hebrew must have felt his soul elevated and rejoiced on the Paschal night. He was " a citizen of no mean city ", and the pedigree which he could look back upon was one, compared with which kings and princes were but of yesterday.

Remembering the fact commemorated by the Paschal supper, Israel might well rejoice. They sang of their nation in bondage, trodden beneath the tyrannical foot of Pharaoh ; they began the Psalm right sorrowfully, as they thought of the bricks made without straw, and of the iron furnace ; but the strain soon mounted from the deep bass, and began to climb

the scale, as they sang of Moses the servant of God,
and of the Lord appearing to him in the burning bush.
They remembered the mystic rod, which became a
serpent, and which swallowed up the rods of the
magicians; their music told of the plagues and
wonders which God had wrought upon Zoan; and of
that dread night when the first-born of Egypt fell
before the avenging sword of the angel of death, while
they themselves, feeding on the lamb which had been
slain for them, and whose blood was sprinkled upon
the lintel and upon the side-posts of the door, had
been graciously preserved. Then the song went up
concerning the hour in which all Egypt was humbled
at the feet of Jehovah, whilst as for His people, He
led them forth like sheep, by the hand of Moses and
Aaron, and they went by the way of the sea, even of
the Red Sea. The strain rose higher still as they
tuned the song of Moses, the servant of God, and of
the Lamb. Jubilantly they sang of the Red Sea, and
of the chariots of Pharaoh which went down into the
midst thereof, and the depths covered them till there
was not one of them left. It was a glorious chant
indeed when they sang of Rahab cut in pieces, and of
the dragon wounded at the sea, by the right hand of
the Most High, for the deliverance of the chosen
people.

But, beloved, if I have said that Israel could so
properly sing, *what shall I say of those of us who are
the Lord's spiritually redeemed?* We have been
emancipated from a slavery worse than that of Egypt:
"with a high hand and with an outstretched arm,"
hath God delivered us. The blood of Jesus Christ,
the Lamb of God's Passover, has been sprinkled on

our hearts and consciences. By faith we keep the
Passover, for we have been spared ; we have been
brought out of Egypt ; and though our sins did once
oppose us, they have all been drowned in the Red Sea
of the atoning blood of Jesus: "the depths have
covered them, there is not one of them left." If the
Jew could sing a "great Hallel", our "Hallel" ought
to be more glowing still ; and if every house in
"Judæa's happy land" was full of music when the
people ate the Paschal feast, much more reason have
we for filling every heart with sacred harmony to-
night, while we feast upon Jesus Christ, who was
slain, and has redeemed us to God by His blood.

III. The time has now come for me to say HOW
EARNESTLY I DESIRE YOU TO "SING AN HYMN."

I do not mean to ask you to use your voices,
but let your hearts be brimming with the essence of
praise. Whenever we repair to the Lord's table, which
represents to us the Passover, we ought not to come
to it as to a funeral. Let us select solemn hymns, but
not dirges. Let us sing softly, but none the less joyfully. These are no burial feasts; those are not
funeral cakes which lie upon this table, and yonder
fair white linen cloth is no winding-sheet. "This is
My body," said Jesus, but the body so represented
was no corpse , we feed upon a living Christ. The
blood set forth by yonder wine is the fresh life-blood
of our immortal King. We view not our Lord's body
as clay-cold flesh, pierced with wounds, but as glorified
at the right hand of the Father. We hold a happy
festival when we break bread on the first day of the
week. We come not hither trembling like bondsmen,
cringing on our knees as wretched serfs condemned to

eat on their knees; we approach as freemen to our
Lord's banquet, like His apostles, to recline at length
or sit at ease; not merely to eat bread which may
belong to the most sorrowful, but to drink wine which
belongs to men whose souls are glad. Let us recognize
the rightness, yea, the duty of cheerfulness at this
commemorative supper; and, therefore, let us "sing
an hymn."

Being satisfied on this point, perhaps you ask,
"*What hymn shall we sing?*" Many sorts of hymns
were sung in the olden time: look down the list, and
you will scarcely find one which may not suit us now.

One of the earliest of earthly songs was *the war-
song.* They sang of old a song to the conqueror, when
he returned from the battle. "Saul has slain his
thousands, and David his ten thousands." Women
took their timbrels, and rejoiced in the dance when the
hero returned from the war. Even thus of old did
the people of God extol Him for His mighty acts,
singing aloud with the high-sounding cymbals: "Sing
unto the Lord, for He hath triumphed gloriously . . .
The Lord is a man of war: the Lord is His name."
My brethren, let us lift up a war-song to-night! Why
not? "Who is this that cometh from Edom, with
dyed garments from Bozrah? this that is glorious in
His apparel, travelling in the greatness of His strength?
I that speak in righteousness, mighty to save." Come,
let us praise our Emmanuel, as we see the head of our
foe in His right hand; as we behold Him leading
captivity captive, ascending up on high, with
trumpets' joyful sound, let us chant the pæan; let us
shout the war-song, "*Io Triumphe!*" Behold, He
comes, all glorious from the war: as we gather at this

festive table, which reminds us both of His conflict
and of His victory, let us salute Him with a psalm of
gladsome triumph, which shall be but the prelude of
the song we expect to sing when we get up—

"Where all the singers meet."

Another early form of song was *the pastoral.* When
the shepherds sat down amongst the sheep, they tuned
their pipes, and warbled forth soft and sweet airs in
harmony with rustic quietude. All around was calm
and still ; the sun was brightly shining, and the birds
were making melody among the leafy branches.
Shall I seem fanciful if I say, let us unite in a pastoral
to-night? Sitting round the table, why should we
not sing, "The Lord is my Shepherd ; I shall not
want. He maketh me to lie down in green pastures :
He leadeth me beside the still waters"? If there be
a place beneath the stars where one might feel
perfectly at rest and ease, surely it is at the table of
the Lord. Here, then, let us sing to our great
Shepherd a pastoral of delight. Let the bleating of
sheep be in our ears as we remember the Good
Shepherd who laid down His life for His flock.

You need not to be reminded that the ancients
were very fond of *festive songs.* When they assembled
at their great festivals, led by their chosen minstrels,
they sang right joyously, with boisterous mirth. Let
those who will speak to the praise of wine, my soul
shall extol the precious blood of Jesus ; let who will
laud corn and oil, the rich produce of the harvest, my
heart shall sing of the Bread which came down from
heaven, whereof, if a man eateth, he shall never hunger.
Speak ye of royal banquets, and minstrelsy fit for a

monarch's ear? Ours is a nobler festival, and our
song is sweeter far. Here is room at this table to-
night for all earth's poesy and music, for the place
deserves songs more lustrous with delight, more
sparkling with gems of holy mirth, than any of which
the ancients could conceive.

> " Now for a tune of lofty praise
> To great Jehovah's equal Son !
> Awake, my voice, in heavenly lays
> Tell the loud wonders He hath done ! "

The *love-song* we must not forget, for that is
peculiarly the song of this evening. " Now will I sing
unto my Well-beloved a song." His love to us is an
immortal theme; and as our love, fanned by the
breath of heaven, bursts into a vehement flame, we
may sing, yea, and we will sing among the lilies, a
song of loves.

In the Old Testament, we find many Psalms called
by the title, "*A Song of Degrees.*" This "Song of
Degrees" is supposed by some to have been sung as
the people ascended the temple steps, or made
pilgrimages to the holy place. The strain often
changes, sometimes it is dolorous, and anon it is
gladsome; at one season, the notes are long drawn
out and heavy, at another, they are cheerful and
jubilant. We will sing a "Song of Degrees" to-night.
We will mourn that we pierced the Lord, and we will
rejoice in pardon bought with blood. Our strain must
vary as we talk of sin, feeling its bitterness, and
lamenting it, and then of pardon, rejoicing in its
glorious fulness.

David wrote a considerable number of Psalms which
he entitled, "*Maschil*," which may be called in English,

"instructive Psalms." Where, beloved, can we find richer instruction than at the table of our Lord? He who understands the mystery of incarnation and of substitution, is a master in Scriptural theology. There is more teaching in the Saviour's body and in the Saviour's blood than in all the world besides. O ye who wish to learn the way to comfort, and how to tread the royal road to heavenly wisdom, come ye to the cross, and see the Saviour suffer, and pour out His heart's blood for human sin!

Some of David's Psalms are called, "*Michtam*" which means "golden Psalm." Surely we must sing one of these. Our psalms must be golden when we sing of the Head of the Church, who is as much fine gold. More precious than silver or gold is the inestimable price which He has paid for our ransom. Yes, ye sons of harmony, bring your most melodious anthems here, and let your Saviour have your golden psalms!

Certain Psalms in the Old Testament are entitled, "*Upon Shoshannim*," that is, "Upon the lilies." O ye virgin souls, whose hearts have been washed in blood, and have been made white and pure, bring forth your instruments of song :—

> "Hither, then, your music bring,
>   Strike aloud each cheerful string!"

Let your hearts, when they are in their best state, when they are purest, and most cleansed from earthly dross, give to Jesus their glory and their excellence.

Then there are other Psalms which are dedicated "*To the sons of Korah.*" If the guess be right, the reason why we get the title, "To the sons of Korah"

—" a song of loves"—must be this : that when Korah, Dathan, and Abiram were swallowed up, the sons of Dathan and Abiram were swallowed up, too ; but the sons of Korah perished not. Why they were not destroyed, we cannot tell. Perhaps it was that sovereign grace spared those whom justice might have doomed ; and "the sons of Korah" were ever after made the sweet singers of the sanctuary ; and whenever there was a special "song of loves", it was always dedicated to them. Ah ! we will have one of those songs of love to-night, around the table, for we, too, are saved by distinguishing grace. We will sing of the heavenly Lover, and the many waters which could not quench His love.

> " Love, so vast that nought can bound ;
> Love, too deep for thought to sound
> Love, which made the Lord of all
> Drink the wormwood and the gall.

> " Love, which led Him to the cross,
> Bearing there unutter'd loss ;
> Love, which brought Him to the gloom
> Of the cold and darksome tomb.

> " Love, which made Him hence arise
> Far above the starry skies,
> There with tender, loving care,
> All His people's griefs to share.

> " Love, which will not let Him rest
> Till His chosen all are blest ;
> Till they all for whom He died
> Live rejoicing by His side."

We have not half exhausted the list, but it is clear that, sitting at the Lord's table, we shall have no lack of suitable psalmody. Perhaps no one hymn will quite meet the sentiments of all; and while we would not write a hymn for you, we would pray the Holy Spirit to write now the spirit of praise upon your hearts, that, sitting here, you may "after supper" sing "an hymn."

IV. For one or two minutes let us ask,—"WHAT SHALL THE TUNE BE?" It must be a strange one, for if we are to sing "an hymn" to-night, around the table, the tune must have all the parts of music. Yonder believer is heavy of heart through manifold sorrows, bereavements, and watchings by the sick. He loves his Lord, and would fain praise Him, but his soul refuses to use her wings. Brother, we will have a tune in which you can join, and you shall lead the bass. You shall sing of your fellowship with your Beloved in His sufferings; how He, too, lost a friend; how He spent whole nights in sleeplessness; how His soul was exceeding sorrowful. But the tune must not be all bass, or it would not suit some of us to-night, for we can reach the highest note. We have seen the Lord, and our spirit has rejoiced in God our Saviour. We want to lift the chorus high; yea, there are some true hearts here who are at times so full of joy that they will want special music written for them. "Whether in the body, I cannot tell; or whether out of the body, I cannot tell:" said Paul, and so have said others since, when Christ has been with them. Ah! then they have been obliged to mount to the highest notes, to the very loftiest range of song.

Remember, beloved, that the same Saviour who will accept the joyful shoutings of the strong, will also receive the plaintive notes of the weak and weeping. You little ones, you babes in grace, may cry,

"Hosanna," and the King will not silence you; and you strong men, with all your power of faith, may shout, "Hallelujah!" and your notes shall be accepted, too.

Come, then, let us have a tune in which we can all unite; but ah! we cannot make one which will suit the dead—the dead, I mean, "in trespasses and sins" —and there are some such here. Oh, may God open their mouths, and unloose their tongues; but as for those of us who are alive unto God, let us, as we come to the table, all contribute our own share of the music, and so make up a song of blended harmony, with many parts, one great united song of praise to Jesus our Lord!

We should not choose a tune for the communion table which is not very *soft*. These are no boisterous themes with which we have to deal when we tarry here. A bleeding Saviour, robed in a vesture dyed with blood—this is a theme which you must treat with loving gentleness, for everything that is coarse is out of place. While the tune is soft, it must also be *sweet*. Silence, ye doubts; be dumb, ye fears; be hushed, ye cares! Why come ye here? My music must be sweet and soft when I sing of Him. But oh! it must also be *strong;* there must be a full swell in my praise. Draw out the stops, and let the organ swell the diapason! In fulness let its roll of thundering harmony go up to heaven; let every note be sounded at its loudest. "Praise ye Him upon the cymbals, upon the high-sounding cymbals; upon the harp with a solemn sound." Soft, sweet, and strong, let the music be.

Alas! you complain that your soul is out of tune. Then ask the Master to tune the heart-strings. Those "Selahs" which we find so often in the Psalms, are supposed by many scholars to mean, " Put the harp-strings in tune : " truly we require many " Selahs ", for our hearts are constantly unstrung. Oh, that to-night the Master would enable each one of us to offer that tuneful prayer which we so often sing,—

> " Teach me some melodious sonnet,
>   Sung by flaming tongues above :
> Praise the mount—oh, fix me on it,
>   Mount of God's unchanging love ! "

V. We close by enquiring,—WHO SHALL SING THIS HYMN ?

Sitting around the Father's board, we will raise a joyful song, but who shall do it ? " I will," saith one ; " and we will," say others. What is the reason why so many are willing to join ? The reason is to be found in the verse we were singing just now,—

> " When He's the subject of the song,
>   Who can refuse to sing ? "

What ! a Christian silent when others are praising his Master ? No ; he must join in the song. Satan tries to make God's people dumb, but he cannot, for the Lord has not a tongue-tied child in all His family. They can all speak, and they can all cry, even if they cannot all sing, and *I* think there are times when they can all sing ; yea, they must, for you know the promise, " Then shall the tongue of the dumb sing." Surely, when Jesus leads the tune, if there should be any silent ones in the Lord's family, they must begin to praise the name of the Lord. After Giant Despair's head had been cut off, Christiana and Mr. Greatheart, and all the rest of them, brought out the best of their pro-visions, and made a feast, and Mr. Bunyan says that, after they had feasted, they danced. In the dance there was one remarkable dancer, namely, Mr. Ready-to-Halt. Now, Mr. Ready-to-Halt usually went upon crutches, but for once he laid them aside. "And," says Bunyan, "I warrant you he footed it well!" This is quaintly showing us that, sometimes, the very sorrowful ones, the Ready-to-Halts, when they see Giant Despair's head cut off, when they see death, hell, and sin led in triumphant captivity at the wheels of Christ's victorious chariot, feel that even *they* must for once indulge in a song of gladness. So, when I put the question to-night, "Who will sing?" I trust that Ready-to-Halt will promise, "I will."

You have not much comfort at home, perhaps; by very hard work you earn that little. Sunday is to you a day of true rest, for you are worked very cruelly all the week. Those cheeks of yours, poor girl, are getting very pale, and who knows but what Hood's pathetic lines may be true of you?—

> "Stitch, stitch, stitch,
>   In poverty, hunger, and dirt,
>   Sewing at once, with a double thread,
>   A shroud as well as a shirt."

But, my sister, you may surely rejoice to-night in spite of all this. There may be little on earth, but there is much in heaven. There may be but small comfort for you here apart from Christ; but oh! when, by faith, you mount into His glory, your soul is glad. You shall be as rich as the richest to-night if the Holy Spirit shall but bring you to the table, and enable you to feed upon your Lord and Master. Perhaps you have come here to-night when you ought not to have done so. The physician would have told you to keep to your bed, but you persisted in coming up to the house where the Lord has so often met with you. I trust that we shall hear your voice in the song. There appear to have been in David's day many things to silence the praise of God, but David was one who would sing. I like that expression of his, where the devil seems to come up, and put his hand on his mouth, and say, " Be quiet." " No," says David, " I will sing." Again the devil tries to quiet him, but David is not to be silenced, for three times he puts it, " I will sing, yea, I will sing praises unto the Lord." May the Lord make you resolve this night that you will praise the Lord Jesus with all your heart!

Alas! there are many of you here to-night whom I could not invite to this feast of song, and who could not truly come if you were invited. Your sins are not forgiven; your souls are not saved; you have not trusted Christ; you are still in nature's darkness, still in the gall of bitterness, and in the bonds of iniquity. Must it always be so? Will you destroy your-selves? Have you made a league with death, and a covenant with hell? Mercy lingers! Longsuffering continues! Jesus waits! Remember that He hung upon the cross for sinners such as you are, and that if you believe in Him now, you shall be saved. One act of faith, and all the sin you have committed is blotted out. A single glance of faith's eye to the wounds of the Messiah, and your load of iniquity is rolled into the depths of the sea, and you are forgiven in a moment!

" Oh!" says one, " would God I could believe!" Poor soul. may God help thee to believe now! God took upon Himself our flesh; Christ was born among

men, and suffered on account of human guilt, being
made to suffer "the Just for the unjust, that He might
bring us to God." Christ was punished in the room,
place, and stead of every man and woman who will
believe on Him. If you believe on Him, He was
punished for you ; and you will never be punished.
Your debts are paid, your sins are forgiven. God
cannot punish you, for He has punished Christ instead
of you, and He will never punish twice for one offence.
To believe is to trust. If you will now trust your soul
entirely with Him, you are saved, for He loved you,
and gave Himself for you. When you know this, and
feel it to be true, then come to the Lord's table,
and join with us, when, AFTER SUPPER WE SING OUR
HYMN,—

> "'It is finished !'—Oh, what pleasure
>   Do these charming words afford !
> Heavenly blessings without measure
>   Flow to us from Christ the Lord :
>   'It is finished !'
>   Saints, the dying words record.
>
> "Tune your harps anew, ye seraphs,
>   Join to sing the pleasing theme ;
> All on earth, and all in heaven,
>   Join to praise Immanuel's name !
>   Hallelujah !
>   Glory to the bleeding Lamb !'"

JESUS ASLEEP ON A PILLOW.

" And He was in the hinder part of the ship, asleep on a pillow: and they awake Him, and say unto Him, Master, carest Thou not that we perish? And He arose, and rebuked the wind, and said unto the sea, Peace, be still. And the wind ceased, and there was a great calm."— *Mark* iv. 38, 39.

JESUS ASLEEP ON A PILLOW.

O UR Lord took His disciples with Him into the ship to teach them a practical lesson. It is one thing to talk to people about our oneness with them, and about how they should exercise faith in time of danger, and about their real safety in apparent peril; but it is another, and a far better thing, to go into the ship with them, to let them feel all the terror of the storm, and then to arise, and rebuke the wind, and say unto the sea, "Peace, be still." Our Lord gave His disciples a kind of Kindergarten lesson, an acted sermon, in which the truth was set forth visibly before them. Such teaching produced a wonderful effect upon their lives. May we also be instructed by it!

In our text there are two great calms; the first is, *the calm in the Saviour's heart*, and the second is, *the calm which He created* with a word upon the storm-tossed sea.

1. WITHIN THE LORD THERE WAS A GREAT CALM, and that is why there was soon a great calm around Him; for what is in God comes out of God. Since there was a calm in Christ for Himself, there was afterwards a calm outside for others. What a wonderful inner calm it was! "He was in the hinder part of the ship, asleep on a pillow."

He had *perfect confidence in God* that all was well. The waves might roar, the winds might rage, but He

was not at all disquieted by their fury. He knew
that the waters were in the hollow of His Father's
hand, and that every wind was but the breath of His
Father's mouth; and so He was not troubled; nay,
He had not even a careful thought, He was as much
at ease as on a sunny day. His mind and heart were
free from every kind of care, for amid the gathering
tempest He deliberately laid Himself down, and slept
like a weary child. He went to the hinder part of the
ship, most out of the dash of the spray; He took a
pillow, and put it under His head, and with fixed
intent disposed Himself to slumber. It was His own
act and deed to go to sleep in the storm; He had
nothing for which to keep awake, so pure and perfect
was His confidence in the great Father. What an
example this is to us! We have not half the confidence in God that we ought to have, not even the
best of us. The Lord deserves our unbounded belief,
our unquestioning confidence, our undisturbed reliance.
Oh, that we rendered it to Him as the Saviour did!

There was also mixed with His faith in the Father
a sweet confidence in His own Sonship. He did not
doubt that He was the Son of the Highest. I may
not question God's power to deliver, but I may sometimes question my right to expect deliverance; and if
so, my comfort vanishes. Our Lord had no doubts of
this kind. He had long before heard that word, " This
is My beloved Son, in whom I am well pleased;" He
had so lived and walked with God that the witness
within Him was continuous, so He had no question
about the Father's love to Him as His own Son.
"Rocked in the cradle of the deep," His Father
keeping watch over Him,—what could a child do

better than go to sleep in such a happy position?
And so He does. You and I, too, want a fuller
assurance of our sonship if we would have greater
peace with God. The devil knows that, and therefore
he will come to us with his insinuating suggestion,
" If thou be the son of God." If we have the Spirit
of adoption in us, we shall put the accuser to rout at
once, by opposing the Witness within to his question
from without. Then shall we be filled with a great
calm, because we have confidence in our Father, and
assurance of our sonship.

Then *He had a sweet way*—this blessed Lord of
ours—*of leaving all with God*. He takes no watch,
He makes no fret ; but He goes to sleep. Whatever
comes, He has left all in the hands of the great Care-
taker ; and what more is needful ? If a watchman
were set to guard my house, I should be foolish if I
also sat up for fear of thieves. Why have a watchman
if I cannot trust him to watch? " Cast thy burden
upon the Lord ; " but when thou hast done so, leave
it with the Lord, and do not try to carry it thyself.
That is to make a mock of God, to have the name
of God, but not the reality of God. Lay down every
care, even as Jesus did when He went calmly to the
hinder part of the ship, and quietly took a pillow, and
went to sleep.

But I think I hear someone say, " I could do that
if mine were solely care about myself." Yes, perhaps
you could ; and yet you cannot cast upon God your
burden of care about your children. But your Lord
trusted the Father with those dear to Him. Do you
not think that Christ's disciples were as precious to
Him as our children are to us ? If that ship had been

wrecked, what would have become of Peter? What would have become of "that disciple whom Jesus loved"? Our Lord regarded with intense affection those whom He had chosen and called, and who had been with Him in His temptation, yet He was quite content to leave them all in the care of His Father, and go to sleep.

You answer, "Yes, but there is a still wider circle of people watching to see what will happen to me, and to the cause of Christ with which I am connected. I am obliged to care, whether I will or no." Is your case, then, more trying than your Lord's? Do you forget that "there were also with Him many other little ships"? When the storm was tossing His barque, their little ships were even more in jeopardy; and He cared for them all. He was the Lord High Admiral of the Lake of Gennesaret that night. The other ships were a fleet under His convoy, and His great heart went out to them all. Yet He went to sleep, because He had left in His Father's care even the solicitudes of His charity and sympathy. We, my brethren, who are much weaker than He, shall find strength in doing the same.

Having left everything with His Father, *our Lord did the very wisest thing possible*. He did just what the hour demanded. "Why," say you, "He went to sleep!" That was the best thing Jesus could do; and sometimes it is the best thing we can do. Christ was weary and worn; and when anyone is exhausted, it is his duty to go to sleep if he can. The Saviour must be up again in the morning, preaching and working miracles, and if He does not sleep, He will not be fit for His holy duty; it is incumbent upon

Him to keep Himself in trim for His service. Knowing that the time to sleep has come, the Lord sleeps, and does well in sleeping. Often, when we have been fretting and worrying, we should have glorified God far more had we literally gone to sleep. To glorify God by sleep is not so difficult as some might think; at least, to our Lord it was natural. Here you are worried, sad, wearied; the doctor prescribes for you; his medicine does you no good; but oh! if you enter into full peace with God, and go to sleep, you will wake up infinitely more refreshed than by any drug. The sleep which the Lord giveth to His beloved is balmy indeed. Seek it as Jesus sought it. Go to bed, brother, and you will better imitate your Lord than by putting yourself into ill humour, and worrying other people.

There is a spiritual sleep in which we ought to imitate Jesus. How often I have worried my poor brain about my great church, until I have come to my senses, and then I have said to myself, " How foolish you are! Can you not depend upon God? Is it not far more His cause than yours?" Then I have taken my load in prayer, and left it with the Lord. I have said, " In God's name, this matter shall never worry me again," and I have left my urgent care with Him, and ended it for ever. I have so deliberately given up many a trying case into the Lord's care that, when any of my friends have said to me, " What about so and so?" I have simply answered, " I do not know, and I am no longer careful to know. The Lord will interpose in some way or other, but I will trouble no more about it." No mischief has ever come through any matter which I have left in the divine keeping. The staying of my hand has been wisdom. " Stand still, and see the salvation of God," is God's own precept. Here let us follow Jesus. Having a child's confidence in the great Father, He retires to the stern of the ship, selects a pillow, deliberately lies down upon it, and goes to sleep; and though the ship is filling with water, and rolls and pitches, He sleeps on. Nothing can break the peace of His tranquil soul. Every sailor on board reels to and fro, and staggers like a drunken man, and is at his wits' end ; but Jesus is neither at his wits' end, nor does He stagger, for He rests in perfect innocence, and undisturbed confidence. His heart is happy in God, and therefore doth He remain in repose. Oh, for grace to copy Him !

II. But here notice, dear friends, THE DIFFERENCE BETWEEN THE MASTER AND HIS DISCIPLES; for while He was in a great calm, they were in a great storm. Here see their failure. They were just as we are, and we are often just as they were.

They gave way to fear. They were sorely afraid that the ship would sink, and that they would all perish. In thus yielding to fear, *they forgot the solid reasons for courage which lay near at hand ;* for, in truth, they were safe enough. Christ is on board that vessel, and if the ship goes down, He will sink with them. The heathen mariner took courage during a storm from the fact that Cæsar was on board the ship that was tossed by stormy winds ; and should not the disciples feel secure with Jesus on board ? Fear not, ye carry Jesus and His cause! Jesus had come to do a work, and His disciples might have known that He could not perish with that work unaccomplished. Could they not trust Him? They had seen Him multiply the loaves and fishes, and cast out devils, and heal all manner of sicknesses; could they not trust Him to still the storm? Unreasonable unbelief! Faith in God is true prudence, but to doubt God is irrational. It is the height of absurdity and folly to question omnipotent love.

And *the disciples were so unwise as to do the Master a very ill turn.* He was sadly weary, and sorely needed sleep; but they hastened to Him, and aroused Him in a somewhat rough and irreverent manner. They were slow to do so, but their fear urged them; and therefore they awoke Him, uttering ungenerous and unloving words: "Master, carest Thou not that we perish?" Shame on the lips that asked so harsh a question! Did they not upon reflection greatly blame themselves? He had given them no cause for such hard speeches; and, moreover, it was unseemly in them to call Him "Master," and then to ask Him, "Carest Thou not that we perish?" Is He to be accused of such hard-heartedness as to let His faithful disciples perish when He has power to deliver them? Alas, we, too, have been guilty of like offences! I think I have known some of Christ's disciples who have appeared to doubt the wisdom or the love of their Lord. They did not quite say that He was mistaken, but they said that He moved in a mysterious way; they did not quite complain that He was unkind to them, but they whispered that they could not reconcile His dealings with His infinite love. Alas, Jesus has endured much from our unbelief! May this picture help us to see our spots, and may the love of our dear Lord remove them!

III. I have spoken to you of the Master's calm and of the disciples' failure; now let us think of THE GREAT CALM WHICH JESUS CREATED. "There was a great calm."

His voice produced it. They say that if oil be poured upon the waters they will become smooth, and I suppose there is *some* truth in the statement ; but there is all truth in this, that if God speaks, the storm subsides into a calm, so that the waves of the sea are still. It only needs our Lord Jesus to speak in the heart of any one of us, and immediately the peace of God, which passeth all understanding, will possess us. No matter how drear your despondency, nor how dread your despair, the Lord can at once create a great calm of confidence. What a door of hope this opens to any who are in trouble! If I could speak a poor man rich, and a sick one well, I am sure I would do so at once; but Jesus is infinitely better than I am, and therefore I know that He will speak peace to the tried and troubled heart.

Note, too, that *this calm came at once.* "Jesus arose, and rebuked the wind, and said unto the sea, Peace, be still. And the wind ceased, and there was a great calm." As soon as Jesus spake, all was quiet. I have met with a very large number of persons in trouble of mind, and I have seen a few who have slowly come out into light and liberty ; but more frequently deliverance has come suddenly. The iron gate has opened of its own accord, and the prisoner has stepped into immediate freedom. "The snare is broken, and we are escaped." What a joy it is to know that rest is so near even when the tempest rages most furiously !

Note, also, that *the Saviour coupled this repose with faith*, for He said to the disciples as soon as the calm came, "Why are ye so fearful? How is it that ye have no faith?" Faith and the calm go together. If thou believest, thou shalt rest; if thou wilt but cast thyself upon thy God, surrendering absolutely to His will, thou shalt have mercy, and joy, and light. Even if we have no faith, the Lord will sometimes give us the blessing that we need, for He delights to do more for us than we have any right to expect of Him; but usually the rule of His kingdom is, "According to your faith be it unto you."

This great calm is very delightful, and concerning this I desire to bear my personal testimony. I speak from my own knowledge when I say that it passeth all understanding. I was sitting, the other night, meditating on God's mercy and love, when suddenly I found in my own heart a most delightful sense of perfect peace. I had come to Beulah-land, where the sun shines without a cloud. "There was a great calm." I felt as mariners might do who have been tossed about in broken water, and all on a sudden, they cannot tell why, the ocean becomes as unruffled as a mirror, and the sea-birds come and sit in happy circles upon the water. I felt perfectly content, yea, undividedly happy. Not a wave of trouble broke upon the shore of my heart, and even far out to sea in the deeps of my being all was still. I knew no ungratified wish, no unsatisfied desire. I could not discover a reason for uneasiness, or a motive for fear. There was nothing approaching to fanaticism in my feelings, nothing even of excitement: my soul was waiting upon God, and delighting herself alone in

Him. Oh, the blessedness of this rest in the Lord! What an Elysium it is! I must be allowed to say a little upon this purple island in the sea of my life: it was none other than a fragment of heaven. We often talk about our great spiritual storms, why should we not speak of our great calms? If ever we get into trouble, what a noise we make of it! Why should we not sing of our deliverances?

Let us survey our mercies. Every sin that we have ever committed is forgiven. "The blood of Jesus Christ, His Son, cleanseth us from all sin." The power of sin within us is broken; it "shall not have dominion over you, for ye are not under the law but under grace." Satan is a vanquished enemy; the world is overcome by our Lord Jesus, and death is abolished by Him. All providence works for our good. Eternity has no threat for us, it bears within its mysteries nothing but immortality and glory. Nothing can harm us. The Lord is our shield, and our exceeding great reward. Wherefore, then, should we fear? The Lord of hosts is with us, the God of Jacob is our refuge. To the believer, peace is no presumption: he is warranted in enjoying "perfect peace"—a quiet which is deep, and founded on truth, which encompasses all things, and is not broken by any of the ten thousand disturbing causes which otherwise might prevent our rest. "Thou wilt keep him in perfect peace whose mind is stayed on Thee; because he trusteth in Thee." Oh, to get into that calm, and remain in it till we come to that world where there is no more sea!

A calm like that which ruled within our Saviour, should we be happy enough to attain to it, will give us in our measure the power to make outside matters calm. He that hath peace can make peace. We cannot work miracles, and yet the works which Jesus did shall we do also. Sleeping His sleep, we shall awake in His rested energy, and treat the winds and waves as things subject to the power of faith, and therefore to be commanded into quiet. We shall speak so as to console others : our calm shall work marvels in the little ships whereof others are captains. We, too, shall say, " Peace ! Be still." Our confidence shall prove contagious, and the timid shall grow brave : our tender love shall spread itself, and the contentious shall cool down to patience. Only the matter must begin within ourselves. We cannot create a calm till we are in a calm. It is easier to rule the elements than to govern the unruliness of our wayward nature. When grace has made us masters of our fears, so that we can take a pillow and fall asleep amid the hurricane, the fury of the tempest is over. He giveth peace and safety when He giveth His beloved sleep.

REAL CONTACT WITH JESUS.

" And Jesus said, Somebody hath touched Me : for I perceive that virtue is gone out of Me."—*Luke* viii. 46.

REAL CONTACT WITH JESUS.

OUR Lord was very frequently in the midst of a crowd. His preaching was so plain and so forcible that He always attracted a vast company of hearers; and, moreover, the rumour of the loaves and fishes no doubt had something to do with increasing His audiences, while the expectation of beholding a miracle would be sure to add to the numbers of the hangers-on. Our Lord Jesus Christ often found it difficult to move through the streets, because of the masses who pressed upon Him. This was encouraging to Him as a preacher, and yet how small a residuum of real good came of all the excitement which gathered around His personal ministry! He might have looked upon the great mass, and have said, "What is the chaff to the wheat?" for here it was piled up upon the threshing-floor, heap upon heap; and yet, after His decease, His disciples might have been counted by a few scores, for those who had spiritually received Him were but few. Many were called, but few were chosen. Yet, wherever one was blessed, our Saviour took note of it; it touched a chord in His soul. He never could be unaware when virtue had gone out of Him to heal a sick one, or when power had gone forth with His ministry to save a sinful one. Of all the crowd that gathered round the Saviour upon the day of which our text speaks,

I find nothing said about one of them except this solitary "somebody" who had touched Him. The crowd came, and the crowd went; but little is recorded of it all. Just as the ocean, having advanced to full tide, leaves but little behind it when it retires again to its channel, so the vast multitude around the Saviour left only this one precious deposit—one "somebody" who had touched Him, and had received virtue from Him.

Ah, my Master, it may be so again this evening! These Sabbath mornings, and these Sabbath evenings, the crowds come pouring in like a mighty ocean, filling this house, and then they all retire again; only here and there is a "somebody" left weeping for sin, a "somebody" left rejoicing in Christ, a "somebody" who can say, "I have touched the hem of His garment, and I have been made whole." The whole of my other hearers are not worth the "somebodies." The many of you are not worth the few, for the many are the pebbles, and the few are the diamonds; the many are the heaps of husks, and the few are the precious grains. May God find them out at this hour, and His shall be all the praise!

Jesus said, "Somebody hath touched Me," from which we observe that, *in the use of means and ordinances, we should never be satisfied unless we get into personal contact with Christ*, so that we touch Him, as this woman touched His garment. Secondly, *if we can get into such personal contact, we shall have a blessing:* "I perceive that virtue is gone out of Me;" and, thirdly, *if we do get a blessing, Christ will know it;* however obscure our case may be, He will know it, and He will have us let others know it; He will speak, and ask such questions as will draw us out, and manifest us to the world.

I. First, then, IN THE USE OF ALL MEANS AND ORDINANCES, LET IT BE OUR CHIEF AIM AND OBJECT TO COME INTO PERSONAL CONTACT WITH THE LORD JESUS CHRIST.

Peter said, " The multitude throng Thee, and press Thee," and that is true of the multitude to this very day ; but of those who come where Christ is in the assembly of His saints, a large proportion only come because it is their custom to do so. Perhaps they hardly know why they go to a place of worship. They go because they always did go, and they think it wrong not to go. They are just like the doors which swing upon their hinges ; they take no interest in what is done, at least only in the exterior parts of the service ; into the heart and soul of the business they do not enter, and cannot enter. They are glad if the sermon is rather short, there is so much the less tedium for them. They are glad if they can look around and gaze at the congregation, they find in that something to interest them ; but getting near to the Lord Jesus is not the business they come upon. They have not looked at it in that light. They come and they go ; they come and they go ; and it will be so till, by-and-by, they will come for the last time, and they will find out in the next world that the means of grace were not instituted to be matters of custom, and that to have heard Jesus Christ preached, and to have rejected Him, is no trifle, but a solemn thing for which they will have to answer in the presence of the great Judge of all the earth.

Others there are who come to the house of prayer,

and try to enter into the service, and do so in a certain fashion; but it is only self-righteously or professionally. They may come to the Lord's table; perhaps they attend to baptism; they may even join the church. They are baptized, yet not by the Holy Spirit; they take the Lord's supper, but they take not the Lord Himself; they eat the bread, but they never eat His flesh; they drink the wine, but they never drink His blood; they have been buried in the pool, but they have never been buried with Christ in baptism, nor have they risen again with Him into newness of life. To them, to read, to sing, to kneel, to hear, and so on, are enough. They are content with the shell, but the blessed spiritual kernel, the true marrow and fatness, these they know nothing of. These are the many, go into what church or meeting-house you please. They are in the press around Jesus, but they do not touch Him. They come, but they come not into contact with Jesus. They are outward, external hearers only, but there is no inward touching of the blessed person of Christ, no mysterious contact with the ever-blessed Saviour, no stream of life and love flowing from Him to them. It is all mechanical religion. Of vital godliness, they know nothing.

But, "somebody," said Christ, "somebody hath touched Me," and that is the soul of the matter. O my hearer, when you are in prayer alone, never be satisfied with having prayed; do not give it up till you have touched Christ in prayer; or, if you have not got to Him, at any rate sigh and cry until you do! Do not think you have prayed, but try again. When you come to public worship, I beseech you, rest not satisfied with listening to the sermon, and so on,—as you all do with sufficient attention ; to that I bear you witness ;—but do not be content unless you get at Christ the Master, and touch Him. At all times when you come to the communion table, count it to have been no ordinance of grace to you unless you have gone right through the veil into Christ's own arms, or at least have touched His garment, feeling that the first object, the life and soul of the means of grace, is to touch Jesus Christ Himself; and except " somebody " hath touched Him, the whole has been a mere dead performance, without life or power.

The woman in our text was not only amongst those who were in the crowd, but she touched Jesus ; and therefore, beloved, let me hold her up to your example in some respects, though I would to God that in other respects you might excel her.

Note, first, she felt that it was of no use being in the crowd, of no use to be in the same street with Christ, or near to the place where Christ was, but *she must get at Him ; she must touch Him.* She touched Him, you will notice, under *many difficulties.* There was a great crowd. She was a woman. She was also a woman enfeebled by a long disease which had drained her constitution, and left her more fit to be upon a bed than to be struggling in the seething tumult. Yet, notwithstanding that, so intense was her desire, that she urged on her way, I doubt not with many a bruise, and many an uncouth push, and at last, poor trembler as she was, she got near to the Lord. Beloved, it is not always easy to get at Jesus. It is very easy to kneel down to pray, but not so easy to reach Christ in prayer. There is a child crying, it is your own, and its noise has often hindered you when you were striving to approach Jesus ; or a knock will come at the door when you most wish to be retired. When you are sitting in the house of God, your neighbour in the seat before you may unconsciously distract your attention. It is not easy to draw near to Christ, especially coming as some of you do right away from the counting-house, and from the workshop, with a thousand thoughts and cares about you. You cannot always unload your burden outside, and come in here with your hearts prepared to receive the gospel. Ah ! it is a terrible fight some-times, a real foot-to-foot fight with evil, with tempta-tion, and I know not what. But, beloved, do fight it out, do fight it out ; do not let your seasons for prayer be wasted, nor your times for hearing be thrown away ; but, like this woman, be resolved, with all your feebleness, that you will lay hold upon Christ. And oh ! if you be resolved about it, if you cannot get to Him, He will come to you, and sometimes, when you are struggling against unbelieving thoughts, He will turn and say, " Make room for that poor feeble one, that she may come to Me, for My desire is to the work of My own hands ; let her come to Me, and let her desire be granted to her."

Observe, again, that this woman touched Jesus *very secretly*. Perhaps there is a dear sister here who is getting near to Christ at this very moment, and yet her face does not betray her. It is so little contact that she has gained with Christ that the joyous flush, and the sparkle of the eye, which we often see in the child of God, have not yet come to her. She is sitting in yonder obscure corner, or standing in this aisle, but

though her touch is secret, it is true. Though she
cannot tell another of it, yet it is accomplished. She
has touched Jesus. Beloved, that is not always the
nearest fellowship with Christ of which we talk the
most. Deep waters are still. Nay, I am not sure but
what we sometimes get nearer to Christ when we
think we are at a distance than we do when we
imagine we are near Him, for we are not always
exactly the best judges of our own spiritual state, and
we may be very close to the Master, and yet for all
that we may be so anxious to get closer that we may
feel dissatisfied with the measure of grace which we
have already received. To be satisfied with self, is no
sign of grace; but to long for more grace, is often a far
better evidence of the healthy state of the soul.
Friend, if thou canst not come to the table to-night
publicly, come to the Master in secret. If thou darest
not tell thy wife, or thy child, or thy father, that thou
art trusting in Jesus, it need not be told as yet. Thou
mayest do it secretly, as he did to whom Jesus said,
"When thou wast under the fig tree, I saw thee."
Nathanael retired to the shade that no one might see
him; but Jesus saw him, and marked his prayer, and
He will see thee in the crowd, and in the dark, and
not withhold His blessing.

This woman also came into contact with Christ
under a very deep sense of unworthiness. I dare say
she thought, "If I touch the Great Prophet, it will be
a wonder if He does not strike me with some sudden
judgment," for she was a woman ceremonially unclean. She had no right to be in the throng. Had
the Levitical law been strictly carried out, I suppose
she would have been confined to her house; but there

she was wandering about, and she must needs go and
touch the holy Saviour. Ah! poor heart, you feel
to-night that you are not fit to touch the skirts of the
Master's robe, for you are so unworthy. You never
felt so undeserving before as you do to-night. In the
recollection of last week and its infirmities, in the
remembrance of the present state of your heart, and
all its wanderings from God, you feel as if there never
was so worthless a sinner in the house of God before.
" Is grace for me?" say you. " Is Christ for me?"
Oh! yes, unworthy one. Do not be put off without
it. Jesus Christ does not save the worthy, but the
unworthy. Your plea must not be righteousness, but
guilt. And you, too, child of God, though you are
ashamed of yourself, Jesus is not ashamed of you;
and though you feel unfit to come, let your unfitness
only impel you with the greater earnestness of desire.
Let your sense of need make you the more fervent to
approach the Lord, who can supply your need.

Thus, you see, the woman came under difficulties,
she came secretly, she came as an unworthy one, but
still she obtained the blessing.

I have known many staggered with that saying of
Paul's, " He that eateth and drinketh unworthily,
eateth and drinketh damnation to himself." Now,
understand that this passage does not refer to the
unworthiness of those persons who come to the Lord's
table; for it does not say, " He that eateth and
drinketh *being unworthy*." It is not an adjective;
it is an adverb: " He that eateth and drinketh un-
worth*ily*," that is to say, he who shall come to the
outward and visible sign of Christ's presence, and
shall eat of the bread in order to obtain money by

being a member of the church, knowing himself to be a hypocrite, or who shall do it jestingly, trifling with the ordinance : such a person would be eating and drinking unworthily, and he will be condemned. The sense of the passage is, not "damnation", as our version reads it, but "condemnation." There can be no doubt that members of the church, coming to the Lord's table in an unworthy manner, do receive condemnation. They are condemned for so doing, and the Lord is grieved. If they have any conscience at all, they ought to feel their sin ; and if not, they may expect the chastisements of God to visit them. But, O sinner, as to coming to Christ,—which is a very different thing from coming to the Lord's table,—as to coming to Christ, the more unworthy you feel yourself to be, the better. Come, thou filthy one, for Christ can wash thee. Come, thou loathsome one, for Christ can beautify thee. Come utterly ruined and undone, for in Jesus Christ there is the strength and salvation which thy case requires.

Notice, once again, that *this woman touched the Master very tremblingly, and it was only a hurried touch, but still it was the touch of faith.* Oh, beloved, to lay hold on Christ! Be thankful if you do but get near Him for a few minutes. "Abide with me," should be your prayer ; but oh, if He only give you a glimpse, be thankful ! Remember that a touch healed the woman. She did not embrace Christ by the hour together. She had but a touch, and she was healed ; and oh, may you have a sight of Jesus now, my beloved ! Though it be but a glimpse, yet it will gladden and cheer your souls. Perhaps you are waiting on Christ, desiring His company, and while

you are turning it over in your mind you are asking,
"Will He ever shine upon me? Will He ever speak
loving words to me? Will He ever let me sit at His
feet? Will He ever permit me to lean my head
upon His bosom?" Come and try Him. Though
you should shake like an aspen leaf, yet come. They
sometimes come best who come most tremblingly, for
when the creature is lowest then is the Creator highest,
and when in our own esteem we are less than nothing
and vanity, then is Christ the more fair and lovely in
our eyes. One of the best ways of climbing to heaven
is on our hands and knees. At any rate, there is no
fear of falling when we are in that position, for—

"He that is down need fear no fall."

Let your lowliness of heart, your sense of utter
nothingness, instead of disqualifying you, be a sweet
medium for leading you to receive more of Christ.
The more empty I am, the more room is there for my
Master. The more I lack, the more He will give me.
The more I feel my sickness, the more shall I adore
and bless Him when He makes me whole.

You see, the woman did really touch Christ, and so
I come back to that. Whatever infirmity there was
in the touch, it was a real touch of faith. She did
reach Christ Himself. She did not touch Peter; that
would have been of no use to her, any more than it is
for the parish priest to tell you that you are regenerate
when your life soon proves that you are not. She did
not touch John or James; that would have been of
no more good to her than it is for you to be touched
by a bishop's hands, and to be told that you are confirmed in the faith, when you are not even a believer.

and therefore have no faith to be confirmed in. She touched the Master Himself; and, I pray you, do not be content unless you can do the same. Put out the hand of faith, and touch Christ. Rest on Him. Rely on His bloody sacrifice, His dying love, His rising power, His ascended plea; and as you rest in Him, your vital touch, however feeble, will certainly give you the blessing your soul needs.

This brings us to the second part of our discourse, upon which I will say only a little.

II. THE WOMAN IN THE CROWD DID TOUCH JESUS, AND, HAVING DONE SO, SHE RECEIVED VIRTUE FROM HIM.

The healing energy streamed at once through the finger of faith into the woman. In Christ, there is healing for all spiritual diseases. There is a speedy healing, a healing which will not take months nor years, but which is complete in one second. There is in Christ a sufficient healing, though your diseases should be multiplied beyond all bounds. There is in Christ an all-conquering power to drive out every ill. Though, like this woman, you baffle physicians, and your case is reckoned desperate beyond all parallel, yet a touch of Christ will heal you. What a precious, glorious gospel I have to preach to sinners! If they touch Jesus, no matter though the devil himself were in them, that touch of faith would drive the devil out of them. Though you were like the man into whom there had entered a legion of devils, the word of Jesus would cast them all into the deep, and you should sit at His feet, clothed, and in your right mind. There is no excess or extravagance of sin which the power of Jesus Christ cannot overcome. If thou canst believe, whatever thou mayest have been, thou shalt be saved. If thou canst believe, though thou hast been lying in the scarlet dye till the warp and woof of thy being are ingrained therewith, yet shall the precious blood of Jesus make thee white as snow. Though thou art become black as hell itself, and only fit to be cast into the pit, yet if thou trustest Jesus, that simple faith shall give to thy soul the healing which shall make thee fit to tread the streets of heaven, and to stand before Jehovah-Rophi's face, magnifying the Lord that healeth thee.

And now, child of God, I want you to learn the same lesson. Very likely, when you came in here, you said,—"Alas! I feel very dull; my spirituality is at a very low ebb; the place is hot, and I do not feel prepared to hear; the spirit is willing, but the flesh is weak; I shall have no holy enjoyment to-day!" Why not? Why, the touch of Jesus could make you live if you were dead, and surely it will stir the life that is in you, though it may seem to you to be expiring! Now, struggle hard, my beloved, to get at Jesus! May the Eternal Spirit come and help you, and may you yet find that your dull, dead times can soon become your best times. Oh! what a blessing it is that God takes the beggar up from the dunghill! He does not raise us when He sees us already up, but when He finds us lying on the dunghill, then He delights to lift us up, and set us among princes. Or ever you are aware, your soul may become like the chariots of Ammi-nadib. Up from the depths of heaviness to the very heights of ecstatic worship you may mount as in a single moment if you can but touch Christ crucified. View Him yonder, with

streaming wounds, with thorn-crowned head, as in all
the majesty of His misery, He expires for you!

"Alas!" say you, "I have a thousand doubts to-
night." Ah! but your doubts will soon vanish when
you draw nigh to Christ. He never doubts who feels
the touch of Christ, at least, not while the touch lasts,
for observe this woman! She felt in her body that
she was made whole, and so shall you, if you will only
come into contact with the Lord. Do not wait for
evidences, but come to Christ for evidences. If you
cannot even dream of a good thing in yourselves,
come to Jesus Christ as you did at the first. Come
as if you never had come at all. Come to Jesus as a
sinner, and your doubts shall flee away.

"Ay!" saith another, "but my sins come to my
remembrance, my sins since conversion." Well,
return to Jesus, when your guilt seems to return.
The fountain is still open, and that fountain, you will
remember, is not only open for sinners, but for saints;
for what saith the Scripture—" There shall be a fountain opened *for the house of David and for the
inhabitants of Jerusalem,*"—that is, for you, church-
members, for you, believers in Jesus? The fountain is
still open. Come, beloved, come to Jesus anew, and
whatever be your sins, or doubts, or heaviness, they
shall all depart as soon as you can touch your Lord.

III. And now the last point is—and I will not
detain you long upon it — IF SOMEBODY SHALL
TOUCH JESUS, THE LORD WILL KNOW IT.

I do not know your names; a great number of you
are perfect strangers to me. It matters nothing;
your name is "somebody", and Christ will know you.
You are a total stranger, perhaps, to everybody in

this place; but if you get a blessing, there will be two who will know it,—you will, and Christ will. Oh! if you should look to Jesus this day, it may not be registered in our church-book, and we may not hear of it; but still it will be registered in the courts of heaven, and they will set all the bells of the New Jerusalem a-ringing, and all the harps of angels will take a fresh lease of music as soon as they know that you are·born again.

> " With joy the Father doth approve
>   The fruit of His eternal love ;
> The Son with joy looks down and sees
>   The purchase of His agonies ;
> The Spirit takes delight to view
>   The holy soul He formed anew ;
> And saints and angels join to sing
>   The growing empire of their King."

" Somebody !" I do not know the woman's name ; I do not know who the man is, but—" Somebody !"—God's electing love rests on thee, Christ's redeeming blood was shed for thee, the Spirit has wrought a work in thee, or thou wouldst not have touched Jesus ; and all this Jesus knows.

It is a consoling thought that Christ not only knows the great children in the family, but He also knows the little ones. This stands fast: "The Lord knoweth them that are His," whether they are only brought to know Him now, or whether they have known Him for fifty years. "The Lord knoweth them that are His," and if I am a part of Christ's body, I may be but the foot, but the Lord knows the foot; and the head and the heart in heaven feel acutely when the foot on earth is bruised. If you have touched Jesus, I tell you that amidst the glories of angels, and the everlasting hallelujahs of all the blood-bought, He has found time to hear your sigh, to receive your faith, and to give you an answer of peace. All the way from heaven to earth there has rushed a mighty stream of healing virtue, which has come from Christ to you. Since you have touched Him, the healing virtue has touched you.

Now, *as Jesus knows of your salvation, He wishes other people to know of it*, and that is why He has put it into my heart to say,—Somebody has touched the Lord. Where is that somebody? Somebody, where are you? Somebody, where are you? You have touched Christ, though with a feeble finger, and you are saved. Let us know it. It is due to us to let us know. You cannot guess what joy it gives us when we hear of sick ones being healed by our Master. Some of you, perhaps, have known the Lord for months, and you have not yet come forward to make an avowal of it; we beg you to do so. You may come forward tremblingly, as this woman did; you may perhaps say, "I do not know what I should tell you." Well, you must tell us what she told the Lord; she told Him all the truth. We do not want anything else. We do not desire any sham experience. We do not want you to manufacture feelings like somebody else's that you have read of in a book. Come and tell us what you have felt. We shall not ask you to tell us what you have not felt, or what you do not know. But, if you have touched Christ, and you have been healed, I ask it, and I think I may ask it as your duty, as well as a favour to us, to come and tell us what the Lord hath done for your soul.

And you, believers, when you come to the Lord's table, if you draw near to Christ, and have a sweet season, tell it to your brethren. Just as when Benjamin's brethren went down to Egypt to buy corn, they left Benjamin at home, but they took a sack for Benjamin, so you ought always to take a word home for the sick wife at home, or the child who cannot come out. Take home food for those of the family who cannot come for it. God grant that you may have always something sweet to tell of what you have experimentally known of precious truth, for while the sermon may have been sweet in itself, it comes with a double power when you can add, " and there was a savour about it which I enjoyed, and which made my heart leap for joy "!

Whoever you may be, my dear friend, though you may be nothing but a poor " somebody ", yet if you have touched Christ, tell others about it, in order that they may come and touch Him, too ; and the Lord bless you, for Christ's sake ! Amen.

CHRIST AND HIS TABLE-COMPANIONS.

"And when the hour was come, He sat down, and the twelve apostles with Him."—*Luke* xxii. 14.

CHRIST AND HIS TABLE-COMPANIONS.

———

THE outward ordinances of the Christian religion are but two, and those two are exceedingly simple, yet neither of them has escaped human alteration; and, alas! much mischief has been wrought, and much of precious teaching has been sacrificed, by these miserable perversions. For instance, the ordinance of baptism as it was administered by the apostles betokened the burial of the believer with Christ, and his rising with his Lord into newness of life. Men must needs exchange immersion for sprinkling, and the intelligent believer for an unconscious child, and so the ordinance is slain. The other sacred institution, the Lord's supper, like believers' baptism, is simplicity itself. It consists of bread broken, and wine poured out, these viands being eaten and drunk at a festival—a delightful picture of the sufferings of Christ for us, and of the fellowship which the saints have with one another and with Him. But this ordinance, also, has been tampered with by men. By some, the wine has been taken away altogether, or reserved only for a priestly caste; and the simple bread has been changed into a consecrated host. As for the table, the very emblem of fellowship in all nations—for what expresses fellowship better than surrounding a table, and eating and drinking together?—this, forsooth, must be put away, and an altar must be erected, and the bread and wine which were to help us to remember the Lord Jesus are changed into an " unbloody sacrifice ", and so the whole thing becomes an unscriptural celebration instead of a holy institution for fellowship. Let us be warned by these mistakes of others never either to add to or take from the Word of God so much as a single jot or tittle. Keep upon the foundation of the Scriptures, and you stand safely, and have an answer for those who question you; yea, and an answer which you may render at the bar of God; but once allow your own whim, or fancy, or taste, or your notion of what is proper and right, to rule you, instead of the Word of God, and you have entered upon a dangerous course, and unless the grace of God prevent, boundless mischief may ensue. The Bible is our standard authority; none may turn from it. The wise man says, in Ecclesiastes, " I counsel thee to keep the King's commandment ;" we would repeat his advice, and add to it the sage precept of the mother of our Lord, at Cana, when she said, " Whatsoever He saith unto you, do it."

We shall now ask you in contemplation to gaze upon the first celebration of the Lord's supper. You perceive at once that there was no altar in that large upper room. There was a table, a table with bread and wine upon it, but no altar; and Jesus did not kneel,—there is no sign of that,—but He sat down, I doubt not, after the Oriental mode of sitting, that is to say, by a partial reclining, He sat down with His apostles. Now, He who ordained this supper knew how it ought to be observed, and as the first celebration of it was the model for all others, we may be assured that the right way of coming to this communion is to assemble around a table, and to sit or recline while we eat and drink together of bread and wine in remembrance of our Lord.

While we see the Saviour sitting down with His twelve apostles, let us enquire, first, *what did this make them?* Then, secondly, *what did this imply?* And, thirdly, *what further may we legitimately infer from it?*

I. First, then, we see the Great Master, the Lord, the King in Zion, sitting down at the table to eat and drink with His twelve apostles,—WHAT DID THIS MAKE THEM?

Note what they were at first. By His first calling of them they became His *followers*, for He said unto them, "Follow Me." That is to say, they were convinced, by sundry marks and signs, that He was the Messias, and they, therefore, became His followers. Followers may be at a great distance from their leader, and enjoy little or no intercourse with him, for the leader may be too great to be approached by the common members of his band. In the case of the disciples, their following was unusually close, for their Master was very condescending, but still their intercourse was not always of the most intimate kind at first, and therefore it was not at the first that He called them to such a festival as this supper. They began with following, and this is where we must begin. If we cannot enter as yet into closer association with our Lord, we may, at least, know His voice by His Spirit, and follow Him as the sheep follow the shepherd. The most important way of following Him is to trust Him, and then diligently to imitate His example.

This is a good beginning, and it will end well, for those who walk with Him to-day shall rest with Him hereafter; those who tread in His footsteps shall sit on His throne.

Being His followers, they came next to be His *disciples*. A man may have been a follower for a while, and yet may not have reached discipleship. A follower may follow blindly, and hear a great deal which he does not understand; but when he becomes a disciple, his Master instructs him, and leads him into truth. To explain, to expound, to solve difficulties, to clear away doubts, and to make truth intelligible, is the office of a teacher amongst his disciples. Now, it was a very blessed thing for the followers to become disciples, but still disciples are not necessarily so intimate with their Master as to sit and eat with him. Socrates and Plato knew many in the Academy whom they did not invite to their homes. My brethren, if Jesus had but called us to be His disciples, and no more, we should have had cause for great thankfulness; if we had been allowed to sit at His feet, and had never shared in such an entertainment as that before us, we ought to have been profoundly grateful; but now that He has favoured us with a yet higher place, let us never be unfaithful to our discipleship. Let us daily learn of Jesus, let us search the Bible to see what it was that He taught us, and then by the aid of His Holy Spirit let us scrupulously obey. Yet is there a something beyond.

Being the Lord's disciples, the chosen ones next rose to become His *servants*, which is a step in advance, since the disciple may be but a child, but the servant has some strength, has received some measure of training, and renders somewhat in return. Their Master gave them power to preach the gospel, and to execute commissions of grace, and happy were they to be called to wait upon such a Master, and aid in setting up His kingdom. My dear brethren and sisters, are you all Christ's servants consciously? If so, though the service may at times seem heavy because your faith is weak, yet be very thankful that you are servants at all, for it is better to serve God than to reign over all the kingdoms of this world. It is better to be the lowest servant of Christ than to be the greatest of men, and remain slaves to your own lusts, or be mere men-pleasers. His yoke is easy, and His burden is light. The servant of such a Master should rejoice in his calling; yet is there something beyond.

Towards the close of His life, our Master revealed the yet nearer relation of His disciples, and uttered words like these : " Henceforth I call you not servants, for the servant knoweth not what his lord doeth, but I have called you *friends*, for all things that I have heard of My Father I have made known unto you." This is a great step in advance. The friend, however humble, enjoys much familiarity with his friend. The friend is told what the servant need not know. The friend enjoys a communion to which the mere servant, disciple, or follower has not attained. May we know this higher association, this dearer bond of relationship! May we not be content without the enjoyment of our Master's friendship! " He that hath friends must show himself friendly ; " and if we would have Christ's friendship, we must befriend His cause, His truth, and His people. He is a Friend that loveth at all times ; if you would enjoy His friendship, take care to abide in Him.

Now note that, on the night before His Passion, our Lord led His friends a step beyond ordinary friendship. The mere follower does not sit at table with his leader ; the disciple does not claim to be a fellow-commoner with his master ; the servant is seldom entertained at the same table with his lord ; the befriended one is not always invited to be a guest ; but here the Lord Jesus made His chosen ones to be *His table-companions ;* He lifted them up to sit with Him at the same table, to eat of the same bread, and drink of the same cup with Himself. From that position He has never degraded them ; they were representative men, and where the Lord placed them, He has placed all His saints permanently. All the Lord's believing people are sitting, by sacred privilege and calling, at the same table with Jesus, for truly, our fellowship is with the Father and with His Son Jesus Christ. He has come into our hearts, and He sups with us, and we with Him ; we are His table-companions, and shall eat bread with Him in the kingdom of God.

Table-companions, then, that is the answer to the question, " What did this festival make the apostles ? " This festival shows all the members of the Church of Christ to be, through divine grace, table-companions with one another, and with Christ Jesus their Lord.

II. So now we shall pass on, in the second place, to ask, WHAT DID THIS TABLE-COMPANIONSHIP IMPLY?

It implied, first of all, *mutual fidelity.* This solemn eating and drinking together was a pledge of faithfulness to one another. It must have been so understood, or otherwise there would have been no force in the complaint: "He that eateth bread with Me hath lifted up his heel against Me." Did not this mean that, *because* Judas had eaten bread with his Lord, he was bound not to betray Him, and so to lift up his heel against Him? This was the seal of an implied covenant; having eaten together, they were under bond to be faithful to one another. Now, as many of you as are really the servants and friends of Christ may know that the Lord Jesus, in eating with you at His table, pledges Himself to be faithful to you. The Master never plays the Judas,—the Judas is among the disciples. There is nothing traitorous in the Lord; He is not only able to keep that which we have committed to Him, but He is faithful, and will do it. He will be faithful, not only as to the great and main matter, but also to every promise He has made. Know ye then, assuredly, that your Master would not have asked you to His table to eat bread with Him if He intended to desert you. He has received you as His honoured guests, and fed you upon His choicest meat, and thereby He does as good as say to you, "I will never leave you, come what may, and in all times of trial, and depression, and temptation, I will be at your right hand, and you shall not be moved, and to the very last you shall prove My faithfulness and truth."

But, beloved, you do not understand this supper unless you are also reminded of the faithfulness that is due from you to your Lord, for the feast is common, and the pledge mutual. In eating with Him, you plight your troth to the Crucified. Beloved, how have you kept your pledge during the past year? You have eaten bread with Him, and I trust that in your hearts you have never gone so far aside as to lift up your heel against Him, but have you always honoured Him as you should? Have you acted as guests should have done? Can you remember His love to you, and put your love to Him side by side with it, without being ashamed? From this time forth, may the Holy Ghost work in our souls a jealous fidelity to the Well-beloved which shall not permit our hearts to wander from Him, or suffer our zeal for His glory to decline!

Again, remember that there is in this solemn eating and drinking together a pledge of fidelity between the disciples themselves, as well as between the disciples and their Lord. Judas would have been a traitor if he had betrayed Peter, or John, or James: so, when ye come to the one table, my brethren, ye must henceforth be true to one another. All bickerings and jealousies must cease, and a generous and affectionate spirit must rule in every bosom. If you hear any speak against those you have communed with, reckon that, as you have eaten bread with them, you are bound to defend their reputations. If any railing accusation be raised against any brother in Christ, reckon that his character is as dear to you as your own. Let a sacred Freemasonry be maintained among us, if I may liken a far higher and more spiritual union to anything which belongs to common life. Ye are members one of another, see that ye love each other with a pure heart fervently. Drinking of the same cup, eating of the same bread, you set forth before the world a token which I trust is not meant to be a lie. As it truly shows Christ's faithfulness to you, so let it as really typify your faithfulness to Christ, and to one another.

In the next place, eating and drinking together was a token of *mutual confidence.* They, in sitting there together, voluntarily avowed their confidence in each other. Those disciples trusted their Master, they knew He would not mislead or deceive them. They trusted each other also, for when they were told that one of them would betray their Lord, they did not suspect each other, but each one said, " Lord, is it I ?" They had much confidence in one another, and the Lord Jesus, as we have seen, had placed great confidence in them by treating them as His friends. He had even trusted them with the great secret of His coming sufferings, and death. They were a trustful company who sat at that supper-table. Now, beloved, when you gather around this table, come in the spirit of implicit trustfulness in the Lord Jesus. If you are suffering, do not doubt His love, but believe that He works all things for your good. If you are vexed with cares, prove your confidence by leaving them entirely in your Redeemer's hands. It will not be a festival of communion to you if you come here with suspicions about your Master. No, show your confidence as you eat of the bread with Him. Let there also be a brotherly confidence in each other. Grievous would it be to see a spirit of suspicion and distrust among you. Suspicion is the death of fellowship. The moment one Christian imagines that another thinks hardly of him, though there may not be the slightest truth in that thought, yet straightway the root of bitterness is planted. Let us believe in

one another's sincerity, for we may rest assured that
each of our brethren deserves to be trusted more than
we do. Turn your suspicions within, and if you must
suspect, suspect your own heart ; but when you meet
with those who have communed with you at this
table, say within yourself, "If such can deceive me,
and alas ! they may, then will I be content to be imposed upon rather than entertain perpetual mistrust
of my fellow-Christians."

A third meaning of the assembling around the table
is this, *hearty fraternity.* Our Lord, in sitting down
at the table with His disciples, showed Himself to be
one with them, a Brother indeed. We do not read
that there was any order of priority by which their
seats were arranged. Of course, if the Grand
Chamberlain at Rome had arranged the table, he
would have placed Peter at the right hand of Christ,
and the other apostles in graduated positions according to the dignity of their future bishoprics, but all
that we know about their order is this, that John sat
next to the Saviour, and leaned upon His bosom, and
that Peter sat a good way off,—we feel sure he did,
because it is said that he "beckoned" unto John ; if
he had sat next to him, he would have whispered to
him, but he beckoned to him, and so he must have
been some way down the table, if, indeed, there was
any "*down*" or "*up*" in the arrangement of the guests.
We believe the fact was, that they sat there on a
sacred equality, the Lord Jesus, the Elder Brother,
among them, and all else arranged according to those
words, "One is your Master, even Christ, and all ye
are brethren." Let us feel, then, in coming to the
table again at this time, that we are linked in ties of

sacred relationship with Jesus Christ, who is exalted in heaven, and that through Him our relationship with our fellow-Christians is very near and intimate.

Oh, that Christian brotherhood were more real! The very word "brother" has come to be ridiculed as a piece of hypocrisy, and well it may, for it is mostly used as a cant phrase, and in many cases means very little. But it ought to mean something. You have no right to come to that table unless you really feel that those who are washed in Jesus' blood have a claim upon the love of your heart, and the activity of your benevolence. What! are ye to live together for ever in heaven, and will ye show no affection for one another here below? It is your Master's new command that ye love one another; will ye disregard it? He has given this as the badge of Christians: "By this shall all men know that ye are My disciples,"—not if ye wear a gold cross, but—"if ye have love one to another." That is the Christian's badge of his being, in very truth, a disciple of Jesus Christ. Here, at, this table, we find fraternity. Whosoever eateth of this sacred supper declares himself to be one of a brotherhood in Christ, a brotherhood striving for the same cause, having sincere sympathy, being members of each other, and all of them members of the body of Christ. God make this to be a fact throughout Christendom even now, and how will the world marvel as it cries, "See how these Christians love one another!"

But this table means more yet: it signifies *common enjoyment.* Jesus eats, and they eat, the same bread. He drinks, and they drink, of the same cup. There is no distinction in the viands. What meaneth this? Doth it not say to us that the joy of Christ is the joy of His people? Hath He not said, "That My joy might remain in you, and that your joy might be full"? The very joy that delights Christ is that which He prepares for His people. You, if you are a true believer, have sympathy in Christ's joy, you delight to see His kingdom come, the truth advanced, sinners saved, grace glorified, holiness promoted, God exalted; this also is His delight. But my dear brethren and fellow-professors, are you sure that your chief joy is the same as Christ's? Are you certain that the main-stay of your life is the same as that which was His meat and His drink, namely, to do the will of the heavenly Father? If not, I am afraid you have no business at this table; but if it be so, and you come to the table, then I pray that you may share the joy of Christ. May you joy in Him as He joys in you, and so may your fellowship be sweet!

Lastly, on this point, the feast at the one table indicated *familiar affection.* It is the child's place to sit at the table with its parents, for there affection rules. It is the place of honour to sit at the table: "Martha served, but Lazarus was one of them that sat at the table." But the honour is such as love and not fear suggests. Men at the table often reveal their minds more fully than elsewhere. If you want to understand a man, you do not go to see him at the Stock Exchange, or follow him into the market; for there he keeps himself to himself; but you go to his table, and there he unbosoms himself. Now, the Lord Jesus Christ sat at the table with His disciples. 'Twas a meal; 'twas a meal of a homely kind; intimate intercourse ruled the hour. Oh, brethren and sisters, I am afraid we have come to this table sometimes, and gone away again without having had intercourse with Christ, and then it has been an empty formality and nothing more. I thank God that, coming to this table every Sabbath-day, as some of us do, and have done for many years, we have yet for the most part enjoyed the nearest communion with Christ here that we have ever known, and have a thousand times blessed His name for this ordinance. Still, there is such a thing as only eating the bread and drinking the wine, and losing all the sacred meaning thereof. Do pray the Lord to reveal Himself to you. Ask that it may not be a dead form to you, but that now in very deed you may give to Christ your heart, while He shall show to you His hands and His side, and make known to you His agonies and death, wherewith He redeemed you from the wrath to come. All this, and vastly more, is the teaching of the table at which Jesus sat with the twelve. I have often wondered why the Church of Rome does not buy up all those pictures by one of its most renowned painters, Leonardo da Vinci, in which our Lord is represented as sitting at the table with His disciples, for these are a contradiction of the Popish doctrine on this subject. As long as that picture remains on the wall, and as long as copies of it are spread everywhere, the Church of Rome stands convicted of going against the teaching of the earlier Church by setting up an altar when she confesses herself that aforetime it was not considered to be an altar of sacrifice but a table of fellowship, at which the Lord did not kneel, nor stand as an officiating priest, but at which He and His disciples sat. We, at least, have no rebukes to fear from antiquity, for we follow, and mean to follow, the primitive method. Our Lord has

given us commandment to do this until He comes,—
not to alter it, but just to " do this," and nothing else,
in the same manner until He shall come.

III. We will draw to a close by asking—WHAT
FURTHER MAY BE INFERRED FROM THIS SITTING
OF CHRIST WITH HIS DISCIPLES AT THE TABLE?

I answer: first, *there may be inferred from it the
equality of all the saints.* There were here twelve
apostles. Their apostleship, however, is not concerned
in the matter. When the Lord's supper was cele-
brated after all the apostles had gone to heaven, was
there to be any alteration because the apostles had
gone? Not at all. Believers are to do this in
remembrance of their Lord *until He shall come.*
There was no command for a change when the first
apostles were all gone from the Church. No, it was
to be the same still,—bread and wine and the surrounding of the table, until the Lord came. I gather, then,
the equality of all saints. There is a difference in
office, there was a difference in miraculous gift, and
there are great differences in growth of grace; but
still, in the household of God, all saints, whether
apostles, pastors, teachers, deacons, elders, or private
members, being all equal, eat at one table. There is
but one bread, there is but one juice of the vine here.

It is only in the Church of God that those words,
so wild politically, can ever be any more than a dream,
" Liberty, Equality, and Fraternity." There you have
them, where Jesus is; not in a republic, but in the
kingdom of our Lord and Saviour Jesus Christ, where
all rule and dominion are vested in Him, and all of
us willingly acknowledge Him as our glorious Head,
and all we are brethren. Never fall into the idea that

older believers were of a superior nature to ourselves. Do not talk of *Saint* Paul, and *Saint* Matthew, and *Saint* Mark, unless you are prepared to speak of *Saint* William and *Saint* Jane sitting over yonder, for if they be in Christ they are as truly saints as those first saints were, and I ween there may be some who have attained even to higher saintship than many whom tradition has canonized. The heights of saintship are by grace open to us all, and the Lord invites us to ascend. Do not think that what the Lord wrought in the early saints cannot be wrought in you. It is because you think so that you do not pray for it, and because you do not pray for it you do not attain it. The grace of God sustained the apostles ; that grace is not less to-day than it was then. The Lord's arm is not shortened ; His power is not straitened. If we can but believe, and be as earnest as those first saints were, we shall subdue kingdoms yet, and the day shall come when the gods of Hindooism, and the falsehoods of Mohammed, and the lies of Rome, shall as certainly be overthrown as were the ancient philosophies and the classic idolatries of Greece and Rome by the teaching of the first ministers of Christ. There is the same table for you, and the same food is there in emblem, and grace can make you like those holy men, for you are bought with the same blood, and quickened by the same Spirit. Believe only, for all things are possible to him that believeth.

Another inference, only to be hinted at, is this, *that the wants of the Church in all ages will be the same, and the supplies for the Church's wants will never vary.* There will be the table still, and the table with the same viands upon it,—bread still, nothing more than bread for food ; wine still, nothing less than wine for drink. The Church will always want the same food, the same Christ, the same gospel. Out on ye, traitors, who tell us that we are to shape our gospel to suit this enlightened nineteenth century ! Out on ye, false-hearts, who would have us tone down the ever-lasting truth that shall outlive the sun, and moon, and stars, to suit your boasted culture, which is but varnished ignorance ! No, that truth which of old was mighty through God to the pulling down of strongholds, is mighty still, and we will maintain it to the death ; the Church wants the doctrines of grace to-day as much as when Paul, or Augustine, or Calvin preached them ; the Church wants justification by faith, the substitutionary atonement, and regeneration, and divine sovereignty to be preached from her pulpits as much as in days of yore, and by God's grace she shall have them, too.

Lastly, there is in this truth, that Christ has brought all His disciples into the position of table-companions, *a prophecy that this shall be the portion of all His people for ever.* In heaven there cannot be less of privilege than on earth. It cannot be that in the celestial state believers will be degraded from what they have been below. What were they, then, below ? Table-companions. What shall they be in heaven above ? Table-companions still, and blessed is he that shall eat bread in the kingdom of God. "Many shall come from the east and from the west, and shall sit down with Abraham, and Isaac, and Jacob in the kingdom of God," and the Lord Jesus shall be at the head of the table. Now, what will His table of joy be ? Set your imagination to work, and think what

will be His festival of soul when His reward shall be
all before Him, and His triumph all achieved. Have
ye imagined it? Can ye conceive it? Whatever it is,
you shall share in it. I repeat those words, whatever
it is, the least believer shall share in it. You, poor
working-woman, oh, what a change for you, to sit
among princes, near to your Lord Jesus, all your toil
and want for ever ended! And you, sad child of
suffering, scarcely able to come up to the assembly of
God's people, and going back, perhaps, to that bed of
languishing again, you shall have no pains there, but
you shall be for ever with the Lord, and the joy of
Christ shall be your joy for ever and ever! Oh, can
you not realize those words of Dr. Watts,—

> " Yes, and before we rise
> To that immortal state,
> The thoughts of such amazing bliss
> Should constant joys create "?

In the anticipation of the joy that shall be yours,
forget your present troubles, rise superior to the
difficulties of the hour, and if you cannot rejoice in
the present, yet rejoice in the future, which shall so
soon be your own.

We finish with this word of deep regret,—regret that
many here cannot understand what we have been
talking about, and have no part in it. There are some
of you who must not come to the table of communion
because you do not love Christ. You have not trusted
Him; you have no part in Him. There is no salvation in sacraments. Believe me, they are but
delusions to those who do not come to Christ with
their heart. You must not come to the outward sign
if you have not the thing signified. Here is the way

of salvation : believe in the Lord Jesus Christ, and thou shalt be saved. To believe in Him is to trust Him ; to use an old word, it is recumbency ; it is leaning on Him, resting on Him. Here I lean, I rest my whole weight on this support before me ; do so with Christ in a spiritual sense : lean on Him. You have a load of sin, lean on Him, sin and all. You are all unworthy, and weak, and perhaps miserable ; then cast on Him the weakness, the unworthiness, the misery and all. Take Him to be all in all to you, and when you have thus trusted Him, you will have become His follower ; go on by humility to be His disciple, by obedience to be His servant, by love to be His friend, and by communion to be His table-companion.

The Lord so lead you, for Jesus' sake ! Amen.

A WORD FROM THE BELOVED'S
OWN MOUTH.

" And ye are clean."—*John* xiii. 10.

A WORD FROM THE BELOVED'S OWN MOUTH.

———

AS Gideon's fleece was full of dew so that he could wring out the moisture, so will a text sometimes be when the Holy Spirit deigns to visit His servants through its words. This utterance of our Saviour to His disciples has been as a wafer made with honey to our taste, and we doubt not it may prove equally as sweet to others.

Observe carefully, dear friends, what *the eulogium* is which is here passed upon the Lord's beloved disciples: "Ye are clean." This is the primeval blessing, so soon lost by our first parents. This is the virtue, the loss of which shut man out of Paradise, and continues to shut men out of heaven. The want of cleanness in heart and hands condemns sinners to banishment from God, and defiles all their offerings. To be clean before God is the desire of every penitent, and the highest aspiration of the most advanced believer. It is what all the ceremonies and ablutions of the law can never bestow, and what Pharisees with all their pretensions cannot attain. To be clean is to be as the angels are, as glorified saints are, yea, as the Father Himself is.

Acceptance with the Lord, safety, happiness, and every blessing, always go with cleanness of heart, and he that hath it cannot miss of heaven. It seems too high a condition to be ascribed to mortals, yet, by the lips of Him who could not err, the disciples were said, without

a qualifying word, or adverb of degree, to be "clean";
that is to say, they were perfectly justified in the sight
of eternal equity, and were regarded as free from
every impurity. Dear friends, is this blessing yours?
Have you ever believed unto righteousness? Have you
taken the Lord Jesus to be your complete cleansing,
your sanctification, your redemption? Has the Holy
Spirit ever sealed in your peaceful spirit the gracious
testimony, "ye are clean"? The assurance is not
confined to the apostles, for ye also are "complete in
Him," "perfect in Christ Jesus," if ye have indeed by
faith received the righteousness of God. The psalmist
said, "Wash me, and I shall be whiter than snow;"
if you have been washed, you are even to that highest
and purest degree clean before the Lord, and clean
now. Oh, that all believers would live up to their condition and privilege; but alas! too many are pining
as if they were still miserable sinners, and forgetting
that they are in Christ Jesus forgiven sinners, and
therefore ought to be happy in the Lord. Remember,
beloved believer, that, as one with Christ, you are not
with sinners in the gall of bitterness, but with the saints
in the land which floweth with milk and honey.

Your cleanness is not a thing of degrees, it is not a
variable or vanishing quantity, it is present, abiding,
perfect, you are clean through the Word, through the
application of the blood of sprinkling to the conscience,
and through the imputation of the righteousness of the
Lord Jesus Christ. Then lift up your head, and sing
for joy of heart, seeing that your transgression is
pardoned, your sin is covered, and in you Jehovah
seeth not iniquity. Dear friends, let not another
moment pass till by faith in Jesus you have grasped

this privilege. Be not content to believe that the priceless boon may be had, but lay hold upon it for yourself. You will find the song of substitution a choice song if you are able to sing it.

> " In my Surety I am free,
> His dear hands were pierced for me ;
> With his spotless vesture on
> Holy as the Holy One."

Much of the force of the sentence before us lies in *the Person praising*. To be certified as clean by the blind priests of Rome, would be small comfort to a true Christian. To receive the approving verdict of our fellow-men is consoling, but it is after all of small consequence. The human standard of purity is itself grossly incorrect, and therefore to be judged by it is but a poor trial, and to be acquitted a slender comfort ; but the Lord Jesus judges no man after the flesh, He came forth from God, and is Himself God, infinitely just and good, hence His tests are accurate, and His verdict is absolute. I wot whom He pronounces clean is clean indeed. Our Lord was omniscient, He would have at once detected the least evil in His disciples ; if there had remained upon them an unpardoned sin, He must have seen it ; if any relic of condemnation had lingered upon them, He must have detected it at once, no speck could have escaped His all-discerning eye ; yet did He say without hesitation of all but Judas, " Ye are clean."

Perhaps they did not catch the full glory of this utterance ; possibly they missed much of that deep joyous meaning, which is now revealed to us by the Spirit ; otherwise, what bliss to have heard with their own ears from those sacred lips, so plain, so positive, so sure a testimony to their character before God !

Yet our hearts need not be filled with regret because we cannot hear that ever-blessed voice with these our earthly ears, for the testimony of Jesus in the Word is quite as sure as the witness of His lips when He spake among the sons of men, and that testimony is, " Whosoever believeth is justified from all things." Yes, it is as certain as if you, dear friends, heard the Redeemer Himself speak, that you are free from all condemning sin if you are looking with your whole heart to Jesus only as your all in all. What a joy is yours and mine! He who is to judge the world in righteousness has Himself affirmed us to be clean. By how much the condemnation of guilt is black and terrible, by so much the forgiveness of sin is bright and comforting. Let us rejoice in the Lord, whose indisputable judgment has given forth a sentence so joyous, so full of glory.

> " Jesus declares me clean,
>   Then clean indeed I am,
> However guilty I have been,
>   I'm cleansèd through the Lamb.
>
> " His lips can never lie,
>   His eye is never blind,
> If he acquit, I can defy
>   All hell a fault to find."

It may cheer us to call to mind *the persons praised*. They were not cherubim and seraphim, but men, and notably they were men compassed with infirmity. There was Peter, who a few minutes after was forward and presumptuous ; and, indeed, it is not needful to name them one by one, for they all forsook their Master, and fled in His hour of peril. Not one among them was more than a mere child in grace ; they had little about them that was apostolic except their commission, they were very evidently men of like passions with us; yet their Lord declared them to be clean, and clean they were. Here is good cheer for those souls who are hungering after righteousness, and pining because they feel so much of the burden of indwelling sin; for cleanliness before the Lord is not destroyed by our infirmities, nor prevented by our inward temptations. We stand in the righteousness of Another. No measure of personal weakness, spiritual anxiety, soul conflict, or mental agony can mar our acceptance in the Beloved. We may be weak infants, or wandering sheep in ourselves, and for both reasons we may be very far from what we wish to be; but, as God sees us, we are viewed as washed in the blood of Jesus, and we, even we, are clean every whit.

What a forcible expression, "clean every whit;" every inch, from every point of view, in all respects, and to the uttermost degree! Dear friend, if a believer, this fact is true to *you*, even to YOU. Hesitate not to drink, for it is water out of your own cistern, given to you in the covenant of grace. Think not that it is presumption to believe the Word, marvellous though it be. You are dealing with a wonderful Saviour, who only doeth wonderful things, therefore stand not back on account of the greatness of the blessing, but rather believe the more readily because the Word is so like to everything the Lord doeth or speaketh. Yet when thou hast believed for thyself, and cast every doubt to the wind, thou wilt not wonder less, but more, and it will be thy never-ceasing cry, "Whence is this to me?" How is it that I, who wallowed with swine, should be made pure as the angels? Delivered from the foulest guilt, is it indeed possible that I am made the possessor of a perfect righteousness? Sing, O heavens, for the Lord hath done it, and He shall have everlasting praise !

> " Yes, thou, my soul, e'en thou art clean,
>   The Lord has wash'd thee white as snow,
>   In spotless beauty thou art seen,
>   And Jesus hath pronounced thee so.

> " Despite thy conflicts, doubts, and fears,
>   Yet art thou still in Christ all fair,
>   Haste then to wipe away thy tears,
>   And make His glory all thy care."

The time when the praise was given is not without instruction. The word of loving judgment is in the present tense, " Ye *are* clean." It is not, " ye were clean," that might be a rebuke for purity shamelessly sullied, a condemnation for wilful neglect, a prophecy of wrath to come ; neither is it, " ye might have been clean," that would have been a stern rebuke for privileges rejected, and opportunities wasted ; nor is it even, " ye shall be clean," though that would have been a delightful prophecy of good things to come at some distant period ; but ye ARE clean, at this moment, in this room, and around this table. Though but just then Peter had spoken so rudely, yet he was even then clean.

What comfort is here amid our present sense of imperfection ! Our cleanness is a matter of this present hour, we *are*, just here in our present condition and our position, " clean every whit." Why then postpone joy ? The cause of it is in possession, let the mirth be even now overflowing. Much of our heritage is certainly future, but if there were no other boon tangible to faith in this immediate present, this one blessing alone should awaken all our powers to the highest praise. Are we even now clothed with the fair white linen which is the righteousness of saints? Yes, 'tis even so, for—

> " We are wash'd in Jesu's blood,
>   We're pardon'd through His name ;
> And the good Spirit of our God
>   Has sanctified our frame."

Then let us sing a new song unto Jehovah-Tsidkenu, the Lord our Righteousness.

May the Holy Ghost now bear witness with every believer, "and ye are clean."

> " Then may your souls rejoice and sing,
>   Then may your voices sweetly ring,
> For if your souls through Christ are clear,
>   What cause have you to faint or fear ? "

THE BELIEVER NOT AN ORPHAN.

"I will not leave you comfortless : I will come to you."—*John* xiv. 18.

THE BELIEVER NOT AN ORPHAN.

———

YOU will notice that the margin reads, "I will not leave you orphans : I will come to you." In the absence of our Lord Jesus Christ, the disciples were like children deprived of their parents. During the three years in which He had been with them, He had solved all their difficulties, borne all their burdens, and supplied all their needs. Whenever a case was too hard or too heavy for them, they took it to Him. When their enemies well nigh overcame them, Jesus came to the rescue, and turned the tide of battle. They were all happy and safe enough whilst the Master was with them ; He walked in their midst like a father amid a large family of children, making all the household glad. But now He was about to be taken from them by an ignominious death, and they might well feel that they would be like little children deprived of their natural and beloved protector. Our Saviour knew the fear that was in their hearts, and before they could express it, He removed it by saying, "You shall not be left alone in this wild and desert world ; though I be absent in the flesh, yet I will be present with you in a more efficacious manner ; I will come to you spiritually, and you shall derive from My spiritual presence even more good than you could have had from My bodily presence, had I still continued in your midst."

Observe, first, here is *an evil averted :* " I will not leave you orphans ; " and, in the second place, here is *a consolation provided :* " I will come to you."

I.   First, here is, AN EVIL AVERTED.

Without their Lord, believers would, apart from the Holy Spirit, be like other orphans, unhappy and desolate.   Give them what you might, their loss could not have been recompensed.   No number of lamps can make up for the sun's absence ; blaze as they may, it is still night.   No circle of friends can supply to a bereaved woman the loss of her husband ; without him, she is still a widow.   Even thus, without Jesus, it is inevitable that the saints should be as orphans ; but Jesus has promised in the text that we shall not be so ; the one only thing that can remove the trial He declares shall be ours, " I will come to you."

Now remember, that *an orphan is one whose parent is dead.*   This in itself is a great sorrow, if there were no other.   The dear father, so well beloved, was suddenly smitten down with sickness ; they watched him with anxiety ; they nursed him with sedulous care ; but he expired.   The loving eye is closed in darkness for them.   That active hand will no longer toil for the family.   That heart and brain will no longer feel and think for them.   Beneath the green grass the father sleeps, and every time the child surveys that hallowed hillock his heart swells with grief.   Beloved, we are not orphans in that sense, for our Lord Jesus is not dead.   It is true He died, for one of the soldiers with a spear pierced His side, and forthwith came thereout blood and water, a sure evidence that the pericardium had been pierced, and that the fountain of life had been broken up.   He died, 'tis certain, but He is not dead now. Go not to the grave to seek Him. Angel voices say, "He is not here, for He is risen." He could not be holden by the bands of death. We do not worship a dead Christ, nor do we even think of Him now as a corpse. That picture on the wall, which the Romanists paint and worship, represents Christ as dead; but oh! it is so good to think of Christ as living, remaining in an existence real and true, none the less living because He died, but all the more truly full of life because He has passed through the portals of the grave, and is now reigning for ever. See then, dear friends, the bitter root of the orphan's sorrow is gone from us, for our Jesus is not dead now. No mausoleum enshrines His ashes, no pyramid entombs His body, no monument records the place of His permanent sepulchre.

> "He lives, the great Redeemer lives,
>   What joy the blest assurance gives!"

We are not orphans, for "the Lord is risen indeed."

The orphan has a sharp sorrow springing out of the death of his parent, namely, that *he is left alone.* He cannot now make appeals to the wisdom of the parent who could direct him. He cannot run, as once he did, when he was weary, to climb the paternal knee. He cannot lean his aching head upon the parental bosom. "Father," he may say, but no voice gives an answer. "Mother," he may cry, but that fond title, which would awaken the mother if she slept, cannot arouse her from the bed of death. The child is alone, alone as to those two hearts which were its best companions. The parent and lover are gone. The little ones know what it is to be deserted and forsaken. But we are not so; we are not orphans. It is true Jesus is not here in body, but His spiritual presence is quite as blessed as His bodily presence would have been. Nay, it is better, for supposing Jesus Christ to be here in person, you could not all come and touch the hem of His garment,—not all at once, at any rate. There might be thousands waiting all the world over to speak with Him; but how could they all reach Him, if He were merely here in body? You might all be wanting to tell Him something, but in the body He could only receive some one or two of you at a time.

But in spirit there is no need for you to stir from the pew, no need to say a word; Jesus hears your thoughts talk, and attends to all your needs at the same moment. No need to press to get at Him because the throng is great, for He is as near to me as He is to you, and as near to you as to saints in America, or the islands of the Southern Sea. He is everywhere present, and all His beloved may talk with Him. You can tell Him at this moment the sorrows which you dare not open up to anyone else. You will feel that, in declaring them to Him, you have not breathed them to the air, but that a real Person has heard you, One as real as though you could grip His hand, and could see the loving flash of His eye and mark the sympathetic change of His countenance.

Is it not so with you, ye children of a living Saviour? You know it is; you have a Friend that sticketh closer than a brother. You have a near and dear One, who, in the dead of the night is in the chamber, and in the heat and burden of the day is in the field of labour. You are not orphans, the "Wonderful, Counsellor, the mighty God, the Everlasting Father, the Prince of Peace," is with you ; your Lord is here ; and, as one whom his mother comforteth, so Jesus comforts you.

The orphan, too, has *lost the kind hand which took care always that food and raiment should be provided, that the table should be well stored, and that the house should be kept in comfort.* Poor feeble one, who will provide for his wants? His father is dead, his mother is gone : who will take care of the little wanderer now? But it is not so with us. Jesus has not left us orphans; His care for His people is no less now than it was when He sat at the table with Mary, and Martha, and Lazarus, whom "Jesus loved." Instead of the provisions being less, they are even greater, for since the Holy Spirit has been given to us, we have richer fare and are more indulged with spiritual comforts than believers were before the bodily presence of the Master had departed. Do your souls hunger to-night? Jesus gives you the bread of heaven. Do you thirst to-night? The waters from the rock cease not to flow.

"Come, make your wants, your burdens known."

You have but to make known your needs to have them all supplied, Christ waits to be gracious in the midst of this assembly. He is here with His golden hand, opening that hand to supply the wants of every living soul. "Oh!" saith one, "I am poor and needy." Go on with the quotation. "Yet the Lord thinketh upon me." "Ah!" saith another, "I have besought the Lord thrice to take away a thorn in the flesh from me." Remember what he said to Paul, "My grace is sufficient for thee." You are not left without the strength you want. The Lord is **your**

Shepherd still. He will provide for you till He leads you through death's dark valley, and brings you to the shining pastures upon the hill-tops of glory. You are not destitute, you need not beg an asylum from an ungodly world by bowing to its demands, or trusting its vain promises, for Jesus will never leave you nor forsake you.

The orphan, too, is *left without the instruction which is most suitable for a child*. We may say what we will, but there is none so fit to form a child's character as the parent. It is a very sad loss for a child to have lost either father or mother in its early days ; for the most skilful preceptor, though he may do much, by the blessing of God very much, is but a stop-gap, and but half makes up for the original ordinance of Providence, that the parent's love should fashion the child's mind. But, dear friends, we are not orphans ; we who believe in Jesus are not left without an education. Jesus is not here Himself, it is true. I dare say some of you wish you could come on Lord's-days, and listen to Him ! Would it not be sweet to look up to this pulpit, and see the Crucified One, and to hear Him preach ? Ah ! so you think, but the apostle says, " Though we have known Christ after the flesh, yet now henceforth know we Him no more."

It is most for your profit that you should receive the Spirit of truth, not through the golden vessel of Christ in His actual presence here, but through the poor earthen vessels of humble servants of God like ourselves. At any rate, whether *we* speak, or an angel from heaven, the speaker matters not ; it is the Spirit of God alone that is the power of the Word, and makes that Word to become vital and quickening to

you. Now, you have the Spirit of God. The Holy
Spirit is so given, that there is not a truth which you
may not understand. You may be led into the deepest
mysteries by His teaching. You may be made to
know and to comprehend those knotty points in the
Word of God which have hitherto puzzled you. You
have but humbly to look up to Jesus, and His Spirit
will still teach you. I tell you, though you are poor and
ignorant, and perhaps can scarcely read a word in the
Bible ; for all that, you may be better instructed in the
things of God than doctors of divinity, if you go to the
Holy Spirit, and are taught of Him. Those who go
only to books and to the letter, and are taught of
men, may be fools in the sight of God ; but those who
go to Jesus, and sit at His feet, and ask to be taught
of His Spirit, shall be wise unto salvation. Blessed be
God, there are not a few amongst us of this sort.
We are not left orphans ; we have an Instructor with
us still.

There is one point in which the orphan is often
sorrowfully reminded of his orphanhood, namely, *in
lacking a defender.* It is so natural in little children,
when some big boy molests them, to say, " I'll tell my
father ! " How often did we use to say so, and how
often have we heard from the little ones since, " I'll
tell mother ! " Sometimes, the not being able to do
this is a much severer loss than we can guess. Unkind
and cruel men have snatched away from orphans the
little which a father's love had left behind ; and in the
court of law there has been no defender to protect the
orphan's goods. Had the father been there, the child
would have had its rights, scarcely would any have
dared to infringe them ; but, in the absence of the

father, the orphan is eaten up like bread, and the wicked of the earth devour his estate. In this sense, the saints are not orphans. The devil would rob us of our heritage if he could, but there is an Advocate with the Father who pleads for us. Satan would snatch from us every promise, and tear from us all the comforts of the covenant; but we are not orphans, and when he brings a suit-at-law against us, and thinks that we are the only defendants in the case, he is mistaken, for we have an Advocate on high. Christ comes in and pleads, as the sinners' Friend, for us; and when *He* pleads at the bar of justice, there is no fear but that His plea will be of effect, and our inheritance shall be safe. He has not left us orphans.

Now I want, without saying many words, to get you who love the Master to feel what a very precious thought this is, that you are not alone in this world; that, if you have no earthly friends, if you have none to whom you can take your cares, if you are quite lonely so far as outward friends are concerned, yet Jesus is with you, is really with you, practically with you, able to help you, and ready to do so, and that you have a good and kind Protector close at hand at this present moment, for Christ has said it : " I will not leave you orphans."

II. Secondly, there is, A CONSOLATION PROVIDED. The remedy by which the evil is averted is this, our Lord Jesus said, " *I will come to you.*"

What does this mean? Does it not mean, from the connection, this—" *I will come to you by My Spirit*"? Beloved, we must not confuse the Persons of the Godhead. The Holy Spirit is not the Son of God ; Jesus, the Son of God, is not the Holy Spirit.

They are two distinct Persons of the one Godhead. But yet there is such a wonderful unity, and the blessed Spirit acts so marvellously as the Vicar of Christ, that it is quite correct to say that, when the Spirit comes, Jesus comes, too, and " I will come to you," means— " I, by My Spirit, who shall take My place, and represent Me, I will come to be with you." See then, Christian, you have the Holy Spirit in you and with you to be the Representative of Christ. Christ is with you now, not in person, but by His Representative, —an efficient, almighty, divine, everlasting Representative, who stands for Christ, and is as Christ to you in His presence in your souls. Because you thus have Christ by His Spirit, you cannot be orphans, for the Spirit of God is always with you. It is a delightful truth that the Spirit of God always dwells in believers ; —not sometimes, but always. He is not always active in believers, and He may be grieved until His sensible presence is altogether withdrawn, but His secret presence is always there. At no single moment is the Spirit of God wholly gone from a believer. The believer would die spiritually if this could happen, but that cannot be, for Jesus has said, " Because I live, ye shall live also." Even when the believer sins, the Holy Spirit does not utterly depart from him, but is still in him to make him smart for the sin into which he has fallen. The believer's prayers prove that the Holy Spirit is still within him. " Take not Thy Holy Spirit from me," was the prayer of a saint who had fallen very foully, but in whom the Spirit of God still kept His residence, notwithstanding all the foulness of his guilt and sin.

But, beloved, in addition to this, Jesus Christ by

His Spirit *makes visits to His people of a peculiar kind*. The Holy Ghost becomes wonderfully active and potent at certain times of refreshing. We are then especially and joyfully sensible of His divine power. His influence streams through every chamber of our nature, and floods our dark soul with His glorious rays, as the sun shining in its strength. Oh, how delightful this is! Sometimes we have felt this at the Lord's table. My soul pants to sit with you at that table, because I do remember many a happy time when the emblems of bread and wine have assisted my faith, and kindled the passions of my soul into a heavenly flame. I am equally sure that, at the prayer-meeting, under the preaching of the Word, in private meditation, and in searching the Scriptures, we can say that Jesus Christ has come to us. What! have you no hill Mizar to remember?—

> "No Tabor-visits to recount,
> When with Him in the Holy Mount"?

Oh, yes! some of these blessed seasons have left their impress upon our memories, so that, amongst our dying thoughts, will mingle the remembrance of those blessed seasons when Jesus Christ manifested Himself unto us as He doth not unto the world. Oh, to be wrapped in that crimson vest, closely pressed to His open side! Oh, to put our finger into the print of nails, and thrust our hand into His side! We know what this means by past experience.

> "Dear Shepherd of Thy chosen few,
> Thy former mercies here renew."

Permit us once again to feel the truth of the promise, "I will not leave you orphans: I will come to you."

And now, gathering up the few thoughts I have uttered, let me remind you, dear friends, that *every word of the text is instructive :* " I will not leave you orphans : I will come to you." Observe the " I " there twice over. " *I* will not leave you orphans ; father and mother may, but *I* will not ; friends once beloved may turn stony-hearted, but *I* will not ; Judas may play the traitor, and Ahithophel may betray his David, but *I* will not leave you comfortless. You have had many disappointments, great heart-breaking sorrows, but *I* have never caused you any ; *I*—the faithful and the true Witness, the immutable, the unchangeable Jesus, the same yesterday, to-day, and for ever, *I* will not leave you comfortless ; *I* will come unto you." Catch at that word, " I," and let your souls say, "Lord, I am not worthy that Thou shouldest come under my roof ; if Thou hadst said, ' I will send an angel to thee,' it would have been a great mercy, but what sayest Thou, ' I will come unto thee ' ? If Thou hadst bidden some of my brethren come and speak a word of comfort to me, I had been thankful, but Thou hast put it thus in the first person, ' *I* will come unto you.' O my Lord, what shall I say, what shall I do, but feel a hungering and a thirsting after Thee, which nothing shall satisfy till Thou shalt fulfil Thine own Word, ' *I* will not leave you comfortless ; *I* will come to you ' " ?

And then notice the persons to whom it is addressed, " I will not leave *you* comfortless, you, Peter, who will deny Me ; *you*, Thomas, who will doubt Me ; I will not leave *you* comfortless." O you who are so little in Israel that you sometimes think it is a pity that your name is in the church-book at all, because you feel yourselves to be so worthless, so unworthy, He will not leave *you* comfortless, not even *you!* "O Lord," thou sayest, "if Thou wouldst look after the rest of Thy sheep, I would bless Thee for Thy tenderness to them, but *I*—I deserve to be left; if I were forsaken of Thee, I could not blame Thee, for I have played the harlot against Thy love, but yet Thou sayest, 'I will not leave *you.*'" Heir of heaven, do not lose your part in this promise. I pray you say, "Lord, come unto me, and though Thou refresh all my brethren, yet, Lord, refresh me with some of the droppings of Thy love; O Lord, fill the cup *for me; my* thirsty spirit pants for it.

> "'I thirst, I faint, I die to prove
> The greatness of redeeming love,
> The love of Christ to me.'

Now, Lord, fulfil Thy word to Thine unworthy handmaid, as I stand like Hannah in Thy presence. Come unto me, Thy servant, unworthy to lift so much as his eyes towards heaven, and only daring to say, 'God be merciful to me a sinner.' Fulfil Thy promise even to me, 'I will not leave you comfortless; I will come to you.'"

Take whichever of the words you will, and they each one sparkle and flash after this sort. Observe, too, *the richness and sufficiency of the text:* "I will not leave you comfortless: I will come to you." He does not promise, "I will send you sanctifying grace, or sustaining mercy, or precious mercy," but He says, what is the only thing that will prevent your being orphans, "I will come to you." Ah! Lord, Thy grace is sweet, but Thou art better. The vine is good, but the clusters are better. It is well enough to have a gift from Thy hand, but oh! to touch the hand itself. It is well enough to hear the words of Thy lips, but oh! to kiss those lips as the spouse did in the Song, this is better still. You know, if there be an orphan child, you cannot prevent its continuing an orphan. You may feel great kindness towards it, supply its wants, and do all you possibly can towards it, but it is an orphan still. It must get its father and its mother back, or else it will still be an orphan. So, our blessed Lord, knowing this, does not say, "I will do this and that for you," but, "I will come to you."

Do you not see, dear friends, here is not only all you can want, but all you think you can want, wrapped up in a sentence, "I will come to you"? "It pleased the Father that in Him should all fulness dwell;" so that, when Christ comes, in Him "all fulness" comes. "In Him dwelleth all the fulness of the Godhead bodily," so that, when Jesus comes, the very Godhead comes to the believer.

> "All my capacious powers can wish
>   In Thee doth richly meet;"

and if Thou shalt come to me, it is better than all the gifts of Thy covenant. If I get Thee, I get all, and more than all, at once. Observe, then, the language and the sufficiency of the promise.

But I want you to notice, further, *the continued freshness and force of the promise.* Somebody here owes another person fifty pounds, and he gives him a note of hand, "I promise to pay you fifty pounds." Very well! the man calls with that note of hand to-morrow, and gets fifty pounds. And what is the good of the note of hand now? Why, it is of no further value, it is discharged. How would you like to have a note of hand which would always stand good? That would be a right royal present. "I promise to pay evermore, and this bond, though paid a thousand times, shall still hold good." Who would not like to have a cheque of that sort? Yet this is the promise which Christ gives you, "I will not leave you orphans: I will come to you." The first time a sinner looks to Christ, Christ comes to him. And what then? Why, the next minute it is still, "I will come to you." But here is one who has known Christ for fifty years, and he has had this promise fulfilled a thousand times a year: is it not done with? Oh, no! there it stands, just as fresh as when Jesus first spoke it, "I will come to you." Then we will treat our Lord in His own fashion, and take Him at His word. We will go to Him as often as ever we can, for we shall never weary Him; and when He has kept His promise most, then is it that we will go to Him, and ask Him to keep it more still; and after ten thousand proofs of the truth of it, we will only have a greater hungering and thirsting to get it fulfilled again. This is fit provision for life, and for death, "I will come to you." In the last moment, when your pulse beats faintly, and you are just about to pass the curtain, and enter into the invisible world, you may have this upon your lips, and say to your Lord, "My Master, still fulfil the word on which Thou hast caused me to hope, 'I will not leave you comfortless: I will come to you.'"

Let me remind you that *the text is at this moment valid,* and for this I delight in it. "I will not leave you comfortless." That means now, "I will not leave you comfortless *now.*" Are you comfortless at this hour? It is your own fault. Jesus Christ does not leave you so, nor make you so. There are rich and precious things in this word, "I will not leave you comfortless: I will come to you, I will come to you now." It may be a very dull time with you, and you are pining to come nearer to Christ. Very well, then plead the promise before the Lord. Plead the promise as you sit where you are: "Lord, Thou hast said Thou wilt come unto me; come unto me to-night." There are many reasons, believer, why you should plead thus. You want Him; you need Him; you require Him; therefore plead the promise, and expect its fulfilment. And oh! when He cometh, what a joy it is; He is as a bridegroom coming out of his chamber with his garments fragrant with aloes and cassia! How well the oil of joy will perfume your heart! How soon will your sackcloth be put away, and the garments of gladness adorn you! With what joy of heart will your heavy soul begin to sing when Jesus Christ shall whisper that you are His, and that He is yours! Come, my Beloved, make no tarrying; be Thou like a roe or a young hart upon the mountains of separation, and prove to me Thy promise true, "I will not leave you orphans: I will come to you."

And now, dear friends, in conclusion, let me remind you that *there are many who have no share in the text.* What can I say to such? From my soul I pity you who do not know what the love of Christ means. Oh! if you could but tell the joy of God's people, you would not rest an hour without it.

> "His worth, if all the nations knew,
> Sure the whole world would love Him too."

Remember, if you would find Christ, He is to be found in the way of faith. Trust Him, and He is yours. Depend upon the merit of His sacrifice ; cast yourselves entirely upon that, and you are saved, and Christ is yours.

God grant that we may all break bread in the kingdom above, and feast with Jesus, and share His glory ! We are expecting His second coming. He is coming personally and gloriously. This is the brightest hope of His people. This will be the fulness of their redemption, the time of their resurrection. Anticipate it, beloved, and may God make your souls to sing for joy !

> "'Mid the splendours of the glory
>   Which we hope ere long to share ;
> Christ our Head, and we His members,
>   Shall appear, divinely fair.
>   Oh, how glorious !
>   When we meet Him in the air !
>
> " Bright the prospect soon that greets us
>   Of that long'd-for nuptial day,
> When our heavenly Bridegroom meets us
>   On His kingly, conquering way ;
>   In the glory,
>   Bride and Bridegroom reign for aye !"

COMMUNION WITH CHRIST AND HIS PEOPLE.

AN ADDRESS AT A COMMUNION SERVICE

AT MENTONE.

"The cup of blessing which we bless, is it not the communion of the blood of Christ? The bread which we break, is it not the communion of the body of Christ? For we being many are one bread, and one body: for we are all partakers of that one bread."—1 *Cor.* x. 16, 17.

COMMUNION WITH CHRIST AND HIS PEOPLE.

I WILL read you the text as it is given in the Revised Version: "The cup of blessing which we bless, is it not a communion of the blood of Christ?" That is to say,—Is it not one form of expressing the communion of the blood of Christ? "The bread," or as it is in the margin, "the loaf which we break, is it not a communion of the body of Christ? seeing that we, who are many, are one loaf, one body: for we all partake of the one loaf." The word "loaf" helps to bring out more clearly the idea of unity intended to be set forth by the apostle.

It is a lamentable fact that some have fancied that this simple ordinance of the Lord's supper has a certain magical, or at least physical power about it, so that, by the mere act of eating and drinking this bread and wine, men can be made partakers of the body and blood of Christ. It is marvellous that so plain a symbol should have been so complicated by genuflexions, adornments, and technical phrases. Can anyone see the slightest resemblance between the Master's sitting down with the twelve, and the mass of the Roman community? The original rite is lost in the super-imposed ritual. Superstition has produced a sacrament where Jesus intended a fellowship. Too many, who would not go the length of Rome, yet

speak of this simple feast as if it were a mystery dark
and obscure.   They employ all manner of hard words
to turn the children's bread into a stone.   It is not the
Lord's supper, but the Eucharist; we see before us
no plate, but a " paten "; the cup is a " chalice ", and
the table is an " altar."   These are incrustations of
superstition, whereby the blessed ordinance of Christ
is likely to be again overgrown and perverted.

What does this supper mean ?   It means communion : *communion with Christ, and communion with
one another.*

What is communion ?   The word breaks up easily
into union, and its prefix *com*, which means *with*,
union with.   We must, therefore, first enjoy union
with Christ, and with His Church, or else we cannot
enjoy communion.   Union lies at the basis of communion.   We must be one with Christ in heart, and
soul, and life ; baptized into His death ; quickened
by His life, and so brought to be members of His
body, one with the whole Church of which He is the
Head.   We cannot have communion with Christ till
we are in union with *Him ;* and we cannot have communion with the Church till we are in vital union
with *it.*

I.   The teaching of the Lord's supper is just this
—that while we have many ways of COMMUNION
WITH CHRIST, yet the receiving of Christ into our
souls as our Saviour is the best way of communion
with Him.

I said, dear friends, that we have many ways of
communion with Christ ; let me show you that it
is so.

Communion is ours *by personal intercourse* with the

Lord Jesus. We speak with Him in prayer, and He speaks with us through the Word. Some of us speak oftener with Christ than we do with wife or child, and our communion with Jesus is deeper and more thorough than our fellowship with our nearest friend. In meditation and its attendant thanksgiving we speak with our risen Lord, and by His Holy Spirit He answers us by creating fresh thought and emotion in our minds. I like sometimes in prayer, when I do not feel that I can say anything, just to sit still, and look up; then faith spiritually descries the Well-beloved, and hears His voice in the solemn silence of the mind. Thus we have intercourse with Jesus of a closer sort than any words could possibly express. Our soul melts beneath the warmth of Jesus' love, and darts upward her own love in return. Think not that I am dreaming, or am carried off by the memory of some unusual rhapsody: no, I assert that the devout soul can converse with the Lord Jesus all the day, and can have as true fellowship with Him as if He still dwelt bodily among men. This thing comes to me, not by the hearing of the ear, but by my own personal experience: I know of a surety that Jesus manifests Himself unto His people as He doth not unto the world.

Ah, what sweet communion often exists between the saint and the Well-beloved, when there is no bread and wine upon the table, for the Spirit Himself draws the heart of the renewed one, and it runs after Jesus, while the Lord Himself appears unto the longing spirit! Truly our fellowship is with the Father, and with His Son Jesus Christ. Do *you* enjoy this charming converse?

Next, we have communion with Christ *in His thoughts, views, and purposes ;* for His thoughts are our thoughts according to our capacity and sanctity. Believers take the same view of matters as Jesus does ; that which pleases Him pleases them, and that which grieves Him grieves them also. Consider, for instance, the greatest theme of our thought, and see whether our thoughts are not like those of Christ. He delights in the Father, He loves to glorify the Father : do not we ? Is not the Father the centre of our soul's delight ? Do we not rejoice at the very sound of His name ? Does not our spirit cry, " Abba, Father " ? Thus it is clear we feel as Jesus feels towards the Father, and so we have the truest communion with Him. This is but one instance ; your contemplations will bring before you a wide variety of topics wherein we think with Jesus. Now, identity of judgment, opinion, and purpose forms the highway of communion ; yea, it is communion.

We have also communion with Christ *in our emotions.* Have you never felt a holy horror when you have heard a word of blasphemy in the street ? Thus Jesus felt when He saw sin, and bore it in His own person : only He felt it infinitely more than you do. Have you never felt as you looked upon sinners that you must weep over them ? Those are holy tears, and contain the same ingredients as those which Jesus shed when He lamented over Jerusalem. Yes, in our zeal for God, our hatred of sin, our detestation of falsehood, our pity for men, we have true communion with Jesus.

Further, we have had fellowship with Christ *in many of our actions.* Have you ever tried to teach the

ignorant? This Jesus did. Have you found it
difficult? So Jesus found it. Have you striven to
reclaim the backslider? Then you were in communion
with the Good Shepherd who hastens into the
wilderness to find the one lost sheep, finds it, lays it
upon His shoulders, and brings it home rejoicing.
Have you ever watched over a soul night and day
with tears? Then you have had communion with
Him who has borne all our names upon His broken
heart, and carries the memorial of them upon His
pierced hands. Yes, in acts of self-denial, liberality,
benevolence, and piety, we enter into communion with
Him who went about doing good. Whenever we try
to disentangle the snarls of strife, and to make peace
between men who are at enmity, then are we doing
what the great Peace-maker did, and we have communion with the Lord and Giver of peace. Where-
ever, indeed, we co-operate with the Lord Jesus in
His designs of love to men, we are in true and active
communion with Him.

So it is *with our sorrows*. Certain of us have had
large fellowship with the Lord Jesus in affliction.
"Jesus wept": He lost a friend, and so have we.
Jesus grieved over the hardness of men's hearts: we
know that grief. Jesus was exceedingly sorry that the
hopeful young man turned away, and went back to the
world: we know that sorrow. Those who have
sympathetic hearts, and live for others, readily enter
into the experience of "the Man of sorrows." The
wounds of calumny, the reproaches of the proud, the
venom of the bigoted, the treachery of the false, and the
weakness of the true, we have known in our measure;
and therein have had communion with our Lord Jesus.

Nor this alone: we have been with our Divine
Master *in His joys*. I suppose there never lived a
happier man than the Lord Jesus. He was rightly
called "the Man of sorrows"; but He might, with un-
impeachable truth, have been called, "the Man of
joys." He must have rejoiced as He called His
disciples, and they came unto Him; as He bestowed
healing and relief; as He gave pardon to penitents,
and breathed peace on believers. His was the joy of
finding the sheep, and taking the piece of money out
of the dust. His work was His joy: such joy that,
for its sake, He endured the cross, despising the
shame. The exercise of benevolence is joy to loving
hearts: the more pain it costs, the more joy it is.
Kind actions make us happy, and in such joy we find
communion with the great heart of Jesus.

Thus have I given you a list of windows of agate
and gates of carbuncle through which you may come
at the Lord; but the ordinance of the Lord's supper
sets forth a way which surpasses them all. It is the
most accessible and the most effectual method of
fellowship. Here it is that we have fellowship with
the Lord Jesus by receiving Him as our Saviour. We,
being guilty, accept of His atonement as our sacrificial
cleansing, and in token thereof we eat this bread and
drink this cup. "Oh!" says one, "I do not feel that
I can get near to Christ. He is so high and holy, and
I am only a poor sinner." Just so. For that very
reason you can have fellowship with Christ in that
which lies nearest to His heart: He is a Saviour, and
to be a Saviour there must be a sinner to be saved.
Be you that one, and Christ and you shall at once be

in union and communion : He shall save, and you
shall be saved ; He shall sanctify, and you shall be
sanctified ; and twain shall thus be one. This table
sets before you His great sacrifice. Jesus has offered
it ; will you accept it ? He does not ask you to bring
anything,—no drop of blood, no pang of flesh ; all is
here, and your part is to come and partake of it, even
as of old the offerer partook of the peace-offering
which he had brought, and so feasted with God and
with the priest. If you work for Christ, that will
certainly be some kind of fellowship with Him ; but I
tell you that the communion of receiving him into your
inmost soul is the nearest and closest fellowship
possible to mortal man. The fellowship of service is
exceedingly honourable, when we and Christ work
together for the same objects ; the fellowship of suffering is exceedingly instructive, when our heart has
graven upon it the same characters as were graven
upon the heart of Christ : but the fellowship of the
soul which receives Christ, and is received by Christ,
is closer, more vital, more essential than any other.

Such fellowship is eternal. No power upon earth
can henceforth take from me the piece of bread which
I have just now eaten, it has gone where it will be
made up into blood, and nerve, and muscle, and bone.
It is within me, and of me. That drop of wine has
coursed through my veins, and is part and parcel of
my being. So he that takes Jesus by faith to be his
Saviour has chosen the good part which shall not be
taken away from him. He has received the Christ
into his inward parts, and all the men on earth, and
all the devils in hell, cannot extract Christ from him.
Jesus saith, " He that eateth Me, even he shall live by

Me." By our sincere reception of Jesus into our hearts, an indissoluble union is established between us and the Lord, and this manifests itself in mutual communion. To as many as received Him, to them has He given this communion, even to them that believe on His name.

II. I have now to look at another side of communion,—namely, the FELLOWSHIP OF TRUE BELIEVERS WITH EACH OTHER. We have many ways of communing the one with the other, but there is no way of mutual communing like the common reception of the same Christ in the same way. I have said that there are many ways in which Christians commune with one another, and these doors of fellowship I would mention at some length.

Let me go over much the same ground as before. We commune by *holy converse*. I wish we had more of this. Time was when they that feared the Lord spake often one to another ; I am afraid that now they more often speak one against another. It is a grievous thing that full often love lies bleeding by a brother's hand. Where we are not quite so bad as that, yet we are often backward and silent, and so miss profitable converse. Our insular reserve has often made one Christian sit by another in utter isolation, when each would have been charmed with the other's company. Children of one family need not wait to be introduced to each other : having eaten of this one bread, we have given and received the token of brotherhood ; let us therefore act consistently with our relationship, and fall into holy conversation next time we meet. I am afraid that Christian brotherhood in many cases begins and ends inside the place of worship. Let it

not be so among us. Let it be our delight to find
our society in the circle of which Jesus is the centre,
and let us make those our friends who are the friends
of Jesus. By frequent united prayer and praise, and
by ministering the one to the other the things which
we have learned by the Spirit, we shall have fellowship
with each other in our Lord Jesus Christ.

I am sure that all Christians have fellowship together
in their *thoughts.* In the essentials of the gospel we
think alike : in our thoughts of God, of Christ, of sin,
of holiness, we keep step ; in our intense desire to
promote the kingdom of our Lord, we are as one. All
spiritual life is one. The thoughts raised by the
Spirit of God in the souls of men are never contrary
to each other. I say not that the thoughts of all
professors agree, but I do assert that the minds of
the truly regenerate in all sects, and in all ages, are in
harmony with each other,—a harmony which often
excites delighted surprise in those who perceive it.
The marks that divide one set of nominal Christians
from another set are very deep and wide to those who
have nothing of religion but the name ; yet living
believers scarcely notice them. Boundaries which
separate the cattle of the field are no division to the
birds of the air. Our minds, thoughts, desires, and
hopes are one in Christ Jesus, and herein we have
communion.

Beloved friends, our *emotions* are another royal
road of fellowship. You sit down and tell your
experience, and I smile to think that you are telling
mine. Sometimes a young believer enlarges upon the
sad story of his trials and temptations, imagining that
nobody ever had to endure so great a fight, when all

the while he is only describing the common adventures of those who go on pilgrimage, and we are all communing with him. When we talk together about our Lord, are we not agreed? When we speak of our Father, and all His dealings with us, are we not one? And when we weep, and when we sigh, and when we sing, and when we rejoice, are we not all akin? Heavenly fingers touching like strings within our hearts bring forth the self-same notes, for we are the products of the same Maker, and tuned to the same praise. Real harmony exists among all the true people of God : Christians are one in Christ.

We have communion with one another, too, in our *actions*. We unite in trying to save men : I hope we do. We join in instructing, warning, inviting, and persuading sinners to come to Jesus. Our life-ministry is the same : we are workers together with God. We live out the one desire,—" Thy kingdom come. Thy will be done in earth, as it is in heaven."

Certainly we have much communion one with the other in our *sufferings*. There is not a poor sick or despondent saint upon the earth with whom we do not sympathize at this moment, for we are fellow-members, and partakers of the sufferings of Christ. I hope we can say,—

> " Is there a lamb in all Thy flock,
>   I would disdain to feed?
> Is there a foe, before whose face,
>   I fear Thy cause to plead? "

No, we suffer with each other, and bear each other's burden, and so fulfil the law of Christ. If we do not, we have reason for questioning our own faith; but if we do so, we have communion with each other.

I hope we have fellowship in our *joys*. Is one happy? We would not envy him, but rejoice with him. Perhaps this is not so universal as it should be among professors. Are we at once glad because another prospers? If another star outshines ours, do we delight in its radiance? When we meet a brother with ten talents, do we congratulate ourselves on having such a man given to help us, or do we depreciate him as much as we can? Such is the depravity of our nature, that we do not readily rejoice in the progress of others if they leave us behind; but we must school ourselves to this. A man will speedily sit down and sympathize with a friend's griefs; but if he sees him honoured and esteemed, he is apt to regard him as a rival, and does not so readily rejoice with him. This ought not to be; without effort we ought to be happy in our brother's happiness. If we are ill, be this our comfort, that many are in robust health; if we are faint, let us be glad that others are strong in the Lord. Thus shall we enjoy a happy fellowship like that of the perfected above.

When I have put all these modes of Christian communion together, no one of them is so sure, so strong, so deep, as communion in receiving the same Christ as our Saviour, and trusting in the same blood for cleansing unto eternal life. Here on the table you have the tokens of the broadest and fullest communion. This is a kind of communion which you and I cannot choose or reject: if we are in Christ, it is and must be ours. Certain brethren restrict their communion in the outward ordinance, and they think they have good reasons for doing so ; but I am unable to see the force of their reasoning, because I joyfully observe that these brethren commune with other believers in prayer, and praise, and hearing of the Word, and other ways : the fact being that the matter of real communion is very largely beyond human control, and is to the spiritual body what the circulation of the blood is to the natural body, a necessary process not dependent upon volition. In perusing a deeply spiritual book of devotion, you have been charmed and benefited, and yet upon looking at the title-page it may be you have found that the author belonged to the Church of Rome. What then ? Why, then it has happened that the inner life has broken all barriers, and your spirits have communed. For my own part, in reading certain precious works, I have loathed their Romanism, and yet I have had close fellowship with their writers in weeping over sin, in adoring at the foot of the cross, and in rejoicing in the glorious enthronement of our Lord. Blood is thicker than water, and no fellowship is more inevitable and sincere than fellowship in the precious blood, and in the risen life of our Lord Jesus Christ. Here, in the common reception of the one loaf, we bear witness that we are one ; and in the actual participation of all the chosen in the one redemption, that unity is in very deed displayed and matured in the most substantial manner. Washed in the one blood, fed on the same loaf, cheered by the same cup, all differences pass away, and " we, being many, are one body in Christ, and every one members one of another."

Now, then, dear friends, if this kind of fellowship be

the best, LET US TAKE CARE TO ENJOY IT. Let us at this hour avail ourselves of it.

Let us take care to *see Christ* in the mirror of this ordinance. Have any of you eaten the bread, and yet have you not seen Christ? Then you have gained no benefit. Have you drunk the wine, but have you not remembered the Lord? Alas! I fear you have eaten and drunk condemnation to yourselves, not discerning the Lord's body. But if you did see through the emblems, as aged persons see through their spectacles, then you have been thankful for such aids to vision. But what is the use of glasses if there is nothing to look at? and what is the use of the communion if Christ be not in our thoughts and hearts?

If you did discern the Lord, then be sure, again, to *accept Him.* Say to yourself, " All that Christ is to any, He shall be to me. Does He save sinners? He shall save me. Does He change men's hearts? He shall change mine. Is He all in all to those that trust Him? He shall be all in all to me." I have heard persons say that they do not know how to take Christ. What says the apostle? "The Word is nigh thee, even in thy mouth, and in thy heart." If you have something in your mouth that you desire to eat, what is the best thing to do? Will you not swallow it? That is exactly what faith does. Christ's word of grace is very near you, it is on your tongue; let it go down into your inmost soul. Say to your Saviour, "I know I am not fit to receive Thee, O Jesus, but since Thou dost graciously come to me as bread comes to the hungry, I thankfully receive Thee, rejoicing to feed upon Thee! Since Thou dost come to me as the fruit of the vine to a thirsty man, Lord, I take Thee, willingly, and I thank Thee that this reception is all that Thou dost require of me. Has not Thy Spirit so put it—' As many as received Him, to them gave He power to become the sons of God, even to them that believe on His name'?"

Beloved friends, when you have thus received Jesus, fail not to *rejoice in Him* as having received Him. How many there are who have received Christ, who talk and act as if they never had received Him! It is a poor dinner of which a man says, after he has eaten it, that he feels as if he had not dined ; and it is a poor Christ of whom anyone can say, " I have received Him, but I am none the happier, none the more at peace." If you have received Jesus into your heart, you *are* saved, you *are* justified. Do you whisper, "I hope so"? Is that all? Do you not know? The hopings and hoppings of so many are a poor way of going ; put both feet down, and say, " I know whom I have believed, and am persuaded that He is able to keep that which I have committed unto Him against that day." You are either saved or lost ; there is no state between the two. You are either pardoned or condemned ; and you have good reason for the highest happiness, or else you have grave causes for the direst anxiety. If you have received the atonement, be as glad as you can be ; and if you are still an unbeliever, rest not till Christ is yours.

Oh, the joy of continually entering into fellowship with Christ, in such a way that you never lose His company ! Be this yours, beloved, every day, and all the day ! May His shadow fall upon you as you rest in the sun, or stray in the gardens ! May His voice cheer you as you lie down upon the sea-shore, and listen to the murmuring of the waves; may His presence glorify the mountain solitude as you climb the hills! May Jesus be to you an all-surrounding presence, lighting up the night, perfuming the day, gladdening all places, and sanctifying all pursuits! Our Beloved is not a Friend for Lord's-days only, but for week-days, too; He is the inseparable Companion of His loving disciples. Those who have had fellowship with His body and His blood at this table may have the Lord as an habitual Guest at their own tables; those who have met their Master in this upper room may expect Him to make their own chamber bright with His royal presence. Let fellowship with Jesus and with the elect brotherhood be henceforth the atmosphere of our life, the joy of our existence. This will give us a heaven below, and prepare us for a heaven above.

THE SIN-BEARER.

A COMMUNION MEDITATION AT MENTONE.

"Who His own self bare our sins in His own body on the tree, that we, being dead to sins, should live unto righteousness: by whose stripes ye were healed. For ye were as sheep going astray; but are now returned unto the Shepherd and Bishop of your souls."—1 Peter ii. 24, 25.

THE SIN-BEARER.

THIS wonderful passage is a part of Peter's address to servants; and in his day nearly all servants were slaves. Peter begins at the eighteenth verse: "Servants, be subject to your masters with all fear; not only to the good and gentle, but also to the froward. For this is thankworthy, if a man for conscience toward God endure grief, suffering wrongfully. For what glory is it, if, when ye be buffeted for your faults, ye shall take it patiently? but if, when ye do well, and suffer for it, ye take it patiently, this is acceptable with God. For even hereunto were ye called: because Christ also suffered for us, leaving us an example, that ye should follow His steps: who did no sin, neither was guile found in His mouth: who, when He was reviled, reviled not again; when He suffered, He threatened not; but committed Himself to Him that judgeth righteously: who His own self bare our sins in His own body on the tree, that we, being dead to sins, should live unto righteousness: by whose stripes ye were healed." If we are in a lowly condition of life, we shall find our best comfort in thinking of the lowly Saviour bearing our sins in all patience and submission. If we are called to suffer, as servants often were in the Roman times, we shall be solaced by a vision of our Lord buffeted, scourged, and crucified, yet silent in the majesty of His endurance. If these sufferings are entirely undeserved, and we are grossly slandered, we shall be comforted by remembering Him who did no sin, and in whose lips was found no guile. Our Lord Jesus is Head of the Guild of Sufferers: He did well, and suffered for it, but took it patiently. Our support under the cross, which we are appointed to bear, is only to be found in Him "who His own self bare our sins in His own body on the tree."

We ourselves now know by experience that there is no place for comfort like the cross. It is a tree stripped of all foliage, and apparently dead; yet we sit under its shadow with great delight, and its fruit is sweet unto our taste. Truly, in this case, "like cures like." By the suffering of our Lord Jesus, our suffering is made light. The servant is comforted since Jesus took upon Himself the form of a servant; the sufferer is cheered "because Christ also suffered for us;" and the slandered one is strengthened because Jesus also was reviled.

> " Is it not strange, the darkest hour
> That ever dawned on sinful earth
> Should touch the heart with softer power
> For comfort than an angel's mirth?
> That to the cross the mourner's eye should turn
> Sooner than where the stars of Christmas burn?"

Let us, as we hope to pass through the tribulations of this world, stand fast by the cross; for if *that* be gone, the lone-star is quenched whose light cheers the down-trodden, shines on the injured, and brings light to the oppressed. If we lose the cross,—if we miss the substitutionary sacrifice of our Lord Jesus Christ, we have lost all.

The verse on which we would now devoutly meditate

speaks of three things : *the bearing of our sins, the changing of our condition,* and *the healing of our spiritual diseases.* Each of these deserves our most careful notice.

I. The first is, THE BEARING OF OUR SINS by our Lord : "Who His own self bare our sins in His own body on the tree." These words in plainest terms assert that our Lord Jesus did really bear the sins of His people. How *literal* is the language ! Words mean nothing if substitution is not stated here. I do not know the meaning of the fifty-third of Isaiah if this is not its meaning. Hear the prophet's words : "The Lord hath laid on Him the iniquity of us all ; " "for the transgression of my people was He stricken ; " "He shall bear their iniquities :" "He was numbered with the transgressors, and He bare the sin of many."

I cannot imagine that the Holy Spirit would have used language so expressive if He had not intended to teach us that our Saviour did really bear our sins, and suffer in our stead. What else can be intended by texts like these—"Christ was once offered to bear the sins of many" (Heb. ix. 28) ; " He hath made Him to be sin for us, who knew no sin ; that we might be made the righteousness of God in Him " (2 Cor. v. 21) ; "Christ hath redeemed us from the curse of the law, being made a curse for us : for it is written, Cursed is every one that hangeth on a tree " (Gal. iii. 13) ; "Christ also hath loved us, and hath given Himself for us an offering and a sacrifice to God for a sweet-smelling savour " (Eph. v. 2) ; "Once in the end of the world hath He appeared to put away sin by the sacrifice of Himself" (Heb. ix. 26)? I say modestly, but firmly, that these Scriptures either

teach the bearing of our sins by our Lord Jesus, or
they teach nothing. In these days, among many
errors and denials of truth, there has sprung up a
teaching of "modern thought" which explains away
the doctrine of substitution and vicarious sacrifice.
One wise man has gone so far as to say that the
transference of sin or righteousness is impossible, and
another creature of the same school has stigmatized
the idea as immoral.

It does not much matter what these modern haters
of the cross may dare to say; but, assuredly, that
which they deny, denounce, and deride, is the cardinal
doctrine of our most holy faith, and is as clearly in
Scripture as the sun is in the heavens. Beloved, as
we suffer through the sin of Adam, so are we saved
through the righteousness of Christ. Our fall was by
another, and so is our rising again: we are under a
system of representation and imputation, gainsay it
who may. To us, the transference of our sin to
Christ is a blessed fact clearly revealed in the Word
of God, and graciously confirmed in the realizations
of our faith. In that same chapter of Isaiah we read,
"Surely He hath borne our griefs, and carried our
sorrows," and we perceive that this was a matter of
fact, for He was really, truly, and emphatically sorrowful; and, therefore, when we read that "He bare our
sins in His own body on the tree," we dare not fritter
it away, but assuredly believe that in very deed He
was our Sin-Bearer. Possible or impossible, we sing
with full assurance—

"He bore on the tree the sentence for me."

Had the sorrow been figurative, the sin-bearing might

have been mythical; but the one fact is paralleled by
the other. There is no figure in our text; it is a
bare, literal fact: "Who His own self bare our sins in
His own body on the tree." Oh, that men would give
up cavilling! To question and debate at the cross, is
an act near akin to the crime of the soldiers when they
parted His garments among them, and cast lots for
His vesture.

Note how *personal* are the terms here employed!
How expressly the Holy Ghost speaketh! "Who
His own self bare our sins in His own body." It was
not by delegation, but "His own self"; and it was not
in imagination, but "in His own body." Observe,
also, the personality from our side of the question, He
"bare *our* sins," that is to say, my sins and your sins.
There is a sort of cadence of music here,—" His own
self," "our sins." As surely as it was Christ's own
self that suffered on the cross, so truly was it our own
sins that Jesus bore in His own body on the tree.
Our Lord has appeared in court for us, accepting our
place at the bar: "He was numbered with the transgressors." Nay, more, He has appeared at the place
of execution for us, and has borne the death-penalty
upon the gibbet of doom in our stead. *In proprià
personà*, our Redeemer has been arraigned, though
innocent; has come under the curse, though for ever
blessed; and has suffered to the death, though He
had done nothing worthy of blame. "He was
wounded for our transgressions, He was bruised for
our iniquities: the chastisement of our peace was
upon Him; and with His stripes we are healed."

This sin-bearing on our Lord's part was *continual*.
The passage before us has been forced beyond its

teaching, by being made to assert that our Lord Jesus bore our sins nowhere but on the cross: this the words do not say. "The tree" was the place where beyond all other places we see our Lord bearing the chastisement due to our sins; but before this, He had felt the weight of the enormous load. It is wrong to base a great doctrine upon the incidental form of one passage of Scripture, especially when that passage of Scripture bears another meaning.

The marginal reading, which is perfectly correct, is "Who His own self bare our sins in His own body *to* the tree." Our Lord carried the burden of our sins up to the tree, and there and then He made an end of it. He had carried that load long before, for John the Baptist said of Him, "Behold the Lamb of God, which taketh away" (the verb is in the present tense, "which taketh away") "the sin of the world" (John i. 29). Our Lord was then bearing the sin of the world as the Lamb of God. From the day when He began His divine ministry, I might say even before that, He bore our sins. He was the Lamb "slain from the foundation of the world;" so, when He went up to Calvary, bearing His cross, He was bearing our sins up to the tree. Yet, specially and peculiarly in His death-agony He stood in our stead, and upon His soul and body burst the tempest of justice which had gathered through our transgressions.

This sin-bearing is *final*. He bore our sins in His own body on the tree, but He bears them now no more. The sinner and the sinner's Surety are both free, for the law is vindicated, the honour of government is cleared, the substitutionary sacrifice is complete. He dieth no more, death hath no more dominion over Him; for He has ended His work, and has cried, "It is finished." As for the sins which He bore in His own body on the tree, they cannot be found, for they have ceased to be, according to that ancient promise, "In those days, and in that time, saith the Lord, the iniquity of Israel shall be sought for, and there shall be none; and the sins of Judah, and they shall not be found" (Jeremiah l. 20). The work of the Messiah was "to finish the transgression, and to make an end of sins, and to make reconciliation for iniquity, and to bring in everlasting righteousness" (Daniel ix. 24). Now, if sin is made an end of, there is an end of it; and if transgression is "finished", there is no more to be said about it.

Let us look back with holy faith, and see Jesus bearing the stupendous load of our sins up to the tree, and on the tree; and see how *effectual* was His sacrifice for discharging the whole mass of our moral liability both in reference to guiltiness in the sight of God, and the punishment which follows thereon. It is a law of nature that nothing can be in two places at the same time; and if sin was borne away by our Lord, it cannot rest upon us. If by faith we have accepted the Substitute whom God Himself has accepted, then it cannot be that the penalty should be twice demanded, first of the Surety, and then of those for whom He stood. The Lord Jesus bore the sins of His people away, even as the scape-goat, in the type, carried the sin of Israel to a land uninhabited. Our sins are gone for ever. "As far as the east is from the west, so far hath He removed our transgressions from us." He hath cast all our iniquities into the depths of the sea; he hath hurled them behind his back, where they shall no more be seen.

Beloved friends, we very calmly and coolly talk about this thing, but it is the greatest marvel in the universe ; it is the miracle of earth, the mystery of heaven, the terror of hell. Could we fully realize the guilt of sin, the punishment due to it, and the literal substitution of Christ, it would work in us an intense enthusiasm of gratitude, love, and praise. I do not wonder that our Methodist friends shout, "Halle-lujah!" This is enough to make us all shout and sing, as long as we live, "Glory, glory to the Son of God !" What a wonder that the Prince of glory, in whom is no sin, who was indeed incapable of evil, should condescend to come into such contact with our sin as is implied in His being "made sin for us"! Our Lord Jesus did not handle sin with the golden tongs, but He bore it on His own shoulders. He did not lift it with golden staves, as the priests carried the ark ; but He Himself bore the hideous load of our sin in His own body on the tree. This is the mystery of grace which angels desire to look into. I would for ever preach it in the plainest and most unmistak-able language.

II. In the second place, briefly notice THE CHANGE IN OUR CONDITION, which the text describes as coming out of the Lord's bearing of our sins : "That we, being dead to sins, should live unto righteousness." The change is a dying and a reviving, a burial and a resurrection : we are brought from life to death, and from death to life.

We are henceforth legally dead to the punishment of sin. If I were condemned to die for an offence, and some other died in my stead, then I died in him who died for me. The law could not a second time lay its charge against me, and bring me again before the judge, and condemn me, and lead me out to die. Where would be the justice of such a procedure? I am dead already: how can I die again? I have borne the wrath of God in the person of my glorious and ever-blessed Substitute; how then can I bear it again? Where was the use of a Substitute if I am to bear it also? Should Satan come before God to lay an accusation against me, the answer is, "This man is dead. He has borne the penalty, and is 'dead to sins,' for the sentence against him has been executed upon Another." What a wonderful deliverance for us! Bless the Lord, O my soul!

But Peter also means to remind us that, by and through the influence of Christ's death upon our hearts, *the Holy Ghost has made us now to be actually "dead to sins"*: that is to say, we no longer love them, and they have ceased to hold dominion over us. Sin is no longer at home in our hearts; if it enters there, it is as an intruder. We are no more its willing servants. Sin calls to us by temptation, but we give it no answer, for we are dead to its voice. Sin promises us a high reward, but we do not consent, for we are dead to its allurements. We sin, but our will is not to sin. It would be heaven to us to be perfectly holy. Our heart and life go after perfection, but sin is abhorred of our soul. "Now, if I do that which I would not, it is no more I that do it, but sin that dwelleth in me." Our truest and most real self loathes sin; and though we fall into it, it is a fall,— we are out of our element, and escape from the evil with all speed. The new-born life within us has no dealings with sin ; it is dead to sin.

The Greek word here used cannot be fully rendered into English ; it signifies " being unborn to sins." We were born in sin, but by the death of Christ, and the work of the Holy Spirit upon us, that birth is undone, " we are unborn to sins." That which was wrought in us by sin, even at our birth, is through the death of Jesus counteracted by the new life which His Spirit imparts. " We are unborn to sins." I like the phrase, unusual as it sounds. Does it seem possible that birth should be reversed : the born unborn ? Yet so it is. The true *ego*, the reallest " I," is now unborn to sins, for we are " born, not of blood, nor of the will of the flesh, nor of the will of man, but of God." We are unborn to sins, and born unto God.

But our Lord's sin-bearing has also *brought us into life*. Dead to evil according to law, we also live in newness of life in the kingdom of grace. Our Lord's object is " that we should live unto righteousness." Not only are our lives to be righteous, which I trust they are, but we are quickened and made sensitive and vigorous unto righteousness : through our Lord's death we are made quick of eye, and quick of thought, and quick of lip, and quick of heart unto righteousness. Certainly, if the doctrine of His atoning sacrifice does not vivify us, nothing will. When we sin, it is the sorrowful result of our former death ; but when we work righteousness, we throw our whole soul into it, " We live unto righteousness." Because our Divine Lord has died, we feel that we must lay ourselves out for His praise. The tree which brought death to our Saviour is a tree of life to us. Sit under this true *arbor vitæ*, and you will shake off the weakness and disease which came in by that tree of knowledge of good and evil. Livingstone in Africa used certain medicines which are known as *Livingstone's Rousers ;* but what rousers are those glorious truths which are extracted from the bitter wood of the cross ! O my brethren, let us show in our lives what wonders our Lord Jesus has done for us by His agony and bloody sweat, by His cross and passion !

III. The apostle then speaks of THE HEALING OF OUR DISEASES by Christ's death : "By whose stripes ye were healed. For ye were as sheep going astray ; but are now returned unto the Shepherd and Bishop of your souls."

We were healed, and we remain so. It is not a thing to be done in the future ; it has been wrought. Peter describes our disease in the words which compose verse twenty-five. What was it, then ?

First, it was *brutishness.* "Ye were as sheep." Sin has made us so that we are only fit to be compared to beasts, and to those of the least intelligence. Sometimes the Scripture compares the unregenerate man to an ass. Man is said to be "born like a wild ass's colt." Amos likens Israel to the "kine of Bashan", and he saith to them, "Ye shall go out at the breaches, every cow at that which is before her." David compared himself to behemoth : "So foolish was I, and ignorant : I was as a beast before Thee." We are nothing better than beasts until Christ comes to us. But we are not beasts after that : a living, heavenly, spiritual nature is created within us when we come into contact with our Redeemer. We still carry about with us the old brutish nature, but by the grace of God it is put in subjection, and kept there; and our fellowship now is with the Father, and with His Son Jesus Christ. We "were as sheep," but we are now men redeemed unto God.

We are cured also of the *proneness to wander* which is so remarkable in sheep. "Ye were as sheep going astray," always going astray, loving to go astray, delighting in it, never so happy as when they are wandering away from the fold. We wander still, but not as sheep wander: we now seek the right way, and desire to follow the Lamb whithersoever He goeth. If we wander, it is through ignorance or temptation. We can truly say, "My soul followeth hard after Thee." Our Lord's cross has nailed us fast as to hands and feet: we cannot now run greedily after iniquity; rather do we say, "Return unto thy rest, O my soul; for the Lord hath dealt bountifully with thee!"

> "My wanderings, Lord, are at an end,
> 　I'm now return'd to Thee:
> Be Thou my Father and my Friend,
> 　Be all in all to me."

Another disease of ours was *inability to return*: "Ye were as sheep going astray; but are now returned." Dogs and even swine are more likely to return home than wandering sheep. But now, beloved, though we wandered, we have returned, and do still return to our Shepherd. Like Noah's dove, we have found no rest for the sole of our foot anywhere out of the ark, and therefore we return unto Him, and He graciously pulls us in unto Him. If we wander at any time, we bless God that there is a sacred something within us which will not let us rest, and there is a far more powerful something above us which draws us back. We are like the needle in the compass : touch that needle with your finger, and compel it to point to the east, or to the south, and it may do so for the moment; but take away the pressure, and in an instant it returns to the pole. So we must go back to Jesus; we must return to the Bishop of our souls. Our soul cries, "Whom have I in heaven but Thee? and there is none upon earth that I desire beside Thee." Thus, by the virtue of our Lord's death, an immortal love is created in us, which leads us to seek His face, and renew our fellowship with Him.

Our Lord's death has also cured us of our *readiness to follow other leaders*. If one sheep goes through a gap in the hedge, the whole flock will follow. We have been accustomed to follow ringleaders in sin, or in error : we have been too ready to follow custom, and to do that which is judged proper, respectable, and usual : but now we are resolved to follow none but Jesus, according to His word, " My sheep hear My voice, and I know them, and they follow Me. A stranger will they not follow, but will flee from him : for they know not the voice of strangers." For my own part, I am resolved to follow no human leader. Faith in Jesus creates a sacred independence of mind. We have learned so entire a dependence upon our crucified Lord that we have none to spare for men.

Finally, beloved friends, when we were wandering we were like sheep *exposed to wolves*, but we are delivered from this by being near the Shepherd. We were in danger of death, in danger from the devil, in danger from a thousand temptations, which, like ravenous beasts, prowled around us. Having ended our wandering, we are now in a place of safety. When the lion roars, we are driven the closer to the Shepherd, and rejoice that His crook protects us. He says, " My sheep hear My voice, and I know them, and they follow Me : and I give unto them eternal life ; and they shall never perish, neither shall any man pluck them out of My hand."

What a wonderful work of grace has been wrought in us ! We owe all this, not to the teaching of Christ, though that has helped us greatly ; not to the example of Christ, though that is charming us into a diligent copying of it ; but we owe it all to His stripes: " By whose stripes ye were healed." Brethren, we preach Christ crucified, because we have been saved by Christ crucified. His death is the death of our sins. We can never give up the doctrine of Christ's substitutionary sacrifice, for it is the power by which we hope to be made holy. Not only are we washed from guilt in His blood, but by that blood we overcome sin. Never, so long as breath or pulse remains, can we conceal the blessed truth that He " His own self bare our sins in His own body on the tree, that we, being dead to sins, should live unto righteousness." The Lord give us to know much more of this than I can speak, for Jesus Christ's sake ! Amen.

SWOONING AND REVIVING AT CHRIST'S FEET.

AN ADDRESS DELIVERED AT THE CLOSE OF ONE OF THE PASTORS' COLLEGE CONFERENCES.

"And when I saw Him, I fell at His feet as dead. And He laid His right hand upon me, saying unto me, Fear not; I am the first and the last: I am He that liveth, and was dead; and, behold, I am alive for evermore, Amen; and have the keys of hell and of death."

Revelation i. 17, 18.

SWOONING AND REVIVING AT CHRIST'S FEET.

———

WE have nothing now to think of but our Lord. We come to Him that He may cause us to forget all others. We are not here as ministers, cumbered with much serving, but we now sit at His feet with Mary, or lean on His bosom with John. The Lord Himself gives us our watchword as we muster our band for the last assembly. "*Remember Me*," is His loving command. We beseech Him to fill the full circle of our memory as the sun fills the heavens and the earth with light. We are to think only of Jesus, and of Him only will I speak. Oh, for a touch of the live coal from Him who is our Altar as well as our Sacrifice!

My text is found in the words of John, in the first chapter of the Revelation, at the seventeenth and eighteenth verses :—

"*And when I saw* HIM, *I fell at* HIS *feet as dead. And* HE *laid* HIS *right hand upon me, saying unto me, Fear not ; I am the first and the last : I am* HE *that liveth, and was dead ; and, behold, I am alive for evermore, Amen ; and have the keys of hell and of death.*"

John was of all men the most familiar with Jesus, and his Lord had never needed to say to him, " Lovest thou Me ? " Methinks, if any man could have stood erect in the presence of the glorified Saviour, it would have been that disciple whom Jesus loved. Love permits us to take great liberties: the child will climb the knee of his royal father, and no man accuses him of presuming. John had such love, and yet even he could not look into the face of the Lord of glory without being overcome with awe. While yet in the body, even John must swoon if he be indulged with a premature vision of the Well-beloved in His majesty. If permitted to see the Lord before our bodies have undergone that wondrous change by which we are made like Jesus that we may see Him as He is, we shall find the sight to be more than we can bear. A clear view of our Lord's heavenly splendour while we are here on earth would not be fitting, for it would not be profitable for us always to be lying in a swoon at our Redeemer's feet, while there is so much work for us to do.

Permit me, dear brethren, to take my text from its connection, and to apply it to ourselves, by bringing it down from the throne up yonder to the table here. It may be, I trust it will be, that as we see Jesus even here, *we shall with John fall at His feet as dead.* We shall not swoon, but we shall be dead in another sense, most sweetly dead, while our life is revealed in Him. After we have thought upon that, we shall come to what my text implies: then, *may we revive with John,* for if he had not revived he could never have told us of his fainting fit. Thus we shall have death with Christ, and resurrection in Him. Oh, for a deep experience of both, by the power of the Holy Spirit!

I. If we are permitted to see Christ in the simple and instructive memorials which are now upon the table, we shall, in a blessed sense, FALL AT HIS FEET AS DEAD.

For, first, here we see *provision for the removal of our sin*, and we are thus reminded of it. Here is the bread broken because we have broken God's law, and must have been broken for ever had there not been a bruised Saviour. In this wine we see the token of the blood with which we must be cleansed, or else be foul things to be cast away into the burnings of Tophet, because abominable in the sight of God. Inasmuch as we have before us the memorial of the atonement for sin, it reminds us of our death in sin in which we should still have remained but for that grace which spake us into life and salvation. Are you growing great? Be little again as you see that you are nothing but slaves that have been ransomed. "God's freed-men" is still your true rank. Are you beginning to think that, because you are sanctified, you have the less need of daily cleansing? Hear that word, "If we walk in the light, as He is in the light, we have fellowship one with another," yet even then "the blood of Jesus Christ, His Son, cleanseth us from all sin." We sin even when in the highest and divinest fellowship, and need still the cleansing blood. How this humbles us before the Lord! We are to be winners of sinners, and yet we ourselves are sinners still, needing as truly the Bread of life as those to whom we serve it out.

Ah! and some of us have been very special sinners; and therefore, if we love much, it is because we have had much forgiven. We have erred since we knew the Saviour, and that is a kind of sinnership which is exceedingly grievous; we have sinned since we have

entered into the highest state of spiritual joy, and
have been with Him on the holy mount, and have
beheld His glory! This breeds a holy shamefacedness. We may well fall at Jesus' feet, though He
only reveals Himself in bread and wine, for these
convey a sense of our sinnership while they remind
us of how our Lord met our sin, and put it away.

Herein we fall as low as the dead. Where is the "I"?
Where is the self-glorying? Have you any left in the
presence of the crucified Saviour? As you in spirit
eat His flesh and drink His blood, can you glory in
your own flesh, or feel the pride of blood and birth?
Fie upon us if there mingles a tinge of pride with our
ministry, or a taint of self-laudation with our success!
When we see Jesus, our Saviour, the Saviour of
sinners, surely self will sink, and humility will fall at
His feet. When we think of Gethsemane and Calvary,
and all our great Redeemer's pain and agony, surely,
by the Holy Ghost, self-glorying, self-seeking, and
self-will must fall as though slain with a deadly wound.
"When I saw HIM, I fell at HIS feet as dead."

Here, also, we learn a second lesson. *Jesus has
placed upon this table food.* The bread sets forth all
that is necessary, and the cup all that is luxurious:
provision for all our wants and for all our right
desires, all that we need for sustenance and joy.
Then, what a poverty-stricken soul am I that I cannot
find myself in bread! As to comforts, I may not
think of them; they must be given me or I shall
never taste them. Brothers, we are Gentlemen Com-
moners upon the bounty of our great Kinsman : we
come to His table for our maintenance, we have no
establishments of our own. He who feeds the sparrows

feeds our souls ; in spiritual things, we no more gather
into barns than do the blessed birds ; our heavenly
Father feeds us from that " all fulness" which it hath
pleased Him to lay up for us in Jesus. We could not
live an hour spiritually without Him who is not only
bread, but life ; not only the wine which cheereth, but
consolation itself. Our life hangs upon Jesus ; He is
our Head as well as our food. We shall never out-
grow our need of natural bread, and spiritually we
shall never rise out of our need of a present Christ,
but the rather we shall feel a stronger craving and a
more urgent passion for Him. Look at yonder vain
person. He feels that he is a great man, and you
own that he is your superior in gifts ; but what a cheat
he is, what a foolish creature to dream of being somebody ! Now will he be found wanting ; for, like ourselves, he is not sufficient even to think anything of
himself. A beggar who has to live on alms, to eat
the bread of dependence, to take the cup of charity,—
what has he to boast of? HE is the great One who
feeds us, who gives us all that we enjoy, who is our
all in all ; and as for us, we are suppliants,—I had
almost said mendicants,—a community of Begging
Frères, to all personal spiritual wealth as dead as the
slain on Marathon. The negro slave at least could
claim his own breath, but we cannot claim even that.
The Spirit of God must give us spiritual breath, or
our life will expire. When we think of this, surely
the sight of Christ in this bread and wine, though it
be a dim vision compared with that which ravished
the heart of John, will make us fall at the Redeemer's
feet as dead.

The "I" cannot live, for our Lord has provided no

food for the vain *Ego*, and its lordliness. He has
provided all for necessity, but nothing for boasting.
Oh, blessed sense of self-annihilation! We have
experienced it several times this week when certain
of those papers were read to us by our brethren; and,
moreover, we shrivelled right up in the blaze of the
joy with which our Master favoured us. I hope this
happy assembly and its heavenly exercises have
melted the *Ego* within us, and made it, for the while,
flow away in tears. Dying to self is a blessed feeling.
May we all realize it! When we are weak to the
utmost in conscious death of self, then are we strong
to the fulness of might. Swooning away unto self-
death, and losing all consciousness of personal power,
we are introduced into the infinite, and live in God.

II. Now let us consider how WE GET ALIVE
AGAIN, and so know the Lord as the resurrection and
the life. John did revive, and he tells us how it came
about. He says of the Ever-blessed One,—" HE laid
HIS right hand upon me, saying unto me, Fear not;
I am the first and the last: I am HE that liveth, and
was dead; and, behold, I am alive for evermore,
Amen; and have the keys of hell and of death."

All the life-floods of our being will flow with renewed force if, first of all, we are *brought into contact
with Jesus :* "He laid His right hand upon me."
Marvellous patience that He does not set His foot
upon us, and tread us down as the mire of the streets!
I have lain at His feet as dead, and had He spurned
me as tainted with corruption, I could not have im-
pugned His justice. But there is nothing here about
His foot! That foot has been pierced for us, and it
cannot be that the foot which has been nailed to the

cross for His people should ever trample them in His wrath. Hear these words, " He laid His right hand upon me." The right hand of His strength and of His glory He laid upon His fainting servant. It was *the hand of a man*. It is the right hand of Him who, in all our afflictions, was afflicted, who is a Brother born for adversity. Hence, everything about His hand has a reviving influence. The *speech* of sympathy, my brothers, is often too unpractical, and hence it is too feeble to revive the fainting ; the *touch* of sympathy is far more effectual. You remember that happy story of the wild negro child who could never be won till the little lady sat down by ner, and laid her hand upon her. Eva won poor Topsy by that tender touch. The tongue failed, but the hand achieved the victory. So was it with our adorable Lord. He showed us that He was bone of our bone and flesh of our flesh ; He brought Himself into contact with us, and made us perceive the reality of His love to us, and then He became more than a conqueror over us.

Thus, *we felt that He was no fiction*, but a real Christ, for there was His hand, and we felt the gentle pressure. The laying on of the right hand of the Lord had brought healing to the sick, sight to the blind, and even life to the dead, and it is no strange thing that it should restore a fainting disciple. May you all feel it at this very moment in its full reviving power ! May there stream down from the Lord's right hand, not merely His sympathy, because He is a man like ourselves, but as much of the power of *His deity* as can be gotten into man, so that we may be filled with the fulness *of God !* That is possible at this instant. The Lord's supper represents the giving of the whole body of Christ to us, to enter into us for food ; surely, if we enter into its true meaning, we may expect to be revived and vitalized ; for we have here more than a mere touch of the hand, it is the whole Christ that enters into us spiritually, and so comes into contact with our innermost being. I believe in "the real presence" : do not you ? The *carnal* presence is another thing : *that* we do not even desire. Lord Jesus, come into a many-handed contact with us now by dwelling in us, and we in Thee !

Still, there was something else wanted, for our Lord Jesus, after the touch, *gave the word :* " Fear not ; I am the first and the last." What does He say ? Does He say, " Thou art " ? Open your Testaments, and see. Does He exclaim, " Fear not ; thou art the beloved disciple, John the apostle and divine " ? I find nothing of the kind. He did not direct His servant to look at himself, but to remember the great I AM, his Saviour, and Lord. The living comfort of every swooning child of God, of everyone who is conscious of a death-wound to the natural " I," lies in that majestic " I," who alone can say " I am." You live because there is an " I am " who has life in Himself, and has that life for you.

" I am the first." " I have gone before you, and prepared your way ; I loved you before you loved Me ; I ordained your whole course in life before you were in existence. In every work of grace for you and within you, I am the first. Like the dew which comes from the Lord, I waited not for man, neither tarried for the sons of men. And I also am the last, perfecting that which concerneth you, and keeping you unto the end. I am the Alpha and the Omega to you, and all the letters in between; I began with you, and I shall end with you, if an end can be thought of. I march in the van, and I bring up the rear. Your final preservation is as much from Me as your hopeful commencement." Brother, does a fear arise concerning that dark hour which threatens soon to arrive? What hour is that? Jesus knows, and He will be with you through the night, and till the day breaketh. If Jesus is the beginning and the end to us, what is there else? What have we to fear unless it be those unhallowed inventions of our mistrust, those superfluities of naughtiness which fashion themselves into unbeliefs, and doubts, and unkind imaginings? Christ shuts out everything that could hurt us, for He covers all the time, and all the space; He is above the heights, and beneath the depths; and everywhere He is LOVE.

Read on,—"I am He that liveth." "Because I live, ye shall live also; no real death shall befal you, for death hath no more dominion over Me,—your Head, your Life." While there is a living Christ in heaven, no believer shall ever see death: he shall sleep in Jesus, and that is all, for even then he shall be "for ever with the Lord."

Read on,—"and was dead." "Therefore, though you die, you shall go no lower than I went; and you shall be brought up again even as I have returned from the tomb." Think of Jesus as having traversed the realm of death-shade, and you will not fear to follow in His track. Where should the dying members rest but on the same couch with their once dying Head?

" And, behold I am alive for evermore." Yes, behold it, and never cease to behold it : we serve an ever-living Lord. Brothers, go home from Conference in the power of this grand utterance ! The dear child may sicken, or the precious wife may be taken home ; but Christ says, " I am alive for evermore." The believing heart can never be a widow, for its Husband is the living God. Our Lord Jesus will not leave us orphans, He will come unto us. Here is our joy, then : not in ourselves, but in the fact that He ever lives to carry out the Father's good pleasure in us and for us. Onward, soldiers of the cross, for our immortal captain leads the way.

Read once more,—" and have the keys of hell and of death." As I thought over these words, I marvelled for the poverty and meanness of the cause of evil ; for the prince of it, the devil, has not the keys of his own house ; he cannot be trusted with them ; they are swinging at the girdle of Christ. Surely I shall never go to hell, for my Lord Jesus turned the key against my entrance long ago. The doors of hell were locked for me when He died on my behalf. I saw Him lock the door, and, what is more, I saw Him hang the key at His girdle, and there it is to this day. Christ has the keys of hell ; then, whenever He chooses, He can cage the devouring lion, and restrain His power for evil. Oh, that the day were come ! It is coming, for the dragon hath great wrath, knowing that his time is short. Let us not go forth alone to battle with this dread adversary ; let us tell his Conqueror of him, and entreat Him to shorten his chain. I admire the forcible words of a dying woman to one who asked her what she did when she was tempted

by the devil on account of her sin. She replied,
" The devil does not tempt me now ; he came to me
a little while ago, and he does not like me well
enough to come again !" "Why not?" "Well, he
went away because I said to him, Chosen, chosen ! "
" What did you mean by that ? " " Do you not remember how it is said in the Scripture, ' The Lord rebuke
thee, O Satan ; even the Lord that hath *chosen* Jerusalem rebuke thee ' ? " The aged woman's text was
well taken, and well does the enemy know the rebuke
which it contains. When Joshua, the high priest,
clothed in filthy garments, stood before the angel, Satan
stood at his right hand to resist him, but he was
silenced by being told of the election of God : " The
Lord which hath chosen Jerusalem rebuke thee." Ah,
brethren, when Christ's right hand is upon us, the evil
one departs! He knows too well the weight of that
right hand.

Conclude the verse,—" and of death." Our Lord
has the keys of death, and this will be a joyful fact
to us when our last hours arrive. If we say to Him,
" Master, whither am I going ? " He answers, " I
have the key of death and the spirit world." Will we
not reply, " We feel quite confident to go wherever
Thou wilt lead us, O Lord " ? We shall then pursue
His track in His company. Our bodies shall descend
into what men call a charnel-house, though it is really
the unrobing-room of saints, the vestibule of heaven,
the wardrobe of our dress where it shall be cleansed
and perfected. We have a fit spiritual array for the
interval, but we expect that our bodies shall rise
again in the likeness of " the Lord from heaven."
What gainers we shall be when we shall take up the

robes we laid aside, and find them so gloriously changed, and made fit for us to wear even in the presence of our Lord! So, if the worst fear that crosses you should be realized, and you should literally die at your Lord's feet, there is no cause for dread, for no enemy can do you harm, since the divine right hand is pledged to deliver you to the end. Let us give the Well-beloved the most devout and fervent praise as we now partake of this regal festival. The King sitteth at His table, let our spikenard give forth its sweetest smell.

C. H. SPURGEON'S COMMUNION HYMN.

(No. 939 in "Our Own Hymn Book.")

AMIDST us our Belovèd stands,
   And bids us view His piercèd hands;
Points to His wounded feet and side,
Blest emblems of the Crucified.

What food luxurious loads the board,
When at His table sits the Lord!
The wine how rich, the bread how sweet,
When Jesus deigns the guests to meet!

If now with eyes defiled and dim,
We see the signs but see not Him,
Oh, may His love the scales displace,
And bid us see Him face to face!

Our former transports we recount,
When with Him in the holy mount,
These cause our souls to thirst anew,
His marr'd but lovely face to view.

Thou glorious Bridegroom of our hearts,
Thy present smile a heaven imparts:
Oh, lift the veil, if veil there be,
Let every saint Thy beauties see!